Date Due

JUL 1 7 '56		
NOV 1 5 1958		
DE 13 '65		
PRINTED IN U. S. A.		

JOHN EVELYN AND HIS FAMILY CIRCLE

Evelyn's confession of his sins (in contracted Latin) with their several totals.
Mainly compiled on his 60th birthday

[*Frontispiece*]

JOHN EVELYN

and his
Family Circle

~~~~~~

by

W. G. HISCOCK

Routledge & Kegan Paul

LONDON

First published 1955
by Routledge & Kegan Paul Limited
Broadway House, Carter Lane, E.C.4.
Printed in Great Britain
by Butler & Tanner Limited
Frome and London

Preface

AFTER the publication of his *Diary*—and certain carefully selected letters appended to it—in 1818, John Evelyn became more or less generally known as the devout Evelyn by reason of his criticism of the Stuart Court, and for his staunch adherence to the Church of England. When Pepys's Diary appeared in 1825 this idea of Evelyn's personality was reinforced by contrast. Again in 1847, on the publication of Evelyn's *The Life of Mrs. Godolphin*, the Victorians readily placed the author in the beams of the halo which he had put upon the head of his saintly friend. Apart from one S. Lumley—a contemporary reader of that work—who said: 'After the death of poor Mrs. Godolphin [1678] I trust if Evelyn is to be believed',[1] nothing disturbed his title until 1920, when Virginia Woolf flashed a rapier in a short essay entitled *Rambling round Evelyn* (reprinted in *The Common Reader*, 1st series). Despite its brevity and some inaccuracies, it was a brilliant little ramble in and out of his hitherto impregnable defences. She carried out no research, for his unpublished manuscripts and letters were then still inaccessible, and she had read little more than the *Diary*. But she read between the lines, and deservedly became Evelyn's first modern critic.

Lord Ponsonby's able biography of Evelyn, 1933, was based on the published works, the *Diary*, and the appended letters, but embodied no fresh research. Sir Geoffrey Keynes's *John Evelyn* (1937) is a first-rate bibliography, but the preface suffers

---

[1] Evelyn Collection: press-mark P.L. A7^a.

from the author's inadequate knowledge of the then still un-published material—though some is used to good effect.[1]

My study of Evelyn's friendship, *John Evelyn and Mrs. Godolphin* (1951), was, in effect, a criticism of *The Life of Mrs. Godolphin*, and based, in part, on the hitherto unpublished material recently made accessible at Christ Church by the kindness of Mr. John Evelyn. The present work is based on the same source, and includes all other relevant Evelyn material. In many instances—particularly in personal matters—the letters of the Evelyn circle provide a necessary and illuminating corrective to the Victorian eulogy of the Diarist; indeed by allowing Evelyn to speak on every possible occasion, it may be said that he has painted his own portrait.

For permission to use and publish the letters and documents from the Evelyn Collection I am indebted to Mr. John Evelyn and the Hon. Sherman Stonor. Mr. F. A. Taylor, Librarian and Student of Christ Church, very generously gave me facilities for writing the book. Mr. Esmond de Beer kindly allowed me to use the proofs of his forthcoming edition of Evelyn's *Diary*: these were invaluable. Messrs. Macmillan have allowed me to reprint certain passages from *John Evelyn and Mrs. Godolphin*. Dr. John P. Kenyon gave me the benefit of his inti-mate knowledge of the Sunderlands. Mr. D. J. Allan and Mr. J. P. A. Gould deciphered the greater part of Evelyn's confes-sion—which is written in contracted Latin. Dr. E. L. Mascall kindly read the passages in my manuscript dealing with this confession. Mr. John Munro has read the whole typescript and made several valuable suggestions. A like service was given by Dr. Claude Jenkins. To all these gentlemen I offer my warmest thanks.

[1] The most glaring error is seen on Plate 3 where Evelyn's specimen title-page of his 1653 Library Catalogue is harnessed to a page from a subject-catalogue written by his grandson, *c.* 1706.

Contents

PREFACE   *Page* v

Chapter I EARLY YEARS   1

II SAYES COURT GARDEN   18

III CREATIVE PERIOD   37

IV PLAGUE AND WAR   55

V MAIDS AND MEN OF HONOUR   74

VI THE GREAT FRIENDSHIP   91

VII MISTRESS GODOLPHIN   106

VIII SORROW AND CONFESSION   119

IX ROD AND REVOLUTION   140

X FILIAL AND FINANCIAL TROUBLES   154

XI UNSETTLED OUTLOOK   170

XII STILL NO RESPITE   185

XIII THE WOTTON SETTLEMENT   197

XIV THE INHERITANCE   212

XV THE FRUITS OF PATRONAGE   225

BIBLIOGRAPHY   241

INDEX   247

Illustrations

EVELYN'S CONFESSION   *Frontispiece*

PLAN OF SAYES COURT GARDEN   *Facing pages* 24-5

EVELYN'S GARDENING TOOLS   32

NOTE

The letters and MSS. referred to in the footnotes are in the
Evelyn Collection unless otherwise stated.

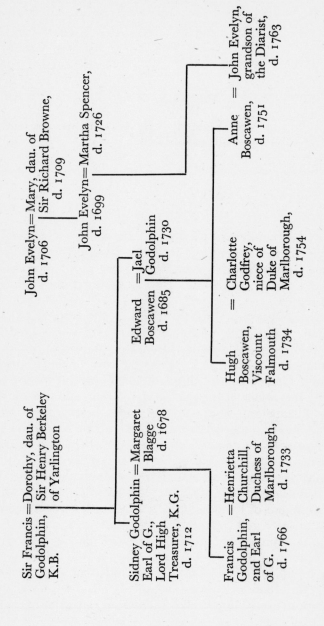

Sir Francis = Dorothy, dau. of
Godolphin,   Sir Henry Berkeley
K.B.   of Yarlington

Sidney Godolphin = Margaret
Earl of G.,   Blagge
Lord High   d. 1678
Treasurer, K.G.
d. 1712

Francis   = Henrietta
Godolphin,   Churchill,
2nd Earl   Duchess of
of G.   Marlborough,
d. 1766   d. 1733

Edward = Jael
Boscawen Godolphin
d. 1685   d. 1730

Hugh   = Charlotte
Boscawen,   Godfrey,
Viscount   niece of
Falmouth   Duke of
d. 1734   Marlborough,
                d. 1754

John Evelyn = Mary, dau. of
d. 1706   Sir Richard Browne,
             d. 1709

John Evelyn = Martha Spencer,
d. 1699   d. 1726

Anne   = John Evelyn,
Boscawen,   grandson of
d. 1751   the Diarist,
             d. 1763

CHAPTER I

Early Years

~~~~~~

T HE Evelyn family had its share of the country's sixteenth
and early seventeenth century prosperity when thrifty yeomen
bought the land which they had farmed, and prosperous mer-
chants—as aspiring gentry—bought the manor houses which
they had rented.

Thus George Evelyn of Surrey, whose wealth came by what
was virtually a monopoly of the manufacture of gunpowder at
his mills at Godstone and Long Ditton, was enabled to buy the
ancient manor of Wotton in 1579. At the turn of the century
he acquired further nearby property including the manor of
Milton. As the woods of the manor of Wotton stretched south
from the Elizabethan house to the woods belonging to the
manor of Abinger (indeed Wotton Wood—or the Manwood to
give its Elizabethan name—was common to both) it was inevitable that the more prosperous owner of Wotton should eventually acquire the other, and this, Richard Evelyn (the son of
George) achieved in 1622. Three years later he bought the
contiguous manor of Paddington in Abinger. (In this property,
there was a water mill converted in 1535 into an ironhammer,
which gave Abinger Hammer its curious name.) Still yet
another manor—Westcott, between Wotton and Dorking—
was bought in 1628, and Gosterwood added in 1636.[1] Surrounding the manors, woods, coppices, farmhouses, heath
and common were hundreds of acres of valuable arable

[1] Evelyn MS. 252 for all references to these properties.

land, productive, from time immemorial, of golden fields of corn.

Wotton House, 'so sweetly environed with those delicious streams and venerable woods' which rise from four hundred feet to nearly a thousand feet at Leith Hill to the south, was the birthplace of John Evelyn, the son of Richard and grandson of George, on 31 October 1620. No wonder he says he was 'wood-born'.

Inevitably the woods have changed with the years. In John's grandfather's time they were of oak, ash, beech, and elm, and great quantities of them were felled and burnt on the hearths, in the manufacture of gunpowder, and in iron-smelting. In the early seventeenth century the timber was consumed only on the hearths of the Evelyns, or by their tenants or labourers who sometimes obtained timber against rent or wages.[1] In 1676 John regretted that there remained—for the most part—but beech, birch and holly.

His father also inherited, by his marriage to Eleanor Stansfield, extensive property in Sussex, mostly on the seaward side of Lewes: the manors of Challenors, Denton, and Northstoke, the rectory of South Malling, and several smaller tenements.

The family income was therefore derived from the rents of the Surrey and Sussex properties and from the timber and corn of the home woods and fields. There was, and indeed is still so named, the cornfield known as the Homefield, bordering Wotton Hatch (the name of the present inn).

John's father was a good husbandman and a considerate landlord who appreciated work well done and knew the value of money. John says his annual estate was esteemed about £4000 (but no accounts survive to enable us to check the statement), and describes him in the opening pages of the *Diary* as 'a thriving, neat, silent, and methodical genius'. He was strong, of low stature, his hair grey, his beard brown and pointed, his complexion fresh, his eyes quick and piercing. John's mother was 'of a brown complexion, but hair of a lovely black, inclined to a religious melancholy or pious sadness', thrifty and prudent, and 'of a rare memory'. John had two brothers, George, the elder by three years, and Richard, the

[1] In 1634 some beech was sold 'to Mr. Brockelsbye for his copper mill' —at present unidentified (Evelyn MS. 131).

younger by two years. There were two sisters: Eliza, six years older than John, who died at the age of twenty, a few months after her marriage; and Jane, who had a great affection for John, four years his senior.

At four years of age John learnt (from one Fryer) 'rudiments' in the porch of Wotton Church. A year later he moved into Sussex where his education was continued at Southover under the indulgent eye of his grandmother. In this easy-going environment he stayed till he was sixteen, admitting that he had learnt little. Eton had been suggested when he was twelve years old, but being 'unreasonably terrified with the report of the severe discipline', he remained with his grandmother. He also confessed that he was too much given to drawing. It is regrettable that these statements[1] afford the only light we have on his early character and proficiency.

Doubtless he absorbed with his eyes, especially when he came home on holiday. Then he would watch with great interest and pleasure the farm labourers at their diverse occupations in his father's woods and fields;[2] the felling of seven years old ash trees in Abinger Shipwalk (perhaps the Flemish variety he mentioned later, in *Sylva*), beech and a small quantity of oak in Pasture Wood, in Heathie Land, and on Wotton Downs; he noted how the men measured the timber in 'stacks', and with what skill they bound the bavins; he was amused at the pigs, grunting and feeding on the mast (though sometimes the mast was sold to a tenant); he watched the loading of oak bark—to be sold at Leatherhead; he would have a word with old Robert Dawe (whose son George also worked for his father) as he quarried stone and chalk on the Downs to repair a house on the estate; perhaps he had a joke with another labourer, Daniel Peter, whose wife—as wet nurse—suckled him; he saw the threshing of wheat which was sold to the Baker of Darking (as it was then called), or maybe at Kingston, and the barley to be sold at Cobham; he noted, particularly, the making of bricks; perhaps he learnt the knack of making ash or beech spitters and corn-shovels, for which his father paid the men two shillings a dozen, and sold them at five shillings a dozen. John noted the versatility of the six or seven labourers his father employed, each of whom could perform any of these tasks; at

[1] *Diary*, 1624-5.   [2] Evelyn MS. 131.

other seasons they went hedging and ditching and spreading denshere (burnt weeds) upon the Downs.

The spelling of Darking is a guide to the local accent; a few years later George asked John for some hertichocks.

John was interested in all tasks and trades of husbandry (and remembered some of them when, later, he attempted to compile a dictionary of crafts and trade secrets).[1] At eleven years of age he says he 'began to observe matters more punctually, which I did use to set down in a blank almanac': that was the beginning of the *Diary*. He learnt that his father usually sold grass to the tenants by the acre: in 1636 the price was fourteen shillings. He was aware that a labourer was often paid in kind: a job of threshing wheat might come to £2 6s. of which the labourer would take twenty-one shillings in money, two bushels of the wheat he had threshed and a peck of rye, leaving the balance of thirteen shillings and fourpence in his master's hands for the half-year's rent of his cottage.[2]

John knew that he could always find happiness in the country. Yet he would ruminate somewhat sadly that, as a younger son, the prospects of his inheritance of the delights of the family estates were inevitably somewhat remote. In due time, he would go to the university; in fact his father was determined that all three sons should acquire degrees (or study long enough) to establish themselves as gentlemen—not as scholars. But the Evelyns were not of the class to countenance any undue expenditure of money at the university; they had too newly acquired the status of gentry for that.

In January 1634 George the elder son left the free school at Guildford to go to William Hobbs, tutor of Trinity College, Oxford. George's father asked Hobbs to take 'special care of him, to read to him as often as possible and to have him lodged in your own chamber',[3] thus mitigating some of the dangers of his son's mixing with bad company. But of such things we learn nothing from the young man's letters. Mrs. Evelyn, perhaps aware of the dangers of Lent when the monotony of the college fare of pike, perch and eels drove the undergraduates to the taverns and ale-houses for meat, and perhaps for too much

[1] Evelyn MS. 65.
[2] Evelyn MS. 131.
[3] Letter, R. Evelyn I to W. Hobbs, 27 Jan. 1633/4.

drink, sent him, to mend his commons at Lent time, a veal pie and a gammon of bacon.

The tuition fees paid to Hobbs were 40s. a quarter. He also received £10 or so to disburse on his pupil's behalf as occasions should require, and a present of 20s. now and then. George matriculated in October, having spent his first ten months as a private pupil of Hobbs—a common procedure at this time—though he continued, after matriculation, to live with him.

In the following month, the risk of smallpox made it expedient for George to go home, but his father, taking no risks, wrote to Hobbs: '. . . but if he has the disease, keep him in Oxford, be sure to get a good tender, and let him have no physic (for that proves fatal to many) till he be well again.'[1]

His wardrobe was not extensive (and we may be certain that it acted as a class distinction); in February 1635 he wrote: 'I want some half shirts, for I wear my black suit which is opened and have but one half shirt.' Hobbs, though devout and God-fearing, was not altogether a satisfactory tutor—in November 1635 he was reading to his pupil once a day, but four months later, George says 'he is only tutor to me *in nomine*, not *re* as the logicians term it; he hath not read to me since I last came [in February 1636][2] sometimes I take occasion to propose questions to him upon which he discourseth cursorily, and when I doubt of any thing, I ask his opinion, and he doth absolve the doubts as solidly as he can. The reason I suppose he is so deficient in reading Logic to me is because he hath been long discontinued from that study, not out of neglect to me—for he hath a conscience.'[3] Admittedly, Hobbs's main subject was theology.

At the suggestion of William Oughtred the mathematician (who was a friend of Evelyn senior) George embarked in his second year on a study of mathematics, during which course he was under the guidance of a B.A. who read astronomy to him in the afternoons.

We hear nothing of George's recreations, only of some sort of remedial athletics: his father had enquired whether he uses his swings, and whether he finds any good of them, concluding

[1] Letter, R. Evelyn I to W. Hobbs, 14 Nov. 1634.
[2] He says quaintly: 'I came safe to Oxford, and in good sanitation.'
[3] Letter, G. Evelyn to R. Evelyn I, 13 March 1636.

with the advice: 'Keep your body straight both in your sitting and walking.' Regarding his swings, he replies: 'I have hung them up for to swing by, in a gentleman's chamber of our college, for my tutor's chamber was too high and had never a beam to hang them on. I use them daily, both morning and evening and I find they do me much good. . . . We have in the same chamber another sort of swings different from these, which they call hand swings; they are made of iron and are hollow to put the hands in . . . sometimes I use mine own and sometimes the other.'[1]

George's third year at Oxford coincided with the new University Statutes compiled by Archbishop Laud. Hitherto it had been possible for Squires' eldest sons and Knights' youngest sons to proceed to a B.A. degree within three years on the completion of the usual B.A. exercise. But now in June 1636, George feared one of the new Laudian statutes, 'that no squire's son except a knight's eldest son shall proceed in 3 years'.[2] It was therefore extremely unlikely that he would be allowed to take the B.A. degree. However, he says his tutor would put his case before the Vice-Chancellor and hopes 'he will be pleased to let me proceed'. As it happened, Laud was to entertain the King in Oxford at the end of August, whose royal presence raised faint hopes in George's mind of an indulgence though 'it will be they only', he writes to his father, 'that can procure friends in Court that shall proceed, if it be not a general dispensation . . . Wherefore, if you have any friend at the Court, I humbly entreat you to crave his favour in it if need shall require.'[3] But he did not proceed for the lack of a friend to speak to Laud, or perhaps George's father was loath to be importunate.

In a later age, a father might have said 'no degree, no clothes', but George persuaded him into providing a new outfit, doubtless against the King's forthcoming visit. 'I want apparel,' wrote George, 'and a hat, also bands and other necessaries for 'tis almost a year since I have had me any. . . . I cannot have less than two suits made me, one to wear (for ordinary occasions) and another for higher days and festivals

[1] Letter, G. Evelyn to R. Evelyn I, 24 Dec. 1635.
[2] Letter, G. Evelyn to R. Evelyn I, 29 June 1636.
[3] Op. cit.

6

. . . to have the doublet of the best suit black silk and the breeches black cloth which will be very handsome, and gentlemen of fashion wear the same habit and I know you will I should be apparelled like such gentlemen . . . for the other suit a plain cloth with a little trimming will do well.'[1] As it turned out he did rather better: he had a black satin doublet, and a white satin doublet with scarlet hose. 'Now for the hat, I want a beaver, you bought me one when I came first to Oxford which is almost 3 years ago . . . the new one will be very genteel.'

In any event, he was well-dressed for the King's visit, when Laud entertained Charles and the Court to plays in Christ Church and to a great feast at St. John's to celebrate the confirmation of Laud's statutes, and his newly completed and beautiful quadrangle; and the young man, if degree-less, could go home for Christmas with no grudge against the university for there was still a chance that he might have his degree at next year's Act.

Meanwhile, John was idling at school in Sussex, making little progress. In 1635 his father had written in admonishment: 'If you do not apply yourself well to your work, you will not be fit for the university a great while, and that will be much disgrace to you.'[2] And again: 'Lay aside your painting and everything else which may hinder you in your learning, for painting and such things will do you no good hereafter . . . you must not lose an hour . . . better to be unborn than untaught.'[3] His father's advice, however, had little effect upon John's studies: 'I went to the university', he says, 'rather out of shame of abiding longer at school than for any fitness as by sad experience I found, which put me to relearn all that I had neglected or but perfunctorily gained';[4] and he was admitted as a Fellow Commoner under the care of the tutor George Bradshaw, at Balliol College on 10 May 1637.

There had been some doubt in his father's mind in sending him to Balliol as a Fellow Commoner, but he was assured that 'in some Houses they have so much liberty as they are the worse for it, but I can assure you that the government of that

[1] Letter, G. Evelyn to R. Evelyn I, 4 Aug. 1636.
[2] Letter, R. Evelyn I to J. Evelyn, 15 Dec. 1635.
[3] Letter, R. Evelyn I to J. Evelyn, n.d. [1635].
[4] *Diary*, 3 April 1637.

7

college is good' and that they are 'careful to hold the fellow Commoner to all kind of exercise so strictly, that I hope that there shall be no fear of any danger herein'.[1] Nor would it be any disgrace to George because he was of another house; in any case, at Trinity they accepted a Fellow Commoner only if he were a knight's eldest son.[2] John must have been rather vague in remembering the circumstances of his admission, for he tells us in the *Diary*[3] that, by presenting on entrance some books to the college library, he ranked as a benefactor; the truth is, at this period it was normal for a Fellow Commoner's £5 admission fee to be disposed of in books—chosen by the tutor—for the library instead of providing a piece of plate.

Thus George's advice and experience were helpful to John, and his frugal father also took advantage of George's impending departure for the Inns of Court: George's bedding, or some of it, could be transferred to John. George was directed to allow his brother as much as could be spared, an economy made possible by George's making use of his chamber-fellow's linen: 'Yet much is not required,' said his father, 'because you lie together.'[4] It is somewhat surprising that John, as a younger son, was more fastidiously bedded than his brother: obviously to escape the Elizabethan practice of double-bedding was now one of the privileges of a Fellow Commoner.

Bradshaw was at once taken with his new pupil: 'I do find him to be a very ingenious young gent.' (The use of the word 'ingenious' was more or less monopolised by John Aubrey, and has acquired considerable virtue; but as Bradshaw also used it later to describe Evelyn's younger brother Richard—who was a particularly colourless person—we must beware of its varying aptness.)

With the approach of the Act in this summer of 1637 the question again arose of George's degree. Hobbs told his father on 5 June that the new Laudian statutes might yet be circumvented and the degree allowed him before the Act and without determining at next Lent, provided the Archbishop was informed of George's status and of his not intending to continue

[1] Letter, Nicholas Bradshaw to R. Evelyn I, 20 March 1637.
[2] Letter, W. Hobbs to Richard Evelyn I, 11 May 1637.
[3] *Diary*, 10 May 1637.
[4] Letter, R. Evelyn I to G. Evelyn, 22 March 1637.

at Oxford as a scholar. But Evelyn senior was still disinclined
or unable to importune the great Laud, and perhaps indifferent
whether his son took or refused it; 'wherefore,' George writes,
'upon mature deliberation I take not the degree, besides it
would have cost me a great sum of money in fees, and a dinner'.
He was now weary of Oxford and disappointed with William
Hobbs: 'I doubt not but I shall profit myself as well with you,'
he writes to his father, 'yea more than I have here, for my
tutor hath not read to me this half year, and all that I have
benefited myself 'tis by my own industry.' Yes, he had done his
part well: 'I thank God I have so carried myself in the House
that I shall go away in the President's love.'¹ No under-
graduate of any generation could say more. Hobbs was indeed
fortunate to receive a 20s. piece from Evelyn senior 'as a
testimony of his love'. In July the honest, critical, tight-fisted
George left Oxford in readiness to take up residence at the
Middle Temple in the following November.

His father now provided an example of a private person's
support of a poor scholar, and showed a desire to keep the
living of Wotton Rectory in one family by contributing towards
the maintenance of John Heigham, son of the rector of Wotton,
and grandson of the former rector. Heigham was thus enabled
to go up to Exeter College in 1638. Evelyn senior continued his
support until 1641,² when the clouds presaging the Civil War
robbed the young man of his degree. In due time—at the
Restoration—Heigham's education bore fruit, and he succeeded
his father at the Rectory. The sending of money entailed a
certain amount of risk, but John and Heigham were regularly
supplied by the Oxford carrier who transported it for Evelyn
senior from London for four shillings in the pound and which
was 'always most safely delivered'.³

For any details of John's residence at Balliol, we must rely
on the *Diary*, for not one letter written to his father at this time
has survived—which is very curious. Unfortunately, the *Diary*
for the period gives us little beyond signs of John's under-
graduate dilettantism: he confesses that he 'was so frequently
diverted, with inclinations to newer trifles'. He was certainly

¹ Letter, G. Evelyn to R. Evelyn I, June 1637.
² Evelyn MS. 131.
³ Letter, N. Bradshaw to R. Evelyn I, 28 March 1638.

interested in dancing and music, and of the latter he even 'began to look upon the rudiments'. He wrote a play; noted the first drinking of coffee; made friends with James Thicknesse who, later, travelled with him abroad; and was confirmed at St. Mary's (although he had previously received the Sacrament on several occasions, confirmations being infrequently held).

In January 1640 he piloted his younger brother Richard (the second 'ingenious' Evelyn) through the ritual of admission and matriculation into Balliol as his chamber-fellow. Although John's inquisitiveness had been applied to inappropriate subjects in Oxford, the same characteristic of disposition was to bear fruit in due time—as we shall discover. He had been up for nearly three years, and now that Richard was settled in Balliol, John was allowed by his father to please his 'own sweet self' as George informed him; either to stay on with Richard or leave the university.

John decided to stay, at least for a while. In March, however, his ageing father became seriously ill, and both brothers returned in haste to Wotton. The illness proved intermittent, the illness of an old man with reserves of strength, and John (having, meanwhile, decided against going back to Oxford) found it convenient in June to begin the new Term with George, to study Law at the Middle Temple.

Always magnifying trifles either for or against himself, John says that the little he had learnt at Oxford was 'of very small benefit'[1] in his new studies. But there is no doubt that he had no interest in the Law, confessing that the very handsome apartment which his father had rented for them 'did not much contribute to the love of that impolish'd study'.[2]

In the meantime George had married Mary, the daughter of Daniel Caldwell of Horndon-on-the-Hill, Essex, the wedding taking place a fortnight before the new Term. The cool, business-like appraisal of his lady at their first meeting is reflected in a letter to his father: 'I had some conference with my love and I find her a good natured gentlewoman, there is such a harmony of our affections. This day I waited on her and the rest of the ladies to a play, but tomorrow I hope I shall have the happiness to enjoy her privately at her grand-

[1] *Diary*, 27 April 1640.   [2] *Diary*, 10 June 1640.

father's chamber that thereby our familiarity may arrive to a better perfection.' This was soon realised and manifested in a gift to her of a 'diamonded jewel' costing £53.[1]

On George's impending marriage, his father had settled on him the two manors of Westcott and Paddington (in Abinger), the former being the nearest residence to Wotton House on the estate, suitable for the new couple. In making the settlement of these two manors Evelyn senior made clear his general intention regarding the inheritance of the whole estate, expressly stating that he was 'content to settle them also' upon George and his issue male 'and for want of such issue to his brother's intail as the others are'.[2] This statement would seem to be of great importance to the two brothers: but it proved to be one that it was characteristic of George to forget or misinterpret, and to be apparently forgotten by John.

When Parliament was dissolved in May 1640 it seemed to the two brothers an evil portent: the King's urgent monetary requirements were blocked by the demurs and procrastination of the Commons. The study of the Law seemed of little account. Evelyn senior, nearing his end, expressed his heartfelt sorrow for the ill news from Westminster: 'but God's will be done and we must frame ourselves to patience to bear what He will have us suffer'. Perhaps the greater fortitude was required for his own poor health, now visibly declining with every day. Yet in June, he undertook the ninety miles journey to Bath: three days on dusty roads, with stopping-places, perhaps, at Basingstoke and Amesbury. Little improvement, however, resulted from the waters, and on December 24, having returned home to Wotton, he 'entered into a dropsy', and died.

John, realising his great loss and fearful of his inability to cope with the social and political murmurings, says, at this time, that it was only by the infinite goodness and mercy of God that he did not make shipwreck of his liberty and virtue.[3] On the other hand, he may have experienced no more than is the usual lot of youth, for he was so given to words.

Of course it was no longer necessary for George to live at Westcott; he remained at Wotton as the new head of the

[1] Letter, G. Evelyn to R. Evelyn I, 15 Nov. 1639.
[2] Letter, R. Evelyn I to G. Evelyn, 4 Feb. 1640.
[3] *Diary*, 2 Jan. 1641.

family. By his father's will John was left £4000 and some land at South Malling; Richard had £1000 and Baynards—a house a few miles south of Wotton; Leigh Farm in Sussex and £2000 went to Jane; the residue to George.[1]

These were indeed unsettled times and especially so for the Evelyns. In addition to his extra responsibilities in the New Year George was at once canvassed to stand in his father's place as High Sheriff of the county; as yet uncertain of his support he would not accept the office, nor even commit himself to support a petition until he knew of 'what number and what persons of quality do meet'. Even a suggested baronetcy did not tempt him 'except he see the times settled and improved'.[2] The office now carried unknown risks and dangerous responsibilities, unsought in the defence of the realm; for in the rumbling of Westminster no man could distinguish friend from potential enemy.

In April, John attended Strafford's trial rather belatedly, missing the most dramatic passages. In the following month he was more successful in satisfying his innate curiosity by witnessing, in company with George, Strafford's execution on Tower Hill: alas, but a temporary bar across the King's sad, obstinate way with Church and Commons.

Shortly afterwards, and perhaps for the first time in his life, John acted with decision: he determined to go abroad—to Holland. Why should he remain in England? There was no call on him to assist his brother in the management of the estate, or indeed any likelihood of his inheritance for many years to come. Moreover, what could he do in these political wranglings? But there was some opposition to his decision; to absent himself, he says, 'from this ill face of things . . . gave umbrage to wiser than myself'.[3]

It is likely that his sister Jane was one to deplore his leaving the country at this juncture; her letters, as we shall see, show that while she loved her brother, she could not applaud his absence. George, too, could hardly hide his thoughts: 'Your letter informs me of a farther design to Flanders, which God bless to you, and when you have perfected that journey, pray

[1] H. Evelyn, *Hist. of the Evelyn Family*, 1915, p. 35.
[2] Letter, G. Evelyn to J. Evelyn, 1 Feb. 1641.
[3] *Diary*, 28 June 1641.

think on your own country and return to your friends who much bewail your absence.'[1]

A parting gift of a new portrait of himself to Jane showed his affection for her; it was by Henrico van der Borcht (then living in the Earl of Arundel's household) and very attractive, depicting John's fine dark eyes and elegant silks—a picture that Jane must have treasured.

In Holland his education began in earnest. Mr. John Stoye has suggested that he went 'to gain a sufficiency of military experience',[2] but such an undertaking would be alien to his temperament. He certainly enrolled and trailed a pike for a few days at Genep in Captain Apsley's English company; but he could not endure the heat of the sun nor the night mists. In other ways for four months he indulged his deepest interests; he saw great pictures and magnificent buildings; he bought books, maps, engravings and pictures, three by Heemskirk and a Lievens. George had asked for 'a good one to hang over my chimney in the dining room', but John bought nothing so large. At Ghent he met the Earl of Arundel who had recently accompanied the Queen Mother from England. This seems to have been his first important contact with the nobility, a meeting of two virtuosi—the great and the promising embryo. Doubtless John made a good impression; in the arts they had much in common, and he returned with the Earl in October 1641.

John spent the next twelve months restlessly, visiting relations and his Sussex property, while keeping an eye on the gathering 'bloody difference between the King and Parliament'. On 12 November he was in some harmless way concerned with the battle of Brentford; he 'came in . . . just at the retreat, but was not permitted to stay longer than the 15th by reason of the Army's marching to Gloucester,[3] which had left both me and my brothers exposed to ruin without any advantage to his majesty'. May we not reasonably enquire: by whom was he not permitted to stay? We are also curious to know the nature of his enlistment, and why it was possible for him to say that nobody knew of his 'having been in His Majesty's army'? It

---

[1] Letter, G. Evelyn to J. Evelyn, 29 Aug. 1641.
[2] J. W. Stoye, *English Travellers Abroad, 1604–67*, 264.
[3] Actually Charles retired to Oxford (*Diary*, de Beer's ed., 79).

would have been wiser—in his case—to have adopted that neutrality observed by many noble families.

In the following summer, he was more happily—and more prudently—engaged in a little landscape gardening at Wotton. In this congenial occupation he could safely review the state of the country and decide upon the part that he would play. In any case he could demonstrate his Royalist sympathies: he sent a horse, complete with harness, as a gift to the King at Oxford. He avoided signing the Covenant, and 'finding it impossible to evade the doing very unhandsome things'[1] (whatever that may mean) obtained a licence from the King to travel again. Was it not imprudent to fight if one lacked soldierly qualities? Perhaps his experience at Brentford was a deciding factor: we cannot all be of the stuff of which commandos are made.

He first visited Paris, and then travelling leisurely by way of Tours, Lyons, Avignon and Cannes, arrived at Genoa; then on to Leghorn, Florence, Sienna, to arrive in Rome in November 1644. He saw everything that lay in his path. He made amends for what he failed to learn at Oxford, demonstrating in some cases that a man's best education is of his own acquiring. On his journey between Rome and Naples he made five small sketches. Then he went on to Venice, Padua, Verona, Milan, and Geneva, developing into an authority, or at least a well-informed connoisseur, on pictures, gardens, engravings, and architecture. To the nucleus of his library bought in Holland he added many more books. He studied physic and anatomy at Padua in the fashion of travelling Englishmen. He collected, arranged, and pressed in a large folio volume hundreds of simples from the Padua Botanic Garden, which are as well-preserved today as when Pepys saw them and said 'it was better than an herball'.[2] Carlo Maratti gave him some of his earliest drawings at Rome in 1645; he bought the same artist's copy of Correggio's *Madonna, Babe, St. Catharine and St. Sebastian*, expressly borrowed for the purpose by Evelyn in 1646 from Cardinal Barbarini, and Maratti's *Church and Reason submitting to Faith*, and the *Cross on a Book*.[3]

Thus Evelyn continued to acquire knowledge and happiness. But at home his brothers and sister were experiencing the

[1] *Diary*, 23 July 1643.   [2] Evelyn MS. d. 16.   [3] Evelyn MS. 53.

miseries of the Civil War which showed no signs of coming
to an end. On 17 June 1644 Jane voices to John, the general,
disturbing feeling: 'God send us peace . . . or else I know not
what will become of us. There are yet no hopes of any, both
sides being strong . . . and we are so wasted through intolerable
taxes that 'tis impossible for us to subsist long.' George suffered
personal sadness, too; early in the year the short life of his wife
came to a painful end by an ulcer in her left kidney. (John was
told in 1644 and recorded it belatedly on 21 May.)

Her death disrupted the domestic happiness of Wotton. Such
a blow it was to George that, with the prevailing smallness of
rents and the heavy taxes, he was forced to live in the Middle
Temple. He took two of his servants to look after his horse,
leaving four at Wotton House to keep the place habitable.
'All the husbandmen are yet at Wotton,' writes Jane, 'but my
brother tells me he will put them away at Christmas, and hire
men by the week.'[1]

Though Jane went for a while to live with her brother
Richard at Baynards, she had no hope of any settled state of
residence: '. . . there are scarce five gentlemen in our county
but have left off house keeping.'[2] And so it proved. By the end
of the year she was living at Twitnam with a widowed landlady
whose husband had been one of the Bed Chamber to the King.
She had little comfort or peace of mind, however, having to
pay twenty shillings a week for herself and maid and find her
fuel and linen: 'There are now so few housekeepers, and those
that do will not board any but to get [profit] by them.' She
was doubtless of a brave, independent spirit: 'I would fain have
been with some of my friends, but I have none that do offer
me any courtesy now, or do so much as invite me to their
houses, and as long as I can live without them I will not seek
them.'[3] Why she left Richard we do not know.

Jane could hardly be expected to refrain from comparing her
economic upheaval with John's sunny paradise of travel under
Italian skies: 'I envied your happiness that have the world so
much at large for pleasure.' Nor must we blame her if she
showed no real interest in Roundhead or Cavalier: 'We through
the necessities of these times are forced to suffer a division (but

[1] Letter, Jane Evelyn to J. Evelyn, n.d. [1644].   [2] Ibid.
[3] Letter, Jane Evelyn to J. Evelyn, 14 Dec. 1644.

will assure you the contrary) but I will say no more lest I be taken for a neuter which you know is criminal';[1] she is merely voicing the country conservatism. So she beguiled. the time with her bed of knots at Twitnam, until the summer of 1645, when 'a great blessing from heaven' enabled her to join George at Wotton—who had begun housekeeping again.

Jane's letters to John now reflected her regained happiness: he had praised their 'harmony', and in modesty she protested that it 'is indeed no music of my own making', and if there was anything 'than the usual plainsong of my former lines, 'twas truly not the hand of Joah, but yours only (that in your answer hath so handsomely played upon me) which made the descant'.

Evelyn, delighted with her style, parades her letters before his fellow-travellers: she protests 'let me entreat you for your own sake to deal no copies, that those who are yet strangers to my defects, may not wonder so complete a man as yourself should have a sister no better accomplished'. She then chides him: 'You have met with fair donnas with whom you have exercised yourself into a habit of eloquence,' and sends the present letter 'to show the infinite difference which is between two, who, I will not say sucked one breast, but I am sure lay in one and the same belly', concluding, 'your completeness is the glass of my imperfections'.[2] He sent her a fan, pendants, rings, some Venice glass, and a watch costing twenty to thirty pounds which Jane considered would 'be far above most that are usually worn even by the best ladies in England'.

'So complete a man' was, of course, the approbation of a loving sister, and one to which Evelyn would hardly yet agree. Nor would he allow her accusation of any traffic with the donnas! But quite soon now he was not to be averse to a bambino! When he arrived back in Paris in 1646, he idled for a while, wrote a little and studied chemistry under Nicasius Le Febure. He also renewed his friendship with Sir Richard Browne the King's resident ambassador, and Mary his daughter, having first met them at the outset of his travels. Perhaps he then fell in love with her when she was but eight years old. But it is more likely that she was eleven when he described her

---

[1] Letter, Jane Evelyn to J. Evelyn, 9 Dec. 1644.
[2] Letter, Jane Evelyn to J. Evelyn, 27 Sept. 1646.

thus in his manuscript, *The Legend of the Pearl*: 'The prettyness and innocence of her youth had something methought in her that pleased me in a gravity I had not observed in so tender a bud: for I could call her woman for nothing, but her early steadiness, and that at the age of playing with babies, she would be at her book, her needle, drawing of pictures, casting accompts and understood to govern the house . . . she began to discourse not impertinently, was gay enough for my humour; and one I believed that might one day grow up to be the agreeable companion of an honest man: but I swear I had no more design to make her my wife, than I had to dive for pearls upon Salisbury Plain, and yet I made this creature my wife, and found a pearl.'[1]

They were married on 27 June 1647, the octave of Corpus Christi when the Paris streets were hung with tapestry and gay with flowers—as it were in their honour.

[1] Evelyn MS. 304.

CHAPTER II

Sayes Court Garden

〜〜〜〜〜〜〜〜〜〜〜〜〜〜〜〜〜〜〜〜〜〜〜〜〜〜〜〜〜〜

Two months later Evelyn returned alone to England, his 'wife being yet very young', he says, 'and therefore dispensing with a temporary and kind separation;[1] in other words, she was content to stay with her mother because her placid temperament was as yet undisturbed by her marriage. Evelyn's estate in Sussex demanded attention; political intelligence was required for his own guidance and for transmission to Sir Richard Browne; there were friendships to be renewed. He was entertained for five days at Wotton by George and Jane, and by George's second wife Mary, daughter of Sir Robert Offley, who was married at a date unknown and whom John was meeting for the first time. He must have noticed, sadly, the derelict garden, and how shamefully overgrown were his little 'improvements'. Perhaps he pondered the fecundity of the new mistress of Wotton as his eyes roamed over the house and woods he loved so well: the thought was as natural as the love for one's birthplace.

Fortunately there were other things to ponder. He was presented to King Charles at Hampton Court, 'one among the multitudes of people who repair to kiss his hands'. He was more fortunate than the crowd; he not only kissed hands, but saw him dine, and reported to Sir Richard that he thought the King 'nothing apparently changed as if he were altogether unconcerned with all those rigours of his adverse fortune', and that

[1] *Diary*, de Beer's ed., 10 Sept. 1647.

'the tranquillity which he enjoys in his own thoughts together with his confidence that God will vindicate his cause, is that which makes him ride out this storm with so much assurance'.[1]

But of all Evelyn's obligations during this visit, the most important was to find a home for himself and his young bride. In the changes of ownership of houses due to sequestration and the frequent inability to compound, the choice was large and varied: 'since my being in town, many gallant seats and reasonable purchases have been asked me,' he told Sir Richard. In other cases, purchase was extremely risky: 'The people cry out so horridly against the Army's quartering, that the sale of the Bishops' lands is virulently in agitation but none that I can hear of buys them; the very Puritan priests themselves now dissuading all their parishioners from meddling with Church lands. There was yesterday proposals touching the selling likewise of all Deans and Chapters lands, which the major part would by no means consent unto . . . in fine, if you believe they will shortly cut one another's throats it is but the sense of the whole kingdom.'[2]

Evelyn, therefore, was wary. Meanwhile, Sir Richard allowed him a *pied à terre* at his former home Sayes Court, at Deptford, now in the tenancy of Sir Richard's brother-in-law William Prettyman. Sayes Court was a modest triple-gabled Elizabethan house of three storeys in a bad state of repair. Deptford, however, was conveniently near London; but a short journey to Lambeth, then a ferry-ride over the Thames, and one was in Whitehall. Convenient as it undoubtedly was, Evelyn was not yet prepared to consider its further advantages; before any decision could be made, many more visits to other possible seats would be necessary. His relatives, too, still had claims upon him after so long an absence. Therefore, he divided his time between his London lodgings, with George and Jane at Wotton, with Richard at Baynards, and resting and writing at Sayes Court— where one day he saw, on the fringe of the garden, a party of insurgents on their way to Colchester siege.

His discordant feelings on George's second marriage had hardly been resolved when Jane told him of her recent marriage to William Glanville, a barrister, who was at Oxford in George's time. The surprise of this information did not prevent John

[1] Letter, J. Evelyn to Sir R. Browne, 25 Oct. 1647. [2] Op. cit.

19

from liking the man; he was witty—perhaps a little too witty. The important thing—that Jane was immensely happy—well-nigh dispersed John's antagonism, indeed it silenced all puritanical criticism of the family's second secret marriage. But it did—in a manner—bring the Civil War very near indeed to Wotton House. Amid John's endless journeyings these marital vagaries were soon forgotten: there was William Ducie (who became Viscount Downe) and Sir Clipsby Crew to dine with at Isleworth, and to discourse on miniatures, pictures, medals, and even flowers with the latest continental scholarship. They voiced, too, their Royalist hopes of the day when the Prince of Wales would show his hand: 'Much is here expected from the Prince,' wrote Evelyn on 4 April 1648; 'pray let us know of his motions.' But the time was not yet propitious.

In the spring of the year John was tempted to buy Bolney Court near Henley, but 'we did not accord', he writes. He sold his South Malling property for three thousand pounds,[1] and rashly bought Hurcott Manor in Worcestershire from George for £3,300, which he re-sold a little later, for a profit of one hundred pounds[2]—probably an unhappy transaction.

In all these comings and goings of business and pleasure his wife was not forgotten. At Sayes Court or in London he stole enough time to compose for her a very strange manuscript entitled *Instructions Œconomique*,[3] being thirteen chapters on the ethics of marriage. It treated of such things as conjugal offices and included Francis de Sales' discourse (in French) touching the nuptial bed. Evelyn considered that his young inexperienced wife stood in need of some enlightenment. 'Thus my dearest,' he wrote in the accompanying letter, 'having now completely furnished you with precepts, I shall rejoice and attend to see the fruits of them.' He sent the manuscript, beautifully bound in red leather and bearing his arms and motto, *Omnia Explorate, meliora retinete*, prove all things, retain the best, with his 'most real unfeigned and inviolable love, and implicit instructions to keep it under lock and key and to let no other eye peruse it', adding: 'for as none but he which had a mind to blemish his honour, would shew his wife naked.'[4] The letter was also to be kept from other eyes. Whether we regard this gift as the mani-

---

[1] *Diary*, 4 May 1648.　　　　[2] *Diary*, 2 Dec. 1648.
[3] Evelyn MS. 143.　　[4] Letter, J. Evelyn to M. Evelyn, 16 Sept. 1643.

festation of preciosity, a worthy token of practical idealism, or
of anything else, the act was typical of him. A portrait of himself
by Robert Walker, painted in July 1648, and which bore the
frank inscription in Greek, 'Repentance is the beginning of
wisdom', went with the manuscript. He would have preferred
a miniature, 'but since the late death of Oliver, and absence of
Hoskins, Johnson and the rest, could meet with none capable',
he says.[1]

What do we find of these marital revelations in the *Diary*?
The answer is nothing. Virginia Woolf said that 'he never used
its pages to reveal the secrets of his heart, and all that he wrote
might have been read aloud in the evening with a calm conscience to his children'.[2] But of course he never intended in the
Diary consciously to reveal himself. When we come to realise
what subjects were omitted, we are forced to conclude that he
constantly bore in mind both propriety and posterity.

It was perhaps fortunate that no other member of the family
was given to these pre-marital precepts. A great belly—as it was
called—gave no trouble to George's wife, who could produce
one with astonishing facility, and repeat the act with commend-
able regularity. In November, she presented George with their
first daughter, Mary, of whom later we shall hear a good deal.
Richard, despite his lack of any outstanding qualities, made an
excellent marriage with Elizabeth, daughter of George Mynne
who had a considerable estate, including the manor of Woodcott (or Woodcote Park) near Epsom,[3] where the couple lived
as comfortably as the times allowed.

There was, however, as yet, little hope of national security,
and John soon despaired of buying any property; in fact, after
hearing Ireton presiding over the 'young, raw, and ill-spoken'
Council of Officers he could not envisage them as the future
governors of the country, 'puffed up (as they are) with success,
interest, corruption'. So desperate was he, he asked Sir Richard
Browne: 'I wish you could advise me how I may prevent an
absolute ruin as to some part of my future, which I would most
willingly dispose of in some more peaceable and sober corner
of the earth; . . . even . . . my best friends . . . have thought

[1] Op. cit.
[2] 'Rambling round Evelyn' (*The Common Reader*, 1st Ser., p. 110).
[3] *Diary*, 16 Aug. 1648.

of leaving this place in a very short time, if these proceedings (of the Council) continue.'[1] These were the fears of a sensitive Royalist as events moved relentlessly forward to the execution of the King.

The great act took place on 30 January, nine days after John had published his first book, a translation, entitled *Of Liberty and Servitude*, from the French of the Sieur de la Mothe le Vayer. Its publication was badly timed; by his references in the preface to the former halcyon days under the King, John might well have risked some penalty, indeed he says he was 'severely threatn'd'. But again he does not say by whom—and we have failed to discover any record that this unimportant book, by its then little-known translator, did ever incur the wrath of the Parliament.

George was present at the execution; John—according to the *Diary*—refused to witness it and kept the day as a fast. By the end of May the office of kingship was disclaimed in the Royal Exchange, 'which could only tend', wrote John to Sir Richard, 'to an arbitrary and tyrannical enslaving of the free people'.[2] He decided to return to France.

In July, having obtained, 'with exceeding difficulty, strict examination, and great jealousy',[3] a pass—of which however there is no account—from Bradshaw (as President of the Council of State) he embarked for France with a one-eyed servant named Richard Hoare whom Sir Richard Browne had left behind at Sayes Court and who had fled to Woodcott where Evelyn found him: 'I shall have now time', Evelyn told Sir Richard, 'to reduce my studies into a method, for which end his [Hoare's] assistance will much ease and please me': an indication that John was ambitious of authorship and in no haste to settle in England. In any event, apart from Sayes Court, he had nowhere to live. When he had spent some months in Paris, Richard gave him no encouragement to return: 'I am resolved to live in so unsettled a condition as that I may pack up and be gone at any time without much trouble. Truly, should you resolve for England I should esteem it as the best way, not to settle in any place, but to live in London, and there

---

[1] Letter, J. Evelyn to Sir R. Browne, 18 Dec. 1648; *Diary*, 1854 ed.
[2] Letter, J. Evelyn to Sir R. Browne, 31 May 1649.
[3] Letter, J. Evelyn to Sir R. Browne, 21 June 1649.

as private as may be, for the country is not habitable during these distractions, which are like to continue a very long time.'[1] The rebel-patriot Cromwell was yet to come to power.

John's round of life in Paris was pleasant enough: his social aspirations were satisfied in the circles of Charles's hopeful Court; he could write, and plan the books he hoped to publish; his wife continued her singing and drawing lessons; he could approve—presumably—her assimilation of the *Instructions Œconomique*; and he delighted in writing to Jane (the letters to his brothers were usually on business matters: that could not be helped). He would tell her of the latest French fashions: 'They dress their locks so far backward that the tips of their ears may be seen, or just as if they were marching against a gentle wind'.[2] (But fashion changes were few: 'the present miseries have bred that strange humour of constancy in their attire,'[2] said Lady Garrett.) He related the sad story of his wife's 'blue satin gown upon which her mother daubed twenty pistoles of lace, and two other fine gowns made against his coming, which were all too short for her, she having never worn any save her mourning habit 'for four months': 'is not that a lamentable thing?'[3] On another occasion Jane was delighted to receive two or three hundred small oranges, dried black, to be strung as beads, bracelets, or into chaplets.

He also told her what 'an incredible comfort Sir Richard's chapel was to them, that during this persecution at home, the Church of England is not utterly lost abroad . . . the English ladies here never miss frequenting every Sunday and holiday.'[4]

To George he sent well-intentioned but lengthy advice on the making of a grotto at Wotton, specifying foreign and almost unprocurable materials with a considerable display of erudition. About this time George was thinking of employing John's cousin, Captain George Evelyn, to build a garden temple at Wotton. John said he overbuilt everything, and perhaps the temple he built—probably in 1652—was a little overwhelming for John's particular taste. Perhaps he thought it dwarfed the Mount against which it stands. George was angry with John when having £500 ready to repay a loan, John refused to

[1] Letter, R. Evelyn II to J. Evelyn, after Aug. 1649.
[2] Letter, J. Evelyn to Jane Evelyn, 5 Nov. 1649.
[3] Letter, J. Evelyn to Jane Evelyn, 27 Nov. 1649.   [4] Ibid.

deliver up the bond unless both principal and interest were paid. George, having the money ready, refused, reasonably enough, to pay any more interest, and insisted that John took the £500. Richard, acting as a go-between, said he 'durst not receive it, because the times are very dangerous' and 'he knew not where to dispose of it safely as none knows now who is whole'.[1] Fortunately, a friend agreed to keep it for fourteen or twenty-one days until John could dispose of it. Money was always less troublesome when put out to interest.

The one-eyed Hoare was kept busy transcribing into a large folio commonplace book passages of his master's reading; copying cookery and medical receipts, some of which came from Jane, 'receipts of our good grandmother, which it were pity', said Jane, 'not to propagate'; supervising the binding[2] of the books, and making John's illuminated books of devotion. He was also making resolutions—only to be broken—to overcome his weakness for the bottle. John's admonitions against this vice must have been driven home with visions of hell-fire—at least Hoare said that they were administered 'with a kind of passion', and that 'the consideration of my own damnation . . . is of force sufficient to terrify me from the committing it, since I am resolved to be your convert'. Not permanently, however. On too little evidence, Hoare has been described by Dr. Keynes as a 'heaven-sent secretary for a bibliophil, and clearly appreciated by Evelyn to the full';[3] for his calligraphy and occasional engraving,[4] perhaps, but not otherwise.

In the new year of 1652, John received news of the death, a fortnight before, of Jane, which cast a heavy gloom on William Glanville, over Wotton, and himself, perhaps heaviest of all on himself: 'there is yet an expedient to render you', he wrote to Glanville, 'as happy in another wife, none to console your poor brother with so dear a sister . . . so great a part even of my better nature and inclinations'. As the sad news coincided with his plans to return to England, the bonds between Wotton and

---

[1] Letter, R. Evelyn II to J. Evelyn, 8 May 1650.

[2] A. Bosse made the drawings for Evelyn's arms and monograph ornament which were engraved by Abraham Symons (of the Mint) for use as binding stamps.

[3] *John Evelyn*, 1937, p. 22.

[4] See H. Walpole, *Catal. of Engravers*, 1763, p. 79.

Part of the

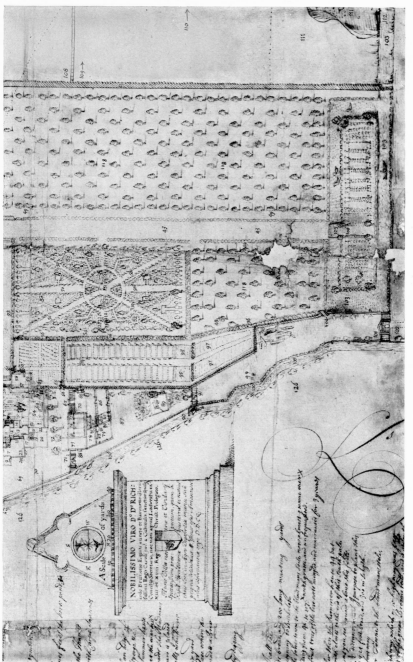

Sayes Court Garden Plan, 1653

Paris must have seemed to him irremediably weakened. It was so true that Jane was a part of his better nature; she had always understood his loftiest aspirations. In March 1650 when she told him how happy she was to be a mother, she touched him deeply—as only she could: 'The best return I can make', she replied to his congratulations, 'is to wish you a father, to beget a son.' It was his greatest wish. And she understood so intimately the finer part of paternity; when he had a son, she said, 'you will quickly perceive that the merits of a good husband are at once recompensed and increased.'[1] He looked forward to the fulfilment of her words; his remembrance of them would be her memorial.

John desired to see for himself whether England was habitable, and to test the amenities of Sayes Court. There was a national resurgence, perhaps not yet definable—except in the Navy's aspirations—but it was promising. If conditions proved tolerable he would send for his wife and Lady Browne.

January 26 was practically a windless day; he left Calais and drifted slowly and tediously across to Dover for thirteen hours —which was a rare experience in winter. Two days later he took horse for Canterbury, having sent a few quaint lines to his wife saying that when they met shortly at Dover she would have 'cod and the best fish this town can afford'.[2] From Canterbury he rode through the Kentish winter scene to Sittingbourne, then on to Rochester for the night. The next day brought him to Gravesend, completing his journey by wherry up the estuary to Deptford, where, in a few months' time, he would witness great naval activity against the Dutchman Tromp. Would it not be strange if a lover of peace should come to live so near a dockyard?

But as yet he had decided nothing. There were many problems to solve. Was his young inexperienced wife to be wrenched from the civilised society of the ambassadorial circle and planted in the purlieus of a dockyard? Could she shoulder the burdens of housekeeping? Her instruction in singing and drawing—still in progress—was hardly a qualification for the still-room. There was a possibility that Uncle Prettyman might marry, share a lease and the cost of housekeeping—but it was

---

[1] Letter, Jane Evelyn to J. Evelyn, 1 March 1650.
[2] Letter, J. Evelyn to M. Evelyn, 27 Jan. 1652.

only a possibility. John reckoned that he and his wife and Lady Browne could live on £300 a year, including the luxury of a coach: in Paris, he said, they spent £400, and in some years, £500. Lady Browne was not at all anxious to be uprooted: persuasion would be required. John reckoned that the old Elizabethan house could be repaired this year, the gardens—neglected and overgrown—the next. He sent his wife a list of necessary plate: it was plainer—and cheaper—in France, and would be 'entertainment enough'. John's economy also forced his wife to forgo a necklace of pearl in favour of a coach.

To these harassing choices and problems, John—little hardened by his travels—added a doubt whether the English air suited him, and concerned himself that his wife's last Paris bill was not 'circumscribed within the sum' he mentioned: 'I beseech my dear wife therefore to exercise her discreet frugality.'

Her health in February was apparently somewhat irregular and her complexion blemished: 'I am not a little sorry', he wrote, 'that the sulphur does not proceed any better . . . exercise and the use of natural waters I am told are most likely to recover you; for unless those accidents be perfectly cured, it is impossible you should make a grandfather.'[1] (Evelyn felt that his wife was still attached to her father.) Fourteen days later, without waiting for any reply on the subject of Sayes Court, he writes that he will expect them some time in May, and—'be careful of your face, my dear'. In March, Lady Browne was still doubtful of her safety in England; Mrs. Evelyn deemed it unwise for John to change the air of Paris for an unkind climate, and criticised his domestic arithmetic: 'If (as you say) you spent four or five hundred pound a year here . . . which I much wonder at, not knowing of above two hundred for diet, my clothes, servants, wages, and masters; for the rest you can best tell.' Womanlike, she justified her estimated expenditure: 'I shall leave out such things as shall bring it within what you desire though truly I do not remember any thing unnecessary.'[2]

Early in May, measures more drastic were taken to alleviate her continued irregularity of health, being let blood in the arm and foot. On the 25th, she or her mother or her doctor at last

[1] Letter, J. Evelyn to M. Evelyn, 8 Feb. 1652.
[2] Letter, M. Evelyn to J. Evelyn, 30 March 1652.

realised that Mrs. Evelyn's condition was none other than the sixth month of a pregnancy: she wrote to her husband: 'I must confess I never was more surprised . . . after all that physic and letting blood, which was enough to have destroyed it.' She was, naturally, apprehensive of the dangerous journey; the longer sea voyage from Dieppe, necessitated by the movement of Condé's troops to the east of Paris; the risks of capture by the picaroons or of being sighted by the Dutch fleet; and to land at Rye (where there was great rigour of search) with seventeen bales of furniture, knowing that Mrs. Windham had all her belongings confiscated 'for having only one piece of new stuff unmade-up'. She had asked her husband (with rare political wisdom for a seventeen-year-old) whether some 'powerful person could get you some favour' at Rye. In fact, Evelyn had already obtained the good offices and a pass for her landing from Colonel Morley of the Council of State (and an old school-fellow).

Although Mrs. Evelyn was to join her husband, she could not forget that she was to leave her father; she tells Evelyn it will cause 'very much grief to part from so good a father', and that 'I scarce have time to assure you of my affection, but I hope you will believe that since I must quit my father for any man living, I should not do it for one that I love more than your self'. His last letter to her before she sailed assured her of his 'exceeding contentments' in her condition, 'the first apparent pledge of our dearest affections, and the expectations of so many years, for all which you have now abundantly gratified your loving husband, who calls incessantly upon God to protect you and his dearest child'.

The packet-boat arrived after being three days at sea. Evelyn exaggerated the risks of their voyage by recording in the *Diary* that they 'hardly escaped the whole Dutch fleet'; in fact, it was lying off the Flemish coast.[1] Doubtless he was overwhelmed with joy when he made up the *Diary* on this day of their reunion.

For a month the ladies stayed at Tonbridge—where Evelyn presented his wife with her new coach—until the dust of the masonry had settled at Sayes Court. On 24 August Evelyn became a proud and exuberant father of a boy 'every way

[1] *Diary*, de Beer's ed., 11 June 1653, *note 3.*

perfect and hopeful', the mother having passed through 'the rudest conflicts of six or seven hours besides the first approaches for twelve before'; the child born 'precisely at the hour of one at noon, as I could calculate by a ring or universal dial which I consulted very carefully at the very point and minute', he informed Sir Richard. Three weeks later it was: 'Your godson is as fine a child as ever I saw.' The *Instructions Œconomique* were justified.

Many a virtuoso of the seventeenth century would have said that Sayes Court was not worth rebuilding and too near the Deptford dockyard to justify any attempt to convert the adjacent grasslands into a show-place. But what was formerly a field of a hundred acres Evelyn transformed into a garden charming in its variety. He had seen the gardens of Italy, France, and England, and would improve on them all. He certainly adopted little of the Tudor uniformity with its interminable and uninspiring geometrical patterns, nor was he desirous of a garden of Bacon's princely dimensions, or content with John Rea's meagre suggestion of 40 yards square of fruit and 20 yards square of flowers.

The plan, drawn up in 1652, was 'the guide of all our designs', he tells Sir Richard in September, and with little alteration adhered to. The aspect was south and west of the house, itself sheltered by a few old hollow elms. Directly to the south he made two walled bowling greens divided by gravel walks and planted with cypress—the walls with fruit trees. Beyond and in line with the bowling green gate he planted an avenue of lime trees, 300 feet long, forming a drive which led to the main entrance gates. On either side of the lime avenue stretched a grass expanse of the field he called the hither Broomefield, the boundaries of its five acres marked by newly planted ash and elm. Beyond this field was a footway, later known as Butt Lane, which led to Deptford.

Beyond the eastern wall of the bowling green he laid down a pleasant grass plot to be called the Milking Close, considerately planted with eight walnut trees under which the cows were milked. Still farther to the east he made a carp pond 'new dug and raild' which was fed by each tide of the river ditch: it also served as a watering-place for the cows and horses.

Immediately to the west of the house, Evelyn had his walled private garden of choice flowers and simples, interspersed with gravel walks and grass alleys. At the end of one of the alleys was an arbour under two old tall elms in the corner; in the centre a fountain played. Here he kept his aviary wherein the Marquis of Argyll, in 1656, mistook the turtle-doves for owls, and the new transparent bee-hive, in which, said Pepys, 'you may see the bees making their honey and combs mighty pleasantly'.[1] It was given to Evelyn by Dr. Wilkins of Wadham College and 'built like castles and palaces, and so ordered one upon another, as to take the honey without destroying the bees . . . adorned with a variety of dials, little statues, vases',[2] which the restored King was later to come especially to see. Except for bowling greens and private gardens of choice plants, Evelyn disapproved of walling; 'rather therefore let such partitions be made of contr'espaliers' and hedges of evergreens and flowering shrubs.[3]

On the western side of his private garden stood the 'elaboratorie' with a pillared portico (where for another five or six years he continued to practise chemistry), and over it a pigeon-house for wild pigeons. This overlooked the nursery garden. Adjoining the nursery garden on the north was the kitchen garden of '38 beds of potherbs, besides borders', with separate plots for melons, peas, and beans. A magnificent lilac hedge formed the western boundary of the kitchen and nursery gardens and the eastern boundary of the Grove.

The Grove was very dear to Evelyn's heart, based, and perhaps an improvement, on Pierre Morin's Paris garden: 'if God prosper us,' Evelyn wrote to Sir Richard, 'my Morin garden . . . will far exceed that both for design and other accommodation';[4] and he used Morin's *Catalogues de quelques plantes à fleurs*, 1651. The Grove was divided by several walks, meanders, and thickets, some in the design of spider claws, planted with a thousand of his favourite evergreen alaternus (which he introduced into England as a hedging plant), French walnuts, and five hundred trees of oak, ash, elm, service, beech,

---

[1] *Diary*, 5 May 1665.
[2] Evelyn's *Diary*, 13 July 1654.
[3] Evelyn MS. 45.
[4] Letter, J. Evelyn to Sir R. Browne, 2 May 1653.

and chestnut; and he said in 1654 that he intended to plant therein another eight hundred.[1]

To the south, bordering the southern end of the nursery garden and the Grove—and overlooking them—was a narrow terrace grass walk or mount in the Bacon style 'of some pretty height to look abroad into the fields', hedged on the south with holly, on the north with berberis. Beyond the Mount on the southern side was the Oval Garden of evergreen thickets 'for birds, private walks, shades, and cabinetts', grass plots set about with flower-pots (as in the essentially Tudor garden at Wilton) and a round parterre of box with twelve beds of flowers, 'and passages betwixt each bed'.

For the management of box—which he clipped into mottoes —he followed Parkinson, though in the flower-garden Evelyn preferred the partridge-eyed or Spanish pink to Box: 'When it comes to blow, the wonderful beauty of the flower will infinitely exceed all other fringes . . . also lavender-cotton does well and any plant which grows thick and is patient of clipping.'[2] Of flowers, the tulip comes first with him, and he benefited by several pages in manuscript on their culture, sent from his friend and neighbour at Lewisham, the flower enthusiast Sir Thomas Hanmer.

Extending along the western edge of the Oval Garden and of the Grove was a long, cool, narrow grass promenade, 526 feet long, and 21 feet broad, palisaded with hedges of codlins and pearmaines. This formed the eastern boundary of the Great Orchard, planted at the 'new moon, wind west', with three hundred fruit trees of the 'best sorts mingled'.

At the southern end of this delightful promenade stood a miniature banqueting-house to be used chiefly by his children for shelter, frolic, and picnic. At the northern end a drawbridge led over a moat—stored with carps, swans, ducks, and a boat —to a small delectable island planted with hedges of fruit, eight beds of asparagus, raspberries, a mulberry tree, and adorned with a summer-house: a treasure island indeed.

Apparently Evelyn disregarded topiary work, except for 'knobbs and pyramids at the corners of beds—which also my Lord Bacon approves', and pleached trunks; in fact, the

---

[1] Letter, J. Evelyn to Sir R. Browne, 23 Jan. 1654.
[2] Evelyn MS. 45.

gardening authorities such as Bacon, Parkinson, Worlidge, and Blake with their insistence on rectangular or geometrical uniformity had little attraction for him: 'at no hand', he says, 'let our workman enforce his plot to any particular fancy, but contrive rather how to apply to it the best shape that will agree with the nature of the place . . . that so the shade and the lights may fall and diversify in sweet and gracious varieties, and which may be effected with a great deal more facility where the site is uneven by Nature or easily made so by Art, than by those starch't and affected designs which we behold in many of our Cockney Plantations that look like gardens of pasteboard and marchpane, and which smell more of paint than of flowers and natural verdue.'[1] George sent quails, pigeons and a pair of turtles 'to alarm you in the morning with their melancholy note and innocent courtship'. Richard presented to his brother one hundred elms and twenty oaks to make a walk from the house to the water, and transferred his gardener— who was to receive six pounds a year from Evelyn.

The garden at Sayes Court was the realisation of an ideal. Or almost so; for when the wind was northerly, Evelyn must have been reminded to remove the hens, the dung pit, the kitchen garden privy, the pigs and the house of office further afield, being all within twenty-five yards of his study. As to the house, he was to confess, later: 'better I had done to have pulled all down at first'. There was no such thing as perfection —though we would not expect him to admit it.

Nevertheless, Evelyn set a new standard in English garden-design. His use of evergreens was particularly admired. Roger North at some time after 1664 says the garden 'was exquisite, being most boscaresque, and as it were, an exemplar of his book of forest trees. They appeared all so thriving and clean that in so much variety no one could be satiated in viewing.' Pepys was another enthusiast, who recorded that the evergreens and hedge of holly were the finest things he ever saw in his life.[2]

For many of his shrubs and evergreens Evelyn was under considerable obligation to Pierre Morin of Paris; not only for his 1651 catalogue of plants, but also for cultural directions— sent on by Sir Richard Browne. Many of Morin's shrubs were little known in England, perhaps only known to Sir Thomas

[1] Evelyn MS. 45.   [2] *Diary*, 5 Oct. 1665.

Hanmer, shrubs such as Cistus, Tragacantha, Cytisus, Jasmin des Indes, and Sedum. These, and several others 'are all unknown to me,' Evelyn says; 'such of them as may be conveyed in seeds I would give any price for; especially the six sorts of phyleria you mention and what other M. Morin shall think proper for our climate.'[1]

Although, by 1652, Evelyn possessed all the important gardening books of the sixteenth and early seventeenth centuries, his general avoidance of Tudor and Jacobean design, apart from twelve flower beds laid in a circle in his Oval Parterre, is the measure of his originality. On the other hand, for *method* and *varieties* he was indebted to many of the leading English authorities, such as Hill, Lawson, Mascall, Markham, Standish, Tusser, Parkinson, Blith, and Blake. He learnt, too, from experience, of course, and in subsequent plantings of apples, pears, and cherries dropped in 1669, or in 1684–86, some of the varieties—chosen in 1653 from Parkinson—in favour of others recommended in Rea's *Flora, Ceres et Pomona*, 1665. And again, Evelyn prefers lilac, berberis, holly, and palisaded fruit trees for hedging rather than the old-fashioned pyracantha recommended by Parkinson and others.[2]

By 1653 or so Evelyn felt himself qualified to make his own contribution to gardening literature; he had seen the finest gardens abroad, he had read widely on the subject and he had had practical experience. He began to write the *Elysium Britannicum*—the title deriving from his definition of a garden as 'a place of all terrestriall enjoyments the most resembling Heaven and the best representation of our lost felicity. It is the common term and the pit from whence we were dug; we all came out of the parsley-bed—at least according to the creed of a poet (Lucretius, V, 807–10). As no man can be very miserable that is master of a garden here; so will no man ever be happy who is not sure of a garden hereafter. From thence we came, and thither we tend; where the first Adam fell, the second arose. Kings, philosophers, and wise men spent their choicest hours in them; and when they would frame a type of Heaven, because there is nothing in nature more worthy and illustrious, they describe a garden, and call it Elysium.'

[1] Letter, J. Evelyn to Sir R. Browne, 18 Oct. 1656.
[2] Evelyn MS. 45.

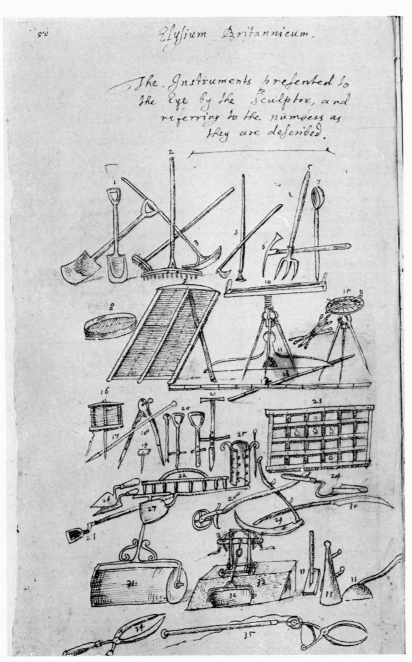

Evelyn's gardening tools as used and drawn by him, *c.* 1660
(From his unfinished gardening MS. *Elysium Britannicum*)

[*Facing p. 32*

Evelyn's gardening tools (*continued*)

This manuscript[1] treated of gardening in all its aspects, and comprised nearly 900 folio pages, of which 342 have survived. Evelyn had this by him for the rest of his life, always expanding, amending, and including new facts, or things read: perfection was unattainable. As time went on, the work got out of hand; the inexhaustible number of insertions put all out of scale and it never got into print.

To return to 1652: his boy was thriving—a joy temporarily clouded in October by the death of Lady Browne. His second publication, *The State of France*, appeared this year, another small slim volume notable for little else but the widely quoted phrase of 'counting steeples', a phrase, however, not Evelyn's but borrowed from his fellow-traveller Thomas Henshaw; writing from Venice on 20 April 1647, he told Evelyn that he was 'so tired with this pilgrim's life of counting steeples'.

In November, Evelyn was saddened by the Dutch victory off Dungeness, and expressed his belief to Sir Richard that only the restored monarchy could stabilise the country. Yet his gloom gradually dispersed, perhaps, as he witnessed Deptford's share in the drastic naval re-organisation which was to lead to Blake's victory over Tromp in February. At least, some sign of republican virtue in the new year persuaded Evelyn to lay out £3,500 for the purchase of Sayes Court; and all former doubts of stability or prowess at sea could be excused as he exclaimed after the victory, to Sir Richard: 'I adore God's judgments, whose ways are past our investigations.'[2] In June Blake's victory off Harwich regained for the Navy complete control of the English Channel. Evelyn was convinced that his money was well spent.

Mrs. Evelyn, whose housekeeping responsibilities were still shared by Uncle Prettyman's servants, spent much time in painting and designing; in May Sir Richard is assured that she is 'improved to admiration; few painters in England being able to design more masterly'; she 'far out designs' her drawing master Monsieur du Guernier of Paris (who was with her every second or third day) 'and will go very near to outpaint him'.[3] She was expecting her second child in October.

---

[1] Evelyn MS. 45.
[2] Letter, J. Evelyn to Sir R. Browne, 28 Feb. 1653.
[3] Letter, J. Evelyn to Sir R. Browne, 2 May 1653.

We are beginning to notice that Evelyn desired posterity to think well of himself, of his wife and family, and of his friends; that all were practically immune to natural frailty. This is particularly noticeable in the *Diary*. Even Richard Hoare must not be allowed to appear as human as the generality of mankind; if he happens to get apoplexy, he gets it in a laudable manner. Therefore, we read in the *Diary*, 17 May 1653, that 'he fell of a fit of apoplexy, caused, as I suppose, by tampering with mercury about an experiment on gold'. But we are not convinced by Evelyn's '*I suppose*', especially as we remember the nature of Hoare's previous experiments. It is remarkable that no volumes written or illuminated by him can be dated after 1653, nor is there any further mention of him after 1654 until 5 July 1658 when Evelyn tells Sir Richard that he is working in an office in London, 'grown very sober'. The inference is that he was sacked for intemperance—a reflection on Evelyn's prescience that went unrecorded in the *Diary*.

In October Mrs. Evelyn duly presented her husband with his second son, and George conveyed to him his congratulations somewhat pointedly, praying 'that God will fill your quiver with such arrows that we may not be ashamed to meet our enemies within our gates'.[1] George said that his wife, too, was 'in the straw';[2] in fact, the fertility at Sayes Court, Wotton and Westcott caused a long succession of begettings and, alas, burials of children; family visits, in consequence, were for the most part either congratulatory or condolatory. George and his wife were mourning their child in November; altogether George lost four sons in infancy by his first wife, and six children by his second wife. Richard also lost four sons, and by 1658 John, too, was to lose the same number.

With the winter planting completed Evelyn could begin to enjoy his garden in the new year of 1654: 'Now in truth the labour and expense over, I find the pleasure of adorning, fitting, and sprucifying the place renders me some return.'[3] He was also thinking in monetary terms of the outskirts of his estate: 'In the Butt Lane, I have already set out and ditching—in some ground which I hope to improve by letting out to

---

[1] Letter, G. Evelyn to J. Evelyn, 4 Oct. 1653.   [2] *O.E.D.*, 1661.
[3] Letter, J. Evelyn to Sir R. Browne, 23 Jan. 1654.

building in time.' The first leases began in 1654—mostly for a few pounds: every few years he let more ground, until his income from this source amounted, in 1690, to £600 yearly. The promise of his environment was reflected in the contemporary political scene—or at least he was just now in optimistic mood: 'We shall see good times again. I despair now less than ever: many eyes are opened,' he wrote to Sir Richard on 23 January. Two days later the household was plunged in sadness when his new baby son died of convulsions.

On 8 June Evelyn and his wife set out in their coach and four on a sightseeing tour of the greater part of England: a respite from building for himself and a change from domestic worries for his wife. During a week at Oxford in July he first met Christopher Wren, 'that miracle of a youth' and 'prodigious young scholar' as he calls him. In later life, they were to meet on many occasions and projects, but there is no evidence of any great friendship between them. Perhaps Wren was a little too professional, too much of a specialist to encourage the versatile Evelyn.

If John appeared to be content with the renovated Sayes Court, George was not so sure that his brother had made a good bargain; in November he had advised him to realise on it 'now you have made it so handsome and convenient', and to buy the estate of Squerryes in Westerham, 'a very complete uniform house and excellent waters where you may make very rare fountains ... water comes into all offices ... wood enough for your fire ... a warren well paled ... excellent fish ponds'. He told John that he could 'compass the money by selling your scattering lands in Sussex and at Wasley in Essex: I believe these may bring you £6000':[1] Westerham would cost £7500 and John could borrow the rest. But he would not be tempted, and continued to turn a blind eye to the menacing dockyard, despite the importunity of Sir Nicholas Crisp who just now was trying to bargain away some of Evelyn's land for the erection of a mole. His heart had gone into the last two years' work, and where his heart was he would remain. With another winter came his third son and the only one to survive—to be named John. Twelve months later Evelyn's political optimism had momentarily faded: 'The Church undone, the new ones flourishing,

[1] Letter, G. Evelyn to J. Evelyn, 25 Nov. 1653.

35

the taxes increasing, and wise men possess themselves in patience.'[1]

In the spring of 1656 Evelyn spent a few days at Wotton: to his wife he wrote the nearest approach to a love-letter which has survived: 'I have been so affected for the loss of your company, that, if you had been within my thoughts, you would there have discovered some tendernesses which I cannot express, and such indeed as I myself have not been so sensible of at other times when we have been less separated . . . You will hardly believe that the history of Artaban[2] (which I finished in the coach) raised such passions in me, as I am almost ashamed to tell you . . .'[3] It is remarkable that the earliest surviving letters to his wife cannot in any sense be termed love-letters.

[1] Letter, J. Evelyn to Sir. R. Browne, 29 Jan. 1656.
[2] La Calprenède: *Cléopâtre*.
[3] Letter, J. Evelyn to Mrs. Evelyn, 16 April 1656.

CHAPTER III

Creative Period

~~~~~~

T HE publication in 1656 of Evelyn's translation of Lucretius
set up a rhythm in his creative work as regular as in, and
perhaps related to, the procreative. His Lucretius, however, was
hardly successful; later he confessed it to be a 'knotty piece
undertaken when he was very young and therefore very rash'.
(But we must remember that he was thirty-five years old when
he allowed it to appear.) In 1658 by translating Nicolas de
Bonnefons' *Le Jardinier François* he gained his first notice in
print as a gardener. Curiously, in the introduction, he almost
disdains the work; although it treats excellently of soil, situation,
and planting, and became very popular, he says he would
rather introduce, out of his own experience, the *appendices* to
gardens. He then cites—as if to advertise—some of the many
chapter headings of the *Elysium Britannicum*—the parterre,
grottoes, fountains, aviaries, vivaries, piscinas, groves, statues,
the palisades and contr'-espaliers of alaternus 'which most incomparable verdure together with the right culture of it [for
the moment he had forgotten Monsieur Morin] I might glory
to have been the first propagator in England'. In the second
edition of 1669—and in the later ones—this enthusiasm for his
manuscript was omitted, perhaps indicating his unwillingness
to put it in order for printing; or simply because he then realised
that it was totally irrelevant to *The French Gardener*. Furthermore, with his obligations to Morin in mind, we can hardly
approve his criticism of monsieurs 'new come over who think

37

we are as much obliged to follow their mode of gardening as we do that of their garments, till we become in both ridiculous'.

Evelyn's next publication was intimately associated with the greatest sorrow he had yet experienced. His son Richard had developed into an extraordinarily clever and beautiful child. At three and a half years of age he could 'repeat above a hundred words in French, and had a prodigious memory and affection to pictures', wrote his father. Three months later he was 'infinitely beyond' his cousin Jack of Wotton 'in his understanding and learning'. At four and a half his father's opinion is that 'he must needs emerge a prodigious learned man'. At four years and eight months having 'most perfectly conquered the active and passive of our grammar verbs, he is now falling upon the nouns'. At five he 'can read this very ugly hand which I write,' says his father, modestly to Sir Richard, 'and any of your letters'. As a gardener, Evelyn may well have feared that such early blossom rarely bore lasting fruit, and on 27 January 1658, at five and a half years of age, his son died 'after six fits of a quartan ague . . . we lost the prettiest and dearest child that ever parents had', mourned his father; 'a prodigy for wit and understanding, for beauty of body a very Angel, and for endowments of mind of incredible and rare hopes.'

This great blow was quickly followed by another; a fortnight afterwards Evelyn wrote to Sir Richard: 'The hand that struck me so severely in that dear child, has also since taken away my other small infant in the arms of its nurse, after a seven weeks languishing in breeding the teeth so that now the cup of our afflictions is full and flowing over. Thus you see me, Sir, reduced to one from four. But I submit, and had therefore these blessings for a punishment, and I have constantly begged of God that I might receive it in this world . . . and obtain mercy hereafter . . . without this consideration I find nothing in all philosophy capable to allay the impression of it.'[1] A month later, Evelyn gives Sir Richard a touching picture of his sorrowing household: 'My losses are so great as I can never hope to see repaired in every instance, and therefore I must mourn as long as I want my children (that dear one especially) and that will be so long as I live . . . I wish my wife were as well fortified as myself, but she is still in tears, and in every corner of this

[1] Letter, J. Evelyn to Sir R. Browne, 15 Feb. 1658.

house she hears the voice, and sees the face of her dear companion, that strangely cheerful and beautiful child: but I begin to be transported . . . but I cannot help it.'[1] We see him—a sad and sombre figure—wearing a black 'studying' cap like a Doctor of the Sorbonne.

He turned for consolation to the translation of a little book by St. John Chrysostom—*The Golden Book concerning the education of children* which he published late in 1658, dated 1659. The *Epistle Dedicatory*, relating his son's prodigious attainments, was addressed to his brothers, whose losses of children were no less affecting. Yet Evelyn almost forfeits our sympathy by making a tiresome comparison: 'You have, brothers, both of you lost children, but none of them for whom you had reason to be so sensible as my self, because they died infants and could not so entirely engage your affections as if they had arrived to years of more maturity.' He had forgotten the simple truth that all parents have affection for their children. George's wife in particular mourned passionately for her children, and was yet to lose her six-year-old son and another twelve months old in 1662, two years before she herself literally died of grief.

Evelyn's next book—another small slim volume—*A Character of England* appeared in 1659. It is a criticism of English habits and manners—an English habit in itself—inspired, in part, by the author's experiences in 1652 on his arrival at Dover and during his journey via Rochester to London. His reception at English inns, the insanitary streets of London, its undistinguished buildings and smoke-laden air, doubtless all seemed somewhat barbarous to him, with Paris and its greater refinements still fresh in his mind.

His next publication was of more importance, born of the changing political temper and the Royalist hopes of the King's return. Although Oliver Cromwell had died in 1658, and Richard Cromwell 'his tame successor decently laid aside', a man hostile to Westminster was still likely to be called a traitor. Nevertheless, republicanism was now like a dismasted ship without a compass, and the moment of Royalist salvage was drawing near. Yet desperately confused seas had to be navigated. The hopes of the Royalists—raised in August 1659 by Booth—were dashed by Lambert's victory over him. To Sir

[1] Letter, J. Evelyn to Sir R. Browne, 11 March 1658.

Richard, Evelyn described this reverse as 'a conjuncture the saddest and the most distracted that ever England saw: Booth proclaimed traitor . . . God of his infinite misericord preserve us.'[1] By November the wavering loyalties to the Parliament and a lack of belief in the might of the sword bred chaos, military and mental; Monck and Lambert bent not on fighting, but fraternisation, caused Evelyn to exclaim: 'We are in the height of all confusion and misery . . . some cessation were like to be 'twixt Monck and Lambert: nothing is certain, every moment produces new changes: O that some person of honour might be sent to demand your Master's restitution.'[2]

This desire was urgent in Evelyn's heart, for six days before—on 4 November—he had chosen to publish 'an Apology for the Royal Party', an attack on the Parliament and a plea for the King's return. Yet, as soon as it was in print he must have had grave doubts whether he had chosen the right moment to voice the general longing for peace and monarchy; there was a report that the King had embraced the Roman Catholic religion and dismissed his Protestant council: Evelyn wrote to Sir Richard, saying that unless 'it be suddenly contradicted, your master is utterly ruined as to his interest here in what ever party, if this be true, though he had never a fairer game than at present'.[3]

But we hear no more of the King's conversion; Evelyn at once approached his old school-fellow Colonel Morley (recently deposed from the Council of State—and therefore likely to be tractable) with a copy of *The Apology* (which was, in fact, addressed to him) to move for the King's restoration. Actually, Evelyn had precipitated the moment for action by Morley, and his like; furthermore, he had overestimated Morley's prestige; the seas were subsiding, though Evelyn chose the wrong pilot. He found his reward by seeing his pamphlet four times printed and the Royalist cause well served thereby.

When the new year opened the right man was not discernible by anyone. Monck was certainly gathering power and an army as he approached London. But to Evelyn there was no consolation in 'the barefaced owning of Monck, the acquiescency of all parties, and the pitiful slavery of the City'; for they gave him reason 'to believe that things are as far off from what most

[1] Letter, J. Evelyn to Sir R. Browne, 11 Aug. 1659.
[2] Letter, J. Evelyn to Sir R. Browne, 10 Nov. 1659.   [3] Op. cit.

here do breathe after, and thought so sure, as ever they were.
It is as apparent as the sun at noon that such opportunities have
been lost, as cannot easily be imagined should ever offer themselves again, when we were here for eight weeks without
Parliament and without Army . . . and when two thousand
men might have as easily marched into London, and put
an end to all this, by seizing on the bone, as I do write this
letter.'[1]

Evelyn was not far wrong; and it was Monck who seized the
bone of the Rump, and having seized it—and the power—
remained inscrutable as to what he would do; 'our pendulous
thoughts concerning Monck', wrote Evelyn. A month later
Monck declared for a full Parliament, for an adequate representation of the nation. Thus ended the Rump Parliament; Evelyn
described to Sir Richard the well-known scene, the two thousand bonfires in London, the music, the shouts, 'the Rump is
beshitten': 'the whole city seemed to be on fire, and the people
besides their wits, in sum such a revolution as after ages will
hardly believe . . . the soldiers were caressed, the sack and
claret was drunk like water in the streets, and whole sides of
mutton with the rump to it roasted at divers of the bonfires.'
Yet Evelyn feared—wrongly—that Monck 'has too much kindness for a Commonwealth', and prayed 'that he may fall into
the councils of honest men'.[2] Monck, by admitting to Parliament the secluded members, needed no other counsel. He
became Captain-General, and slowly but inevitably the nation
looked to him to recall the King. Terms for his return were
thrashed out by Monck and his Presbyterian supporters. The
Long Parliament—dissolved on 16 March—would enable the
next, free, Parliament to negotiate with Charles: Sir John
Greenville sailed to arrange the preliminaries.

Evelyn, undeterred by his failure to cast Morley for the chief
role, soon had another opportunity to demonstrate his Royalist
sympathies. In March, Marchamont Needham attacked the
King's character in *News from Brussels*, to which Evelyn—
though ill at the time—at once replied in the King's defence
with *Late News from Brussels unmasked*. This reply, written
'sitting up long in my bed', says Evelyn, 'had caused a small

[1] Letter, J. Evelyn to Sir R. Browne, 5 Jan. 1660.
[2] Letter, J. Evelyn to Sir R. Browne, 13 Feb. 1660.

relapse', and in April he was advised to recuperate in his 'sweet and native air at Wotton', staying with his brother George.

John's absence from Deptford added to his wife's burdens of housekeeping the task of rent-collecting: 'I am sorry our tenants put us to these shifts,' he begins a bullying letter: 'you must dun and quicken the tenants and send often to them. I would have you write earnestly . . . that you want your money and that I made you rely on it . . . it cannot but have some opera-tion for very shame.' As to his own health, 'I hope there is a good progress for I have never exceeded your orders, yet I continue hot after meals, and this morning rose in a great sweat . . . the hemerroids much afflict me, so that I cannot take the rhubarb as I intended.' He concludes by reminding her, in his characteristic manner, of her duties: 'I know you visit all things about the house, and it much rejoices me.'[1]

His letters—addressed to the *Hawk and Pheasant* on Ludgate Hill, and thence via London Bridge to Deptford—travelled slowly, and when they crossed his wife's letters, seemed to her somewhat infrequent; and she feels his absence: 'I must not doubt of your health amongst such excellent friends as you are with, yet I should be glad to hear from you oftener and receive a confirmation of it . . . do but imagine how we designed to live in our cells and you may judge of my life from the time I rise to my going to bed, as regularly and as pleasantly as I could propose if I might add the contentment of visiting you in your solitude which is the only want I find, my ambition being not so great as it is believed.'[2] Evelyn went on to Woodcott, where Mrs. Evelyn—having travelled in the Greenwich coach —joined him, her murmurs dispelled.

To return from the domestic scene to the political, the Com-missioners appointed in May to invite the King—now at Breda —to return included Lord Berkeley, who invited Evelyn to accompany him in a private capacity—'accidentally to accom-pany' him is the way Evelyn puts it. This invitation was undoubtedly a recognition of his recent services on behalf of the King; however, he would not accept; he says that his 'newly-repaired health has excused me that ceremony which (as I am infinitely impatient of journey by sea) the ill accom-

[1] Letter, J. Evelyn to Mrs. Evelyn, 23 April 1660.
[2] Letter, Mrs. Evelyn to J. Evelyn, 27 April 1660.

modation which is to be expected would have much prejudice'. In any case, Evelyn believed 'that His Majesty will prevent even this expedition by a greater one of his own upon the arrival of Sir John Greenville who is gone to hasten his coming'.[1] But he was wrong; the Commissioners duly sailed, and on 29 May returned with the King. As regards Greenville's commission to convey Monck's terms, Evelyn was lamentably out-of-date with the news, for it had been completed by early April.

Now that the political seas were so calm, it was a little unfortunate that Evelyn disliked sleeping in a hammock; he missed hearing from Charles's own lips the compliments for his recent pamphlets—but as it turned out, the pleasure was one merely to be deferred. Modestly, Evelyn told Sir Richard (just before the King sailed) the Court news he had heard, that he 'spake such things of me as are too glorious a record for greater services than it has lain in my humble sphere to perform, who have done but my duty and that in so few instances'.[2]

Evelyn advised Sir Richard to return. Even if we make allowances for a privileged son-in-law, Evelyn adopts a curiously dictatorial manner to the erstwhile Ambassador; but perhaps he needed a goad. 'I wish . . . that you now lay fast hold on the opportunity, and to be about your Master and return to your native country . . . but you can best judge what addresses and what choice to make, and I will not presume to direct you . . .' Then he gives a broad 'directing' hint: 'His Majesty will be here within a very few days and his Council one of the first things to be established.'[3] Four days later, his health now recovered, he gave more advice: 'You have so many friends about His Majesty that it will be your own fault if you miscarry in anything that you shall desire. However, considering how incessantly H.M. is already beset with clients, suitors, and candidates for all places and offices of advantage, and remembering how often you have been neglected by such as you esteem your fastest friends, it is our general advice to come over your self, and to join your own industry to the endeavours of your friends; time being so precious, and all men so eagle-eyed upon every opportunity of the least advancement which

---

[1] Letter, J. Evelyn to Sir R. Browne, 10 May 1660.
[2] Op. cit. [3] Op. cit.

appears; besides, what can you signify in the station you are?'

Poor Sir Richard was already superseded, Lord Jermin being declared to be H.M.'s ambassador in France. Evelyn suggested the London possibilities: 'Offices of the clerks, Treasurer of the Navy, Secretary of State, a thousand other honourable and lucrative places may be found out . . . you may decently beg leave to revisit your native country once in 20 years, both to settle your remainder here, and to solicit the reparation of your losses and recompences of your service in some thing worthy of you.'[1] Evelyn certainly lost no time; the King had not yet landed.

Three days later he again advised Sir Richard: 'Expedite your coming over, and mind your own business; it would be happy that you did appear before everybody have put in their suites; so many pretenders in such a hurry of affairs, and a necessity of obliging the first comers,' and suggested that he sought the office of Treasurer of the Navy: 'one of the most comfortable and lucrative of the nation, very fitting for you', and in which Sir Richard's ancestor Benjamin Gunson had served in Henry VIII's time. 'It is certain that in this affair the Duke of York, and Montagu the present Vice-Admiral are to be made your friends.'[2] In June, Sir Richard returned and was content to remain a Clerk of the Council.[3]

In many spheres, Evelyn's credit was rising; by his knowledge of the arts he was welcome in the circles and at the tables of the nobility; by his regular adherence to the Church and his constant attendance at its services and sacraments he was qualified to share the counsels of the hopeful prelacy; he was friendly with men like Lord John Mordaunt (who was now in close touch with the King and since March 1659 the Chief Commissioner to manage his affairs in England); his recent literary efforts pleased the King. The squirearchy of Wotton must have seemed of little importance, remote from the life he led in and about the purlieus of Whitehall.

Doubtless at his suggestion, and perhaps with Mordaunt's help, even the homely Mrs. Evelyn was induced to leave house-

[1] Letter, J. Evelyn to Sir R. Browne, 14 May 1660.
[2] Letter, J. Evelyn to Sir R. Browne, 17 May 1660.
[3] 'In Charles I's time worth £1500 per annum, since hardly £500': Letter, J. Evelyn to S. Godolphin (Letter Book, Evelyn MS. 39, p. 28).

keeping to become a Lady of the new, exciting Court—though apparently with some hesitation—and on probation. Ten days before the King arrived, Evelyn informed his wife that as the Princess Royal would accompany His Majesty, 'the presence of the Ladies will be requisite at Court, and amongst them especially you . . . be of good cheer'.[1] George was passed over when the office of Sheriff of Surrey was filled by Henry Weston of Ockham. Doubtless George's refusal of the office at the outbreak of the Civil War was remembered.

Mrs. Evelyn also emulated—at her husband's instigation— his busy pen. In December she presented *The Picture of the Princess Henrietta*, which described in fulsome prose the character of Henrietta Anne, Duchess of Orleans and daughter of Charles I—who had returned to England at the Restoration. It was probably written by Evelyn; we seem to recognise his style: 'Her eyes I begin with; as with those twin-stars which illustrate that Orbe of beauty. It is the part we usually examine first, and censure most; but it were here to loose our own lights, not to confess hers so sparkling, and yet so benigne, as at once both to dazle, and refresh the beholder. Her Forehead is majesticall and serene; her Nose of a becoming shape; But her Mouth so rarely proportion'd, as if all the Graces had been in consultation, to fit it for the Charmes, which of necessity must pass through those ranks of Pearl, before they approach her lips, which are full, and of a fresh incarnate . . .'

The Princess gave Mrs. Evelyn 'an extraordinary compliment', says Evelyn; and the piece was printed as a large folio broadsheet.

A compliment was at least something received, but a promise might fail to materialise; three months later the King promised to make Mrs. Evelyn 'Lady of the Jewels', a post which Evelyn characteristically described as 'a very honourable charge'; the office, however, is unknown, and probably became a perquisite of the Second Dresser, enjoyed—or if we believe Evelyn, bribed for—by that great wit, Lady Scrope.[2] There is little doubt that, in this instance of being passed over, Mrs. Evelyn suffered the misfortunes of her husband's ambition. In September 1661 she tells him that 'the King is sufficiently satisfied with her'—

[1] Letter, J. Evelyn to Mrs. Evelyn, 19 May 1660.
[2] *Diary*, de Beer's ed., 31 March 1661.

but in what capacity is unknown. Her duties, however, can hardly have been regular; if they had been so, Evelyn would have put them on record for posterity. A year later the Earl of Chesterfield (the Lord Chamberlain) told Evelyn that another application was necessary in which she was to mention her being long in suspense, if she wished to be in the Queen's service. But by this time Mrs. Evelyn had had enough of the Court. Nine months later she was breeding again, which nullified all social ambitions.

Evelyn's next—his ninth—publication was a prose *Panegyric to Charles II* which he presented in person to the King on the day after his coronation. Charles had feared an oration, saying to Lord Mordaunt, 'I hope it will not be very long.'[1] It comprised fourteen closely printed pages—and Evelyn must have relented. None the less, some of his words arose from the same emotion that supported an all-night wait for a view of Elizabeth the Second in her Coronation Coach: 'The very little children pointed to you, the striplings and young men exulted, the Ancient men stood amazed, and those who were under the empire of a cruel disease leaped out of their beds, to have the sight of you that were the safety of the People.'

The *Panegyric* was the first of four works published by Evelyn in 1661. With the others, the virtuoso was getting into his stride; he gave advice on smoke-abatement in *Fumifugium*; *Instructions concerning erecting of a Library*, translated from Gabriel Naudé; and a protest against Englishmen wearing French fashions in *Tyrannus*. *Fumifugium* was a suggestion for the abatement of the smog of London by removing the noisome trades of brewers, dyers, and soap-boilers to the outskirts of the city, and making strategic plantations of fragrant trees, shrubs, and flowers: Londoners were to breathe the scent of pinks, carnation, clove, stock-gillyflower, primrose, auricula, violet, cowslip, lily, narcissus, strawberry, musk, lemon, mint, marjoram, thyme, spike, camomile, balm, mastick, pimpernel and serpillum (wild thyme). The King liked Evelyn's charming idea, and they discussed it on board the royal yacht on 1 October when the King went racing the Duke of York from Greenwich to Gravesend and back. But nothing came of it.

While he was afloat, Evelyn was commanded by the King to

[1] Letter, Mordaunt to Evelyn, 23 April 1661.

write an account of a 'bloody encounter' near the Tower when the French and Spanish ambassadors contended for precedence: this appeared as *A faithful and impartial narrative of what pass'd at the Landing of the Swedish Ambassador*. Evelyn said that it was published, and collectors, taking him to mean that it appeared as a separate item, have looked for it in vain. In fact it is in Sir Richard Baker's *Chronicles of the Kings of England*, 1665, and reprinted in various editions of the *Diary*.

All this literary activity increased his prestige as a virtuoso, which was duly acknowledged by the newly founded Royal Society in August 1662 when he was elected to be one of the Council.

The same year saw the publication of his *Sculptura, or, the history and art of chalcography and engraving in copper*. This dull, difficult book—little more than a compilation of artists' names—received the blessing of the Royal Society, perhaps chiefly for Evelyn's account—however inadequate—of the new art of engraving in mezzotint, and of its announcement of the invention—however inaccurate—by Prince Rupert; it also contained a mezzotint plate of the Executioner specially made for the book by Prince Rupert.

Evelyn has been severely criticised for not describing the new method in detail; he preferred to leave it 'enigmatical' lest it be 'prostituted at so cheap a rate'. Furthermore, in view of his inadequate description he has been charged with claiming too much in the *Diary* (13 March 1661) of its promoting the growth of mezzotint; he says 'this after noone his highnesse Prince Rupert shewed me with his owne hands the new way of Graving call'd mezzo tinto, which afterwards I by his permission publish'd in my Historie of Chalcographie, which set so many artists on worke, that they soone arrived to that perfection it is since come, emulating the tenderest miniature'. The truth is, he did not publish it in *Sculptura*; but the method is described in a manuscript[1] of his.

In this manuscript he described the use of the hatcher to 'give the dark shades, and the use of the scraper to "scrape away the ground" . . . at such places as the lights and tendernesses should appear . . . and if needs require, polishing it also with

[1] Evelyn MS. 52, pp. 307–8: it—or a similar MS—is briefly referred to in A. M. Hind, *Hist. of Engraving and Etching*, 258–9.

the Burnisher where you would have the light—as in the white of the eye, top of the nose, eminences of the chin, cheeks, fore-head, and the plaits of garments most elevated: this you shall execute with a great deal more tenderness and assurance if you place before you the design washed with Indian ink on paper, or some other colour of *Mezzo Tinto* to direct your lights by . . .' To obtain proofs to your liking, 'you must frequently have recourse to the Rolling-presse . . . abating and polishing for the deep or faint touches . . .' Evelyn then refers to another method which is possibly akin to Ludwig von Siegen's use of the roulette: 'there is another way of engraving, by rowelling a plate with an instrument made like that which scriveners use to direct their ruler by on parchment, only the points are thicker set: and when the plate is sufficiently freckled with it, abated and wrought as we shewed above', that is, preparing the 'darks' with the hatcher; 'of this kind I have seen an head of the Queen of Sweden, made as big as the life; it was pretty, but not comparable to the mezzo-tinto of Prince Rupert described above'. Very late in his life, in a hand shaking with old age, Evelyn added a note to the above to the effect that, instead of the name of mezzo-tinto, Chiaro Oscuro 'had been more proper'.

Against the first charge of falsely crediting Prince Rupert with this invention, one of Evelyn's critics acknowledges 'the obscurity which still shadows the early development of mezzo-tint'.[1] Another critic says that Prince Rupert 'more than any other of its earlier practitioners perceived and enlarged the capacities of the new process'.[2] Well, then, is there not a possibility that Prince Rupert honestly believed his work was new, and justifiably forbade Evelyn to divulge—in public—any details? But he was ready—by Rupert's permission—to give a demonstration to any qualified person. It is true that Evelyn records in his manuscript that Prince Rupert told him that the method 'was the device of a common soldier in Germany by observing something which had scraz'd his musquett'—but that old story does not amount to very much. However, six years after the publication of *Sculptura*, Evelyn—perhaps with fuller knowledge of the invention—was not too happy about his announcement and would have made amends if he had been

[1] A. M. Hind, *Hist. of Engraving and Etching*, 1923, 260.
[2] C. F. Bell, ed. Evelyn's *Sculptura*, 1906, xii.

allowed to; his friend John Beale of the Royal Society wrote: 'perhaps Prince Rupert will (by this time) allow you to speak out . . . truly I do side with your deaf ear'.[1] Admittedly this too is somewhat 'enigmatical', and Evelyn made no amends for his mystification until 1697 when in his *Numismata*, he rightly ascribed the invention to Ludwig von Siegen.

But *Sculptura* had some virtues; it inspired men like Ashmole, Aldrich, and Pepys to begin print-collecting (though we cannot imagine that Pepys ever waded through the book); and it was the first printed on the subject in English. There was one piece of contemporary criticism: Beale pointed out to Evelyn that Sir Henry Wotton was the first to bring Italian engravings of pictures and architecture into the English Court, and that formerly we had been content with the work of the Dutch and French engravers.[2]

From time to time Sir Richard Browne sent Evelyn some interesting Court gossip; on 11 February 1663, he told him that the Queen suffered a Portuguese to draw one of her teeth, which broke, and the stump 'remains in her head until another tooth-drawer comes out of her own country who is purposely sent for. She is not willing to trust herself in the hands of any other.'

Evelyn's spate of work went on; in fact, there was no slackening in his creative efforts until 1669 when his main publications were to come to a curiously abrupt stop.

In the meantime, let us regard the procreative, which had for some years been unproductive—since the miscarriage in the autumn of 1660. Evelyn, naturally, was not content to rest with one son, though the respite from births—and deaths—must have been welcomed by 'the sweet, solid' Mrs. Evelyn; a respite, moreover, that undoubtedly gave her blossoming, matronly personality an added attraction.

It was apparently in the early 1660's that she became in the handsome widower William Glanville's eyes, an object of admiration. He was 'well spoken, of good natural parts',[3] says Evelyn. Unfortunately the family letters throw no light on the genesis of his friendship, and the earliest known letter to Mrs.

[1] Letter, 21 Oct. 1668.
[2] Letter, J. Beale to J. Evelyn, 30 Aug. 1662.
[3] *Diary*, de Beer's ed., 12 April 1702.

Evelyn from him, written in 1663 when he was about forty-four years old and very ill, indicates that our evidence is incomplete: '. . . but whether I live or die let this assure you that no person ever more honoured you than I do for very many reasons. The latter end of your letter is a cordial which I hope will make me sleep this night . . . I seriously profess that I love you with all my heart and am more than I ever yet expressed your affectionate brother and servant William Glanville.'

On 17 January 1664 Mrs. Evelyn gave birth to a son: and Evelyn recorded in the *Diary* 'blessed be God for this mercy to her who had ceased from bearing some years'. Glanville sent his congratulations, implying that this time she wanted a daughter: 'I hope your next great belly may give you a daughter who shall inherit your virtues and no less adorn the sex than you do.'[1] He also sent her some Rhenish and Canary wine, dried citron, Lima oranges and two canaries. Nine weeks later the child died, and Evelyn 'suspected much the Nurse had overlain him'. At such a time distraction is pardonable; he recorded in the *Diary* that the child was but a month old when it died.[2] The following day he recorded: 'After Evening prayer was my child buried near the rest of his brothers, my dear children.'

In February, Evelyn published the book which gave him his high contemporary reputation (for it must be remembered that the *Diary* remained in manuscript until the early nineteenth century): *Sylva, or a discourse of Forest-trees and the propagation of timber in H.M.'s Dominions*, a piece of propaganda for the reafforestation of the country, which proved to be his most successful book. In his mock-modest fashion, he says it is the work of 'a plain husbandman and a simple forester'. But it had a tremendous effect. In his own words 'he incited a world of planters to repair their broken estates'—estates largely impoverished by the Civil War. Woods and avenues sprang up everywhere to the great advantage of the nation. Although the timber woods have long been cut down, throughout the eighteenth century the hearts of oak carried the British flag all over the world. It is not too much to say that the battle of Trafalgar was won in Evelyn's study at Deptford. Two appendices of great interest were included in *Sylva*: *Pomona*, which gave

[1] Letter, W. Glanville to Mrs. Evelyn, Jan. 1664.
[2] *Diary*, 26 March 1664.

the latest technique for making cider, and *Kalendarium Hortense*, which gave in calendar form the gardener's work for the year. This also became an often reprinted and popular work. It is true Sir Thomas Hanmer included in his *Garden Book* 'remembrances of what is to be done in a garden every month of the year' but these concerned only flowers and shrubs, so Evelyn's *Kalendarium*—which dealt with fruit and vegetables as well— was original, and written in a style that is very popular today.

In the dedication of the second edition of the *Kalendarium* to his friend Abraham Cowley (who with a gardener's enthusiasm had previously transcribed the work from Evelyn's manuscript), Evelyn envies the poet, living quietly, and in retirement enjoying the 'glorious recess' of his garden. Cowley prefaced a commendatory poem to Evelyn with words that find an echo in every gardener's heart: 'I never had any other desire so strong, that I might be master at last of a small house and large garden . . . and there dedicate the remainder of my life, only to the culture of them, and study of nature.' Cowley ends his poem with a picture of Evelyn enticed to Court by some noble friends to whom he is showing his garden (a picture somewhat difficult to reconcile with Evelyn's aptitude for waylaying courtiers in the antechambers of Whitehall):

> If I, my friends (said he) should to you show
> All the contents which in this garden grow,
> 'Tis likelier much that you should with me stay
> Than 'tis that you should carry me away.

Cowley also gave publicity to Evelyn's out-of-hand *Elizium Britannicum*, an attention the author did not welcome. The manuscript was out of hand with numerous insertions, and he was in despair of its ever seeing the light, and realised how unwise it was to breathe a word about a projected book; in fact, it had become like a thorn in the flesh. He had had prods from other friends, too, from Jeremy Taylor, and particularly from Beale, who advertised the promised work among his friends in the west country, who were, he says on 30 August 1662, 'impatient for your dispatch'. Beale was even thinking of the prefatory poems for it; 'I hope the royal Denham and my old friend Mr. Waller will paint your *Elizium* with all the felicities of their poetical pencils.' Two years later, Evelyn acknowledged defeat—or whatever he would have called it: when John Rea published in November 1664 his *Flora, Ceres et Pomona*, Evelyn wrote to Robert Boyle: 'It does in nothing reach my long since attempted design of that entire subject which I had shortly hoped to perfect, had God given me opportunity.'[1] Let us hope that he found some consolation in the reflection that he was doing pretty well, and that one man cannot write on all subjects.

Eight months later it was the turn of architecture (and a very successful one too), the *Parallel between Ancient and Modern Architecture*, a translation from the French of Fréart de Chambray (perhaps the best work on Renaissance architecture written in the seventeenth century), to which Evelyn added *An Account of Architects and Architecture*. This fine book, a plea for the general resuscitation of classical architecture, coincided with Wren's first full Renaissance buildings, Pembroke College, Cambridge, and the design of the Sheldonian Theatre, Oxford. Evelyn diagnosed the malaise of the unlearned masons who had been brought up in the medieval tradition; that they were suffering from architectural indigestion as a result of faulty assimilation of such works as Serlio and Sir Henry Wotton's *Elements of Architecture*; it was the *grammar* of architecture that Evelyn prescribed. When he restated in the *Account of Architects and Architecture* the qualities of an architect as laid down in Vitruvius, he made in effect the first call for the individual architect. Evelyn understood that the buildings and scholarship of Inigo Jones and Wren meant that there was no going back to the unlettered mason. The book provided Evelyn with one of the many opportunities of a chat with the King, who complimented him; and they doodled together in the Privy Gallery on the plot for the future building of Whitehall.

On the same day Evelyn was made a Commissioner for the care of sick and wounded prisoners—in readiness for the war now imminent, with the Dutch; he was to be in charge—in this regard—in all the ports of Kent and Sussex, at a salary of £300 a year, with expenses. Before we watch Evelyn in his new and strange occupation, let us glance at George and Wotton, where in September Evelyn paid one of his rare visits, attending the funeral of his brother's wife who had died worn out with losing

[1] *Diary*, 1854 ed., Vol. III, p. 149.

her children. George felt her loss in the upbringing of the survivors. Two of them were in constant need of reproof; his son George—now twenty years old and a prodigal—was travelling in Italy under the care of Dr. Walter Pope. The young spendthrift kept a coach in Rome, 'having no other motive to it that I saw some of my countrymen give me that example who had as mean fortunes as I'.[1] Evelyn was thanked by George for giving his son 'excellent advices', though his father doubted whether 'they may make any impression on him'. He was right; in September 1664 young George stoutly rebutted Evelyn's remonstration about the cost of his Italian journey: 'I have a greater expense upon me than you had, a companion you know equals two servants (and a servant besides) and . . . living now in Italy is dearer than in your days.'[2]

George's daughter Mary (called Moll) had grown into a trying adolescent of sixteen; she never wanted to go to bed, nor to get up, carried herself badly, loathed exercise and writing letters. Sir Richard called her a 'fat squob'. When George was attending Parliament and she was left in charge—under the housekeeper Mrs. Heigham, the rector's wife—advice on her failings made up the greater part of his letters. George seemed more thrifty than ever—perhaps in relation to his son's extravagance: at the cook's wedding, 'take care', he wrote to Moll, 'that the people do not drink out above a barrel of beer'.[3] Medicines were sent from Wotton, their ingredients generally bought in London: a bottle of Mumford's water 'of the strongest sort'[4] was sent up for Lady Herbert's sister Aunt Gerrard, and snail water 'for a lady very far gone in a consumption'.[5] When engaging a new cook in 1665 at £12 a year, his remark that 'the profits of the kitchen they are inconsiderable: I know of none but what comes of conny skins'[6] goes to show that he lived in no great style.

Ten months after the death of his wife George lost his two-year-old daughter Elizabeth, and sent Evelyn the details of her

[1] Letter, G. Evelyn, jun., to J. Evelyn, Sept. 1664.
[2] Op. cit.
[3] Letter, G. Evelyn to Moll Evelyn, 29 Oct. 1664.
[4] Letter, G. Evelyn to Moll Evelyn, 30 Nov. 1664.
[5] Letter, G. Evelyn to Moll Evelyn, 26 Nov. 1664.
[6] Letter, G. Evelyn to Moll Evelyn, 7 July 1665.

death: 'She was never sick; all her complaint was difficulty of breathing . . . I had the advice of a very able physician Dr. Hailey . . . let her blood four ounces and gave her other things inwardly . . . His judgment was that her iron bodice was her pain, and had hindered the lungs to grow, and truly the surgeon that surclothed her body found her breast bone pressed very deeply inwardly, and he said two of her ribs were broken, and the straightness of the bodice upon the vitals occasioned this difficulty of breathing and her death . . . Both the Doctor and Surgeon did conclude that going into the bodice so young, before her lungs had their growth, and the depression of those parts hastened her death.'[1]

[1] Letter, G. Evelyn to J. Evelyn, July 1665.

CHAPTER IV

Plague and War

~~~~~~

T HE new year of 1665 saw the publication of Evelyn's anti-
papal *The Mysterie of Jesuitism*, a translation, in two parts, of
works by Antoine Arnauld and Pierre Nicole; copies of the
originals had been presented to Evelyn by Sir Robert Moray, a
Fellow of the Royal Society, who asked Evelyn to translate them.
Evelyn expressly omitted his own name from the publication,
and said to his friend Robert Boyle: 'so little credit there is in
these days in doing anything for the interest of religion',[1] surely
an inverted virtue, or it may have been mere prudence; perhaps he smelt the smouldering Roman Catholicism about the
Court. Moray probably gave King Charles a copy and revealed
Evelyn's anonymity. The King told Evelyn that he had carried
the book two days in his pocket, read it, and encouraged him,
at which Evelyn records in the *Diary*: 'I did not a little wonder'[2]
—an ambiguity illustrating Evelyn's doubts of the King's
religion.

Evelyn's duties with the sick and wounded prisoners (war
having been declared in February) were rendered still more
heavy and hazardous by the Plague which, by June, had
seriously increased. Deptford was as yet practically immune,
though the fever was flowing eastwards. A month later, Richard
told Evelyn of the risk of contagion at Woodcott; 'since the
concourse to the [Epsom] waters . . . is such that we are in as

[1] *Diary*, 1854 ed., Vol. III, 148.
[2] *Diary*, 25 Jan. 1665.

great danger as any place whatever . . . we can by no possible means keep back the daily recourse of strangers from London'.[1] William Glanville stayed on at Greenwich. By September Evelyn had to make frequent journeys to the ports. Deptford was now infected, and (for safety and company) he had evacuated his wife (who was expecting another baby), his son, and the tutor Ralph Bohun, to Wotton: there were tears in Mrs. Evelyn's eyes when she left her husband thus exposed to danger. Some years previously, on Christmas Day 1657, in Exeter House Chapel, Evelyn had shown that he could be physically brave when he persisted in receiving the Holy Communion with the muskets of Commonwealth troops pressed against his body. Now he was morally brave, sustained by a belief that God would protect him. He wore, on his arm, a leather amulet—the size of a postage stamp—secured by thin strips of silk which probably contained some devotional words.

It was not long before Mrs. Evelyn tried to persuade him to take a rest at Wotton, but he could not break away from his urgent, pressing work: 'I am full of business, have an hundred letters to write and a thousand things to do, for the contagion being sadly broken in amongst my sick-men I must settle pest-ships before I stir . . . we bury here thirty and forty a week . . . look not for me till you see me.'[2]

But two days later came an opportunity for relaxation and even for sheer merriment—though it was no part of his design to inform his wife or to record it in the *Diary*. On Sunday, 10 September, he heard Dr. Plume's sermon at Greenwich which is duly entered in the *Diary*. After the service came the news of Lord Sandwich's capture of a small part of De Ruyter's ships: an occasion for rejoicing. At supper at Captain Cocke's at Greenwich (the Navy Office temporarily transferred there) Evelyn joined Pepys, Lord Brouncker and his mistress, Sir W. Doyly and Sir John Mennes. The wine flowed, and Evelyn was in tremendous form making comic verses. Pepys says that Evelyn 'did not stop the mouth of Sir J. Mennes in the middle of all his mirth (and in a thing agreeing with his own manner of genius) that I never saw any man so out done in all my life'; giving them 'verses made up of nothing but the various accepta-

[1] Letter, R. Evelyn II to J. Evelyn, 17 July 1665.
[2] Letter, J. Evelyn to Mrs. Evelyn, 8 Sept. 1665.

tions of *may* and *can* . . .'[1] 'and Sir J. Mennes's mirth too to see himself out-done was the crown of all our mirth'. It was wonderful what wine could do—even to the 'gentle' Evelyn; but conscious of the Sabbath and the propriety of his *Diary*, he concludes the day's entry: 'I dined with the Commissioners of the Navy, retreated hither, and with whom I had business.' So in the midst of dangers and the making of naval history Evelyn could be merry, whilst Pepys—with other opportunities— enjoyed his light skirmishing with Mrs. Bagwell. A week later Evelyn wrote to his wife: 'You may be sure I will hasten to you as soon as I have any relaxation; in the interim wherever I am or whatever becomes of me, I shall pray for your happy delivery and that we may meet with more joy than we parted.'[2]

But there is no doubt that his work was a continual strain, physical and mental; long, tiring journeys to Dover and elsewhere—he fainted on one occasion—and from September onwards insufficient public funds caused him constant anxiety: 'The impossibilities of my charge', he wrote to his wife, 'to keep and maintain 3000 prisoners with nothing. I pray God to deliver me from the infinite hazards I am running into . . . yet be not you in the least discouraged, you have a gracious God to trust in . . . if it were not for my confidence in God, and your sincere affection to me, my heart would plainly break.'[3]

He urged Lord Cornbury (to whom he says he is more engaged than to any person living) to read an account of his difficulties to Clarendon his father, and to bring it to the attention of the King and the Lord Treasurer.[4] In reply Sir Philip Warwick expressed the official sympathy and sent him a bleak analysis of the spending of the £2,500,000 voted towards the war—and promised £5000[5]—a sum regarded by Evelyn as a drop in the ocean when his daily expenditure was £200 and likely to increase. But he did not rest satisfied with a promise; Coventry —a fortnight later—also received a recital of his financial plight.[6] Sir Richard—now at Oxford with the Court, seeking

---

[1] Pepys, 10 Sept. 1665.
[2] Letter, J. Evelyn to Mrs. Evelyn, 17 Sept. 1665.
[3] Letter, J. Evelyn to Mrs. Evelyn, 22 Sept. 1665.
[4] Letter, 9 Sept. 1665; *Diary*, 1854 ed.
[5] Letter, 16 Sept. 1665; *Diary*, 1854 ed.
[6] Letter, 2 Oct. 1665; *Diary*, 1854 ed.

safety—had a version of the same sad story of the sick and wounded prisoners: 'We have no money to feed them, nor can I procure officers to govern them; so as I am well at my wits end, and will with all my heart thank His Majesty on my bare knees to place the honour he has conferred on me by this service upon some other that can do miracles, for I can do none . . . The Sickness . . . does so rage at Chelsea that I have lost all my officers there save poor Sandys our Deputy Marshal, who came to me on Wednesday with it upon him and ready to sink down before my door: what is become of him I know not . . .'

The Plague was now all around Evelyn at Deptford, and his tenants were dying: 'Daniel's child is sick, Tom Tucky is sick, if not dead; the gentlewoman at Mrs. Spight's dead, and the brewer who lives at Broomfield's Gate dead; all the houses about the Doctor swept away, and at the least fifty more shut up. The truth is, I dare not enquire, for it ever affrights me, and our bell never lies still.' The Doctor was Dr. Bretton, the Deptford incumbent, who also stayed in his parish throughout the Plague. It was the same at Greenwich and at Chatham, 'so as I am environed with danger,' says Evelyn, 'and have nothing to trust to but your prayers. No money should hire me to this hazard—which I see every man fly from that has any asylum.'[1]

Evelyn's first daughter was born on 1 October with the help of the country midwife, two neighbours evacuated from Deptford, and Mrs. Heigham. Evelyn's stress of work engendered some indifference in the choice of her name: he says, 'Let the name be what you will.' In fact, he was in a poor state of health and suffered more fainting fits, 'but none', he says, 'will counsel me to take any physick'. (Physic was never advisable if the Plague was feared.) Partly on account of his health, and as a protest against the conditions he was subjected to, he was now resolved to lay down his commission—and his fellow commissioner Sir W. D'Oyley would do likewise.[3] Yet Evelyn could jest for his new daughter: 'Let the midwife and goships model her nose betimes that she do not want a handle.'[2] To Sir Richard he unburdened more tales of woe: 'With 24000 prisoners and 2000 sick . . . 'tis not an employment for a slave.'[3]

[1] Letter, J. Evelyn to Mrs. Evelyn, 23 Sept. 1665.
[2] Letter, J. Evelyn to Mrs. Evelyn, 2 Oct. 1665.
[3] Letter, J. Evelyn to Sir R. Browne, 2 Oct. 1665.

The accommodation at some of the ports being full, he was compelled to use force, as at Rochester and Erith (where he saw the prizes from which Pepys, Captain Cocke, and the Earl of Sandwich were drawing such fat profits): well might Evelyn say: 'The war is governed like children play . . . the King is wretchedly abused and all will come to nothing for want of better economy . . . H.M. has lost his seamen's hearts and his credit'; with hyperbolean flourish he goes on: 'there is not a man here within many miles but the Duke of Albemarle, two pitiful Commissioners of the Navy and myself on whom depends the whole stress of the nation's sea affairs . . . let me tell you who know perfectly well how the royal aid has been disposed of . . . they at Court no more minding us as if there were not a Navy in nature . . . pardon this subject: my head is so tormented with it that I cannot forbear to impart it.'[1] At Oxford Charles borrowed money from all his servants; £2000 from Arlington, £500 from Williamson, and £500 from Chiffinch.[2] Even the £5000 assigned to Evelyn was totally owing before he had touched one penny. He applied for further help to Coventry and asked Sir Richard to make the Parliament at Oxford sensible of his plight.[3] The last straw was the diversion to another use of the £5000 assigned to him; however on 10 October his protests at last brought forth £10,000.

Surgeon-General John Pearse knew the conditions of the sick prisoners and agreed with Evelyn 'that the King would not have a man serve him shortly'. The Mayor of Rochester swore to Evelyn that 'they would throw our sick-men in the streets if I did not send them money'; he was also told that things were better managed under Cromwell's naval administration.[4] All this news was sent on to Sir Richard.

Toward the end of October Evelyn was unable to write to his wife; she forgave him, however, 'upon condition that you never keep me in pain so long again'. On 31 October he commemorated his birthday in the *Diary*: 'I was this day 45 years of age, wonderfully preserved, for which I blessed His infinite goodness.'

[1] Op. cit.
[2] Letter, Sir R. Browne to Evelyn, 18 Jan. 1666.
[3] Letter, J. Evelyn to Sir R. Browne, 14 Oct. 1665.
[4] Letter, J. Evelyn to Sir R. Browne, 23 Oct. 1665.

On 5 November he relaxed for an hour or two when Pepys paid him a visit at Sayes Court. In his diary, Pepys gives us our best portrait of Evelyn: 'He read me part of a play or two of his making, very good, but not as he conceits them, I think, to be . . . In fine a most excellent person he is, and must be allowed a little for a little conceitedness; but he may well be so, being a man so much above others. He read me, though with too much gusto, some little poems of his own, that were not transcendent.' Perhaps he struck a chord in Pepys's heart, with that youthful effusion, when, in 1645, tired of travel, he wrote of his yearning for marital comforts:

> A Lovely bride the youth enchains:
> In whose smooth arms no sooner hurl'd
> But he surveys another world
> Where he, enfranchised may stray
> O'er the warm snow or milky way
> And thence as oft as he declines
> Towards those more rich and hidden mines.[1]

Captain Cocke came in 'as drunk as a dog but could stand and talk and laugh'. On this day Evelyn records the text of Dr. Plume's sermon at Greenwich, and of his receiving the Sacrament. The next day Cocke entertained both Pepys and Evelyn to dinner, when they were all 'very merry', records Pepys; Evelyn's diary is blank. A week later when Evelyn had had a few days' rest at Wotton—the Dutch having somewhat eased his burden by maintaining their own prisoners—he told Sir Richard that his wife and brother George 'are breaking my heart, by importuning me not to return to my charge—but duty to the King and honour obliges me to adventure all'.[2] His visit was not only a joy to his wife; it brought news of the great world to George who was for 'want of good neighbours without all intelligence'. But he would add, philosophically, 'as our affairs are managed I may account it a piece of felicity not to hear of our misfortunes and miscarriages'.

Evelyn was now asked to prevail with George's son in the matter of marriage, in which he could have had no easy task, George junior being given to 'impoliteness in manners', and of

---

[1] Evelyn MS. 124, p. 46.
[2] Letter, J. Evelyn to Sir R. Browne, 10 Nov. 1665.

an 'unsettled head in matters of importance'. He was obviously beyond his father's control. George asked Evelyn to advise him to settle down and to be obedient to his father; 'a lady of your choice I shall esteem above all, knowing your judgment', and £1500 a year could be settled on him.[1] This amount was probably less than George could reasonably afford; he was always excessively thrifty. Even Mrs. Evelyn was a paying guest at Wotton: at the end of September Evelyn instructed her to pay George £20 'upon account; at least it will encourage them not to repent of their kindness to us'. But in the *Diary*, of course, Evelyn refers to my 'hospitable brother'.

In the midst of heart-breaking work at the ports, little courtesies were not forgotten: John Bullack, Evelyn's deputy Commissioner at Dover, would send him samphire seeds, French history and plays for his son, and two Italian soap balls for Mrs. Evelyn.

In early December, when Evelyn returned to Wotton with a supply of trees for the Grove at Sayes Court, the Plague was decreasing and the city already almost as full as ever: he felt it safe to dine at *The Sun* (behind the Exchange), 'out of which', he says, 'divers had perished'. He would experience the calm after the storm, and bask in the sunshine of the King's smile: 'I have gotten immortal credit at Oxford,' he wrote to his wife, 'and have upon two businesses at Council received public eulogies from all the Great-ones . . . your father tells me they all say handsome things of me . . . burn the letter.'[2]

Still there remained many sick and wounded prisoners at Chelsea and in Leeds Castle (in Kent)—for whom Evelyn was imploring aid from Oxford in the latter part of December. The Plague—though temporarily decreasing in London—was little less severe in Deptford. To these anxieties, was added in December some exasperating nocturnal thefts of a number of his newly-planted trees. They were identified—replanted—in Greenwich Park—and thus to be regarded as the King's property. Evelyn related the sad story to Sir Richard. The Royal gardeners had bought them for little from the thieves, and pocketed up the King's money. These Royal gardeners actually sold Evelyn some trees one year and stole (or 'received')

---

[1] Letter, G. Evelyn to J. Evelyn, 5 Dec. 1665.
[2] Letter, J. Evelyn to Mrs. Evelyn, 4 Dec. 1665.

them the next. He tried the expedient of a secret nail or brad knocked in at a certain distance from the root—but with what success we do not know. There were disadvantages in possessing a famous garden.

The new year of 1666 found Evelyn in a happier mood—despite a new increase in the Plague in late December—after a few days' rest at Wotton over Christmas. The prisoners in Leeds Castle are 'in excellent order, and they have never been without fire and clean straw with an allowance of near 3*d.* a day . . . coals are now at 33*s.*' The carrier to Dorking was back in service, plying regularly every week; in the matter of letters Mrs. Evelyn was saved further anxiety.

Perhaps Evelyn shared something of the Duke of Albemarle's joyful anticipation to 'have a bout with the Hogens'—Albemarle being now 'most intimately and friendly kind' to him. Great new ships were almost ready at Deptford and Woolwich to be launched by the King. Since his appointment in December—displacing Sandwich—to the supreme sea command (jointly with Prince Rupert) Albemarle had met and dined with Evelyn at the Sheriff's and at the Cockpit in Whitehall. Sir Richard remarked how fortunate Evelyn was in possessing his favour, and doubted not but he would 'cultivate it with care and industry'. Under Sandwich there had been three classes of officers, the 'tarpaulins' who sailed the ships, the army officers turned naval tacticians, and the volunteers—young men who went to sea for the joy of it. Albemarle 'will admit of no volunteers,' says Evelyn to Sir Richard, 'but only my rich countryman Sir Daniel Harvey' (who lived near Nonsuch); 'their great familiarity springs from his love to Greyhounds and coursing, the Duke frequently visiting him':[1] doubtless Evelyn, in this case on Harvey's behalf, successfully cultivated Albemarle's favour.

Towards the end of January there were definite signs that the Plague was decreasing in London—though Evelyn still ran risks: and in the same letter he tells Sir Richard (not yet returned from Oxford) that he had, against his will, been 'engaged with two women of Wapping about exchange of prisoners, who at last confessed they had newly had the Plague, one of them twice: she gave me papers out of a very foul cloak,

[1] Letter, J. Evelyn to Sir R. Browne, 20 Jan. 1666.

which smelt very unpleasingly, but it being an order from his Grace [Albemarle] I was fain to receive it; yet my people were to blame to admit them into my house; but this is but a small instance of my very comfortable employment: they had buried all their children I think they said.' On the 22 January most of the shops were open, the coaches were rattling, and the crowds began to appear: the King and Court were expected to return with the 'miracle' of their Oxford health to Hampton Court—an event that Evelyn could await with justifiable pleasure.

Just now he had worked out his new project for a Naval Infirmary which so impressed Albemarle that he was commanded to wait on him to Hampton Court where the Duke would promote it with the King, and let His Majesty know how much he owes to him: certainly the sun was beginning to shine.

But the war was still much in his mind, and Albemarle's fighting spirit so infectious that on the same day, Evelyn—ever alert and sensitive to danger—told his wife 'there will certainly be landings in Kent and Sussex before summer be spent'.[1]

But whatever else was afoot, his garden was never neglected, and his wife—still at Wotton—received a seasonable hint in the usual manner: 'I shall not need to remind you of getting my trees ready.' There was the question, on leaving Wotton, whether Mrs. Evelyn should pay for her board or shower tips among the staff, 'only', says Evelyn, 'let us not be prodigal'. He suggested that she should consult with George's bailiff, and then 'we might do all things handsomely'. Obviously, Mrs. Evelyn had no enviable task.

On 29 January Evelyn was duly presented by Albemarle to the King; Evelyn described the scene to his wife, how the King gave him 'so kind a reception as I could not have desired a more gracious . . . he ran to me and giving me his hand to kiss told me he was heartily glad he had me safe . . . using this expression, I have been in care for you, I have pitied you . . .' He had the honour 'to entertain him quite alone . . . for near 3 quarters of an hour and after that twice more in private'. Then the Duke of York gave him his hand to kiss, Lord Arlington, Coventry, 'and a full crowd of other great persons to salute

[1] Letter, J. Evelyn to Mrs. Evelyn, 25 Jan. 1666.

me, but none with more ceremony, compliment and wonderful
expressions of kindness, than my Lord of St. Albans who is wont
(you know) to overlook all the world. Thus I passed from one
to another, half pulled to pieces for joy . . . I was once or twice
afraid of making you a Lady; but (I thank God) I got most
dextrously off.'[1]

The project of the Infirmary was not discussed; he was, however, commanded to wait upon the King in a few days' time,
when Evelyn read it to him 'with great approbation'. Pepys,
too, was appreciative, and took it a stage further—to the Navy
Commissioners and to the Duke of York. Chatham was selected
as a possible site, and Evelyn went so far as to set out the
ground; 400 or 500 patients were to be accommodated. After
the end of March the project was shelved, and never saw day-
light again for nearly thirty years. What did Evelyn think of
Arlington who told Sir Richard that the signed 'shall be
speedily put in hand whatever shift is made for money'?[2]

In March was published another short, anonymous translation by Evelyn from the French of Pierre Nicole: *The Pernicious
consequences of the new heresie of the Jesuites against the King and the
State*, dedicated to Clarendon. As usual, Evelyn presented a
copy to the King. (If not found in collections of seventeenth-
century pamphlets catalogued under Evelyn's name, it may
well be found under *Jesuits*.) By this time Evelyn's friendship
with Lord Cornbury had made considerable progress, and
Clarendon himself sought Evelyn's advice on the planting of
the new garden at Cornbury Park. Clarendon was a desirable
patron, though there is no evidence that, when appealed to by
Evelyn in the previous autumn he did more than urge Sir
Philip Warwick to express the Treasury view against Evelyn's
financial demands. Yet, in September he protested that he was
'more engaged to his Lordship than to any person living in
this world'. In suitable language, Evelyn writes himself down
as a 'plain country gentleman; yet hear, and see and observe,
as those in the valleys best discern the mountains'. Alas, for
Evelyn's hopes, this mountain was soon to subside.

Sir Richard continued to provide Evelyn with all the Court
news, and in April related his account of the well-known story

[1] *Seven Letters of John Evelyn*, 1914, p. 7.
[2] Letter, Sir R. Browne to Evelyn, 17 Feb. 1666.

of the mad Sir John Denham's visit to Whitehall, of Denham telling the King 'that he himself was Jesus Christ and that the King should have a very good place in Heaven; but before he came to enjoy it he must live a better life. He saith the Queen and his own wife shall have very good places there also (his wife was the Duke of York's mistress). But his wife must stay a while before she came there. He saith he . . . can go into Heaven when he please: the King willed him to try; whereupon he displayed his arms like wings, but the King told him he was still on earth: the Knight replied that he had one vision more to see, whereupon the King told him the best way to see it was to go to bed . . . the Knight replied he would lie upon the bed, but not dressed to hinder his journey.'

On the 18 April Mrs. Evelyn had her second miscarriage of a son, 'being but young with child'. The Plague—now decreasing in London—had spread to the Surrey countryside. George reported to Evelyn that there were many deaths in East Horsley, Kingston, and Reigate, because the covetous tradesmen 'offer infected goods'. At Deptford it was as serious as ever, and George remained at Wotton though anxious to pay his brother a visit: 'My little courage to adventure so near the town unwillingly keeps me from you,' he said; 'we have here dreadful apprehensions of it, though you and London little regard it.'[1] However, George allowed his own son to visit Deptford 'to see this gallant Navy that is going out', and by the end of the month Moll was staying with her aunt Lady Gerrard in King Street, Covent Garden—for frocks and a husband might be more easily found in London.

During the Plague, Moll was rather uselessly advised by her father not to run into danger of infection; if the Plague increases, she is to buy what she wants and come home. At the beginning of May there were twenty deaths a week in Deptford: Moll was therefore instructed that if she visited Mrs. Evelyn she must notstay the night; if she saw George jun. in London, she is to tell him to hasten home on account of the infection. Moll was also instructed to pay Lady Gerrard thirty shillings for a week's board for herself and her maid. Young George was apparently roaming more or less at leisure in London. I wonder, writes his father, 'he stays in town so long to spend all his money.

[1] Letter, G. Evelyn to J. Evelyn, 19 April 1666.

He hath taken a new man: if he be not to be footman and groom he hath done very ill, for I advised him to take a boy that would both be foot boy and look to his horses: desire him to have a care of his safety and that neither he or his men run into danger.'[1] By 4 June he was safe at Wotton, and writing to Evelyn: 'We are all very impatient here to know what those guns may be we hear so perfectly.'

They were, of course, the guns of the Four Days Battle in the straits of Dover, when Albemarle, although inflicting severe losses on De Ruyter, lost twenty ships and 8000 men through his faulty tactics—ships and men that we were to find hard to replace. Pepys called Albemarle a blockhead but only in his private shorthand diary. None the less, the resilience with which the Dutch had to contend was shown by the fleet's sailing again on 18 July, to gain, this time, a victory, though a modest one. The militia had been mustered in early July against a landing in the Isle of Thanet—so nearly did Evelyn's fears materialise.

To return to Moll. She was now eighteen years old. Good matches had been proposed to her, even suitors with as much as £1800 a year, but she would have none of them. When Evelyn in August put forward for her a man with an estate of £1200, George was impelled to defend Moll's elevated notions of a comfortable marriage—though he would sometimes describe the same notions as 'perverse obstinacy' or a 'foolish resolution against marriage'. It was doubtful whether Evelyn would try again.

Evelyn's son John was eleven years old, learning his Latin from Ralph Bohun and pleasing everyone by his gentle manner. He was a particular favourite of Sir Richard, who would never allow any scene of pageantry in London to pass by without the presence of 'Young Jack'. In June he had been presented to the King, and at his father's request he wrote his first Latin letter this year to Henry Howard (afterwards Duke of Norfolk) who was in Paris. Even the young must be brought up to think of patrons.

In April the King desired Evelyn to be a Justice of Peace, but by nominating another to act, he escaped the obligation: this was reasonable as he was still fully engaged with his sick

[1] Letter, G. Evelyn to Moll Evelyn, 13 May 1666.

prisoners. For the same reason he was excused from, though elected to, the Council of the Royal Society. In July, however, he was made one of the Commissioners for the making of salt-petre, and in the following month appointed one of the surveyors to consider a plan for the new building of St. Paul's. He agreed with Wren that building anew was preferable to patching. Busy though he was, Evelyn published this year a little book on vine-growing, the matter of which came from the King's gardener John Rose. Evelyn characteristically defeated his use of the pseudonym of Philocepos, by referring, at the end of the book, to his *Sylva*.

After the Plague, the Fire—at the beginning of September—of which Evelyn gave a fine account in the *Diary*, although at the finish he was rather like a spectator from some other world . . . 'there I left this smoking and sultry heap, which mounted up in dismal clouds night and day, the poor inhabitants dispersed all about St. George's, Moorfields, as far as Highgate, and several miles in circle, some under tents, others under miserable huts and hovels, without a rag, or any necessary utensils, bed or board, who from delicateness, riches and easy accommodations in stately and well furnished homes were now reduced to extremest misery and poverty: in this calamitous condition I returned with a sad heart to my house, blessing and adoring the distinguishing mercy of God to me and mine, who in the midst of all this ruin, was like Lot, in my little Zoar, safe and sound.'[1]

Wren's new plan for London was in the King's hands by 11 September; two days later Evelyn submitted his. He tells us that Fleet Street was among the streets destroyed; but at least the western half was intact on 13 September, when his brother George stayed at *The Black Lion*, in readiness to attend Parliament. A fortnight later, impressed by the black ruin around him he says it 'hath given us a subject of humiliation'. The lingering risks of the Plague deterred the obstinate Moll from coming to town in the autumn to stay with Sir Henry and Lady Herbert in Tuttle Street, Westminster; "tis not very safe,' writes her father, 'because the barber's house next to Sir H. Herbert's is visited: I think there is danger in it, but Sir Henry and my Lady apprehends none, because all are removed to the

[1] *Diary*, de Beer's ed., 1666, p. 457.

pesthouse';[1] on this occasion, Moll was obedient, deferring her visit until the new year. But she had many opportunities between 1667 and 1670 of staying in town, either with the Herberts or with her cousin Sanders in Covent Garden. If her father was attending Parliament, she remained at Wotton; during the recesses, she was often in London.

By coach it was a six hours' journey from Wotton to the inn at Lambeth; and—leaving the coach at the Inn with a servant to return the next day—there was always someone to see her across the ferry to Westminster. Now she was to offer her aunt forty shillings weekly for board for herself, her nurse, and her boy—and her father was somewhat disappointed when rather surprisingly her aunt accepted it; and there was forty-five shillings to be paid to her dancing master for a month's lessons. When she had a fortnight at Sayes Court, decorum and prestige demanded that every servant received five shillings. In May 1668—she was then with the Herberts—her father wanted her to return to Wotton 'unless she has a servant', he says; 'I suppose Aunt Herbert hath proposed one; you have liberty from me to make your own choice and when a good match is offered not to refuse it.' But her father's board and lodging money as yet brought no reward; and to make an impression he allowed her the use of his best coach. It is remarkable that he gave her little advice beyond 'take care of your necklace when you go to plays' when she was in town; perhaps he had trust in the Herberts. But even they found her lacking in early rising and punctuality at meals. In November 1669 the usual invitation was not forthcoming; instead, she stayed with cousin Sanders in Covent Garden.

At Wotton there was, apparently, no change for the better in her habits; at least her father showered advice and instruction upon her. He hopes his absence will alter her foolish resolution against marriage; she must receive the Holy Communion at Christmas and at Easter—and in preparation read *The Practice of Piety* by Lewis Bayley and *The Whole Duty of Man* (upon the Sacrament); she is to instruct Mrs. Heigham to take in each week no more beef than 25 stone; Moll's sister is to have no supper; to see the servants keep order; she is to 'be a good hussy—for moneys are very hard to get'; she is to take

[1] Letter, G. Evelyn to Moll Evelyn, 24 Oct. 1666.

physic to clear her stomach; to have only a joint of mutton for supper when there is no company; in Lent the servants 'may spare Wednesday, Friday and Saturday suppers as to meat, only cheese, butter, or porridge'; she is not to rub her face, but to rise at seven, walk and take the fresh air which will 'infallibly take away the pimples in your face'; and 'do not use slops to your fare'.[1] Whatever else she did, she continued to rise late and retire late.

George's bottled beer was judged to be excellent by Aunt Gerrard; and she obtained the receipt from Mrs. Heigham. Mrs. Evelyn appreciated it, too; George would send it up to *The Greyhound* near Whitehall Steps where she would call for it, or George would send it down the river to Deptford by his own waterman. He sometimes drank some Wotton-brewed juniper berry ale; this may have been similar to the Hollander's juniper water, or an early kind of ebulum. Saffron was sent down to Wotton from London in small quantities—probably for medicinal purposes and for flavouring the common ale. Mrs. Heigham sent preserved sloes, medlars, and cornelian cherries to stop Dick Herbert's looseness; Cousin Mary Herbert wanted a bottle of Broome water for her swollen feet.

Clothes for George and his family were made by one Cobb, who apparently lived in Wotton. Before choosing material for Moll, George would seek the advice of Aunt Gerrard or Mrs. Evelyn; in 1666 for a petticoat and waistcoat suitable for country wear eleven and a half yards of dark farandine were sent down with six and a quarter yards of striped lutestring; silver buckles now fashionable for her brother's shoes instead of shoestrings; a lutestring hood and scarf; clasps for her brother's girdle and French shalloon to trim his tunic and vest, taffety to face the sleeves.

Moll's reading was not confined to devotional books; her father sent her plays, and in 1670, the memoirs of the famous highwayman Claude Duval—just executed—'to make you merry'. Moll's father disapproved of Valentines except when a likely suitor was involved; 'Sir Ambrose Brown's son hath drawn you,' writes her father in March 1669; 'him you may present with some slight present', but he forbids her to buy one for William Glanville's son—who was not at all an eligible

[1] Letter, G. Evelyn to Moll Evelyn, v.d., 1666–72.

young man; 'I have told him he must expect no present from you, for you gave none to any and he expects none I do assure you . . . you may buy none for any but young Mr. Ambrose. I would not have you so foolishly lay out your moneys, and truly such presents are all laid aside . . . therefore think no more of such fooleries.'

In February 1670 when Moll was nearly twenty-two years old her continual lazy habits caused her father to write: 'Until I hear you do what I desire I am resolved never to see you, but leave you to yourself.' Doubtless a temporary improvement ensued, for no further serious rift between them is recorded. But trying as she was, youth showed by half—as we shall discover.

To return to Evelyn: in March 1667 he published a small essay entitled *Public employment and an active life prefer'd to solitude*, in reply to *A moral essay, preferring solitude to public employment*, written by George Mackenzie.

Students of Evelyn have found this defence of activity unconvincing, and that, being a lover of country tranquillity, he is accused of writing with his tongue in his cheek. But surely, he was the most active of men, and his own life, as we have so far seen it, a complete reply to Mackenzie and a demonstration that he meant every word he said. His garden, bred of ambition, brought reputation, not solitude. In the essay he acknowledges that 'there is more of ambition and empty glory in some solitude and affected retreats than in the most exposed and conspicuous actions whatsoever'. Did Evelyn despise glory? Certainly not; 'this despising of glory is the mother of sloth', he says. We have seen that he had not yet come to retirement in any sense. Was he not as active and as well-preserved as ever? 'Men', he says, 'begin to praise retirement . . . when they cannot otherwise attain to what they aspire.' He was in his forty-seventh year— in the prime of life.

In June the Dutch took audacious advantage of our temporary naval inactivity by capturing Sheerness fort, burning some of our finest ships, sailing up the Medway, and 'stopping up the Thames', as Evelyn puts it. So great—and natural— was the panic, he sent his plate and treasures away for safety. Looking back, on 7 July 1680, Evelyn might well say to Pepys: 'Pray, what have we gotten by our late war with the Hollanders, whom Albemarle did so despise.'

Plague and War

In August, Evelyn's 'mountain' Clarendon subsided under the King's intolerance of his personal criticism; he was also made a scapegoat for the mishandling of the war. In Clarendon's removal, Evelyn lost a patron.

He gained the gratitude of Oxford University in the autumn by persuading Henry Howard, later Duke of Norfolk, to present the Arundel Marbles, which Evelyn 'saw miserably neglected and scattered up and down about the gardens and other places of Arundel House'. About 130 stones bearing inscriptions of Greek history thus found a permanent home through Evelyn's scholarly foresight. Nine years later the University presented him with an attractive Oxford-bound copy of the *Marmora Oxoniensia*, 1676,[1] carried to him by Humphrey Prideaux, the editor of the work. Evelyn 'wholly declined' to allow his name to appear in a commemorative Latin inscription. In September 1667, Howard allowed Evelyn to lay out the beautiful grass terraces at Albury in Surrey—which remain a monument to his skill in garden design.

If Evelyn was happily active so was his wife; indeed we have surmised that her personality was in the ascendant, an ascent perhaps not unconnected with the rhythm of her child-bearing in the 1660's, and possibly the determining factor of their sex. Instead of the disturbing effort of yearly conceptions and infant male deaths, she was now about to enjoy the more reasonably spaced begetting of two more daughters—Elizabeth this year, and Susan in 1669. Indeed her ascendant personality may well have become the dominant.

William Glanville was not the only gallant who wrote to her *con amore* or with that charming raillery which often springs from the true admirer's heart. There were Sir Samuel Tuke the dramatist of 'The Adventures of Five Hours', and Ralph Bohun, her son's tutor. Tuke, who was twice married, had such confidence in Mrs. Evelyn's judgment that his own estimation of a prospective wife was subject to her approbation. When at Norwich as tutor to the Howards, he often recalled in his undated letters to her, their late, delightful conversation at Sayes Court in 'the wooden parlour' or in the 'cypress grove'. Bohun was evidently in his mind when he said, 'You see . . . how naturally I entertain you, leaving the tropes for the learned

[1] Press-mark d. 29, Evelyn Library.

71

whose epistles are dictated by their heads and not their hearts.'
He gives an unusual picture of Restoration wooing at Norwich:
'Here is a young creature whose beauty is as simple as her soul,
who charms by her silence more than the rhetoric of the Circle.
But the spite of it is she has so many out-works, father, mother,
uncles, aunts, cousins, who must all be taken in before one ever
approach her, that I believe it will be the next Spring before
I can speak to her, and it may be the Summer will be past
before she answers.' In 1663 he gives a picture of Newmarket
and its 'great assembly of nobles' who, in the winter, 'will be
given to natural philosophy and Greek with the citizens' wives.'
Writing from Paris in 1666, he says that, on returning to England the following spring, 'I must conform to the fashion of the
country, which as I am told, is a mixture betwixt the Turk and
the Christian.' He was in thought liberal: 'Remember that in
the Farce of this world the actors are not to be valued by the
quality of those personages which they represent, but by their
good acting of those parts which providence has allotted them
to play.'[1] Tuke died in 1674 leaving the field poorer, though a
little clearer, to William Glanville and Ralph Bohun.

Glanville—who was now forty-seven—reappeared at Sayes
Court after the Plague on 10 November 1666—a visit which
Evelyn recorded in the *Diary*. He is not mentioned again in
the *Diary* for twenty-five years. His subsequent visits may have
been too frequent or unimportant to record, though when we
come to appreciate the degree of his friendship for Mrs. Evelyn
we may rightly judge that omission may well have been a
matter of propriety. Indeed we may arrive at the opinion that
had Evelyn succumbed to the Plague, Mrs. Evelyn—who in
1667 was no more than thirty-two years old—would have
become Mrs. Glanville. While Tuke's letters were amusing,
Bohun's flattering, Glanville's were amusing, flattering and
disturbing.

By his pursuits and journeys Evelyn left his wife open to
attack as it were. The Plague and the war were over, but he
was still often absent, engaged with sick prisoners at the ports
or in and around Whitehall on business or pleasure. We may
even discern indications that he needed relaxation or diversion
away from his wife and family: he could not go on writing books

[1] Letter, Sir S. Tuke to Mrs. Evelyn, 4 Dec. 1666.

for ever. His son's health had caused anxiety, even disappointment; at nine years of age he had had specially fitted boots,
armature and bodice to rectify his crooked legs. It was fortunate
that he was well enough to go up to Trinity College, Oxford, in
January 1667; it was only a little over a year before that Tuke
was enquiring 'how poor Jack does in his limbs'. The President
of Trinity, Dr. Bathurst, reported his late rising and neglect of
prayers. In 1669 his father removed him. It is also possible that
the Tuke-Bohun-Glanville attack caused Evelyn to retreat and
to do a little reconnoitring on his own account; not, of course,
in any way comparable to the light skirmishing of Pepys.

Whatever the cause, dissatisfaction, disappointment, lack of
inspiration, or need of recreation, we find him on 29 August
dining at Whitehall with the Maids of Honour and making a
Pepysian entry in his diary: 'and so late home'. (And a dinner
implies an invitation given at a previous, unrecorded, meeting.)
It must not be supposed that anything was hidden from Mrs.
Evelyn, and even in Restoration England Maids of Honour
could be maids of honour. Moreover, Mrs. Evelyn gave her
husband complete freedom—or so he says—for friendship with
the sex. But it is important that the first of such meetings that
led to friendship should be noted.

None the less Mrs. Evelyn—now in the last month of carrying
her second daughter Elizabeth—would find some compensation,
if any were needed, in being able to smile at Glanville's words:
'Women usually say (but 'tis only in private among themselves
they talk so waggishly) that 'tis for the husband's credit when
the great bellied wife can make no certain reckoning.' And
again: 'When you grow light, to atone for leaving Deptford
when I was last there without your permission, I shall make
bold to kiss your hands, and my brother without looking yellow
may permit us to divert ourselves for an hour or two, provided
it be in a place no more convenient than is the edge of a tub.'[1]
With such delightful letters to read, Mrs. Evelyn would not be
unduly perturbed by her husband's appointment with the
Maids of Honour.

[1] Letter, W. Glanville to Mrs. Evelyn, 6 Aug. 1667.

CHAPTER V

Maids and Men of Honour

~~~~~~

BEFORE we relate the progress of Evelyn's quest for friendship in 1669 here is his wife's picture of a Sayes Court winter from which he would, whenever possible, escape, and in which she had to remain: 'The flowers and greens . . . are candying in snow to be preserved for the Spring, and our delights confined to the little wooden room, which could your perspective reach would for variety be no unpleasing diversion, than to see a dull fire, circled with a philosopher, a woman, and a child, heaps of books, our food, and entertainment, silence our law so strictly observed that neither dog nor cat dares transgress it, the crackling of the ice, and whistling winds are our music which if continued long in the same quarter may possibly freeze our wits as well as our pens . . . so stupid hath the congealed Air rendered us . . . I am inclined to believe myself a tortoise, a good secure invention.'[1]

Mrs. Evelyn was not only a critic of scenes and persons, she was a dramatic critic. After seeing Dryden's *The Siege of Granada* she described it to Bohun on 27 February 1668, saying, 'Love is made so pure and valour so nice that one would imagine it designed for an Utopia rather than our stage: I do not quarrel with the poet, but admire one born in the decline of morality should be able to feign such exact virtue; and as poetic fiction has been instructive in former ages, I wish this the same event in ours. As to the strict law of Comedy I dare not pretend to

[1] Letter, to Sir S. Tuke, Dec. 1669.

judge: some think a division of the story not so well, as if it would have been all comprehended in one day's action: truth of history, exactness of time, possibility of adventures are niceties the ancient critics might require; but those who have outdone them in fine notions, may be allowed the liberty to express them their own way; and the present world is so enlightened that the Old Dramatic must bear no sway. This account is perhaps not sufficient to do Mr. Dryden right; yet is as much as you can expect from the leisure of one who has the care of a nursery.' In an earlier letter she had dismissed Cowley's *The Cutter of Colman Street* with 'the Prologue and Epilogue good, the rest may equal some plays which pass well enough, but it did not answer the expectation which Mr. Cowley's wit has given him'.[1]

She gives Bohun her view of Restoration comedy: 'Plays now are but long farces, epitomes of the folly of life, great and noble parts laid aside, the desire of transmitting virtue to posterity does not torment the minds of the living, and what we read of the dead seems a fable, so different is the present practice of the world . . . yet . . . though it be an erring, it is a discerning Age we live in which does not a little add to our condemnation, that we fail by consent.'[2]

Bohun would praise her letters and her skill in kitchen and still-house, yet, at times, the former wellnigh bewildered him, being 'something of kindness and a mixture of reproof' or 'so full of intrigue that I can make myself sure of nothing but good language'; yet he was reassured by her 'essential talent in preserving friendships and never losing any one friend you thought worth owning at first'. No virtue, no favour, was her motto—and his consolation.

If Bohun owed her a letter—from Oxford—she would banter him: 'I suppose your college affairs take up much of your time and will believe your diversions in Oxford are very charming, but neither should make you so absolutely forget Deptford and those in it, as not to impart some of your pleasant thoughts at spare moments as especially knowing how well we receive your letters and how naturally our sex loves novelty, that I cannot but accuse you of unkindness.'

[1] Letter, Mrs. Evelyn to J. Evelyn, 27 Sept. 1661.
[2] Letter, Mrs. Evelyn to R. Bohun, 23 June 1668.

Glanville wrote a letter—which is damaged—to Mrs. Evelyn from Paris, but a most significant ending survives: 'I conclude my letter . . . but with how much of my heart dear sister I dare not tell you, because I am more than I must express your affectionate brother and humble servant W. G. . . .'[1] In another letter (which is undated) he shows Bohun as a rival: apparently the latter had fallen into Mrs. Evelyn's disfavour, and on the status quo Glanville remarks: 'I congratulate Mr. Bohun's being restored . . . but cracked coxcombs are seldom soddered, and I fear by living again one Spring or Fall at Deptford, he would relapse into his old distemper and become as incurable and incorrigible an ass as his brother.' In fact Bohun was a person whose kindness and snivelling melancholy she suffered, but whose esteem she valued.

A downright statement of favour or dislike was rarely made in any letter Mrs Evelyn wrote. Perhaps it was as well; Glanville was pursuing the Roman Catholic widow Lady Lewkenor of Dorking in the autumn of 1670.

But there were ways of knowing how one stood with Mrs. Evelyn. About the time when Evelyn had completed his reconnoitre and was fully engaged with the Maids of Honour, Glanville thought he saw into her heart: 'I confess I have resolved never to be concerned either with women's tears or smiles; both being most commonly employed to deceive; yet there are some few whose tears move me, because from a particular manner (which pleases me) of letting them fall, I fancy their natures are good, if there be any such thing to be found in your sex. There is a certain lady in the world with whose way of weeping I am infinitely pleased, and yet it works so much upon me, that I can hardly refrain from being guilty of the like weakness: methought, sister, at our parting, you wept very like this woman, and that was the reason [I was so] much pleased as to laugh when you cry. It would be a strange vanity in me to believe that my interest in your heart is considerable enough to cause the fall of one tear from your eye; you are too wise to be so weak . . .'[2]

So the delicate raillery went on. He would say that it was abundance rather than want of respect that kept him sometimes

---

[1] Letter, W. Glanville to Mrs. Evelyn, 17 Nov. 1668.
[2] Letter, W. Glanville to Mrs. Evelyn, 30 Sept. 1670.

silent; 'I never yet knew any man fare the better for discovery to a woman the power she had over him.' He assumed that her attachment to him was greater than she dared express: 'Ingenious as you are, I think 'twould puzzle you to write to a person whom you would not importune with hackney compliments or formal civilities, and for whom you had a greater kindness than you dared to let him know . . . you are a great mistress of your passions.' On her defensive tactics he would comment: 'I smile to hear you so often say you are only upon the defensive, pray whence come those by and reverse blows wherewith you usually hit so home?'

Just now Evelyn was enthusiastic over his discovery of young Grinling Gibbons and his incomparable wood carving; in February he took Pepys and Wren—after entertaining them to dinner at Sayes Court—to see Gibbons' copy of Tintoretto's Crucifixion. Later, in gratitude for bringing his work to the notice of Wren and Charles II Gibbons presented Evelyn with a beautiful carved table in limewood and walnut.[1]

Glanville had little success with the Dorking widow, and surprisingly revealed to Evelyn the progress of his suit: 'If I do not prosper, nothing but a thing worse than the Devil, that is his dam, can defeat me: if the widow do not make me her husband, I am sure she can marry no other man while I live, if she have but one grain either of honour or truth. I am now with my lady at Woodcott, where I steal now and then from her lips three or four kisses, just as the dogs are reported to drink in Nilus for fear of the crocodiles, lap twice or thrice and away . . . I know what will be said, if I prevail G is a cunning fellow, if I fail, a coxcomb. But the most dexterous gamester at conny catching would be put to his trumps, to save himself from being bested, had he such a counterer to cope with as I have.'[2]

Mrs. Evelyn at last went over to the offensive, encouraging his courtship of the widow. However, his regard for Mrs. Evelyn in particular and his dislike of widows in general (by this time) inspired the rejoinder: . . . 'should I discover that I am in love with my friend, it cannot justly offend her, or any other person, provided my passion be but platonique. Give my

[1] Now in Evelyn Collection, Christ Church.
[2] Letter, W. Glanville to J. Evelyn, 14 April 1671.

respects what name you please, I am very well satisfied, that never were any professed to the most meritorious of your sex, upon better grounds than are mine to you . . . If prepossession render me incapable of being your adorer, how can you that know my heart was long since devoted to a Sussex saint, propound offering it up to a New Shrine?' His allegiance to a Sussex saint, of whom we know nothing, comes as a surprise to us, and a measure of his raillery; he goes on, 'certainly you tempt me with the Darking widow, at once to make trial both of my faith and discretion. To make a new choice would be inconstancy, and an ill one imprudent. Can you imagine that she . . . will bestow her beauty or her wealth upon any but an active, vigorous gallant, who by works of supererogation must thresh himself into her affections; beside, could she and I join bodies upon equal terms, yet our souls could never unite, since her religion condemns me for heresy, and mine hers for idolatry; to speak truth I think widows a sort of cattle so odd that the best of the kind with all the perfections of nature and advantages of fortune, are seldom an equal exchange for any man's peace and liberty; for my own part, I had much rather die a martyr to a coy and cruel mistress than live a slave to a proud and peevish wife; for in spite of fortune, I can make myself rich in being contented, and maugre all other womens disdain, you alone can make me happy by your friendship, which I hope I shall enjoy so long as I perform Articles.'[1]

Let us leave this 'platonique' dissembling and return to Whitehall—and Evelyn. But before we proceed to more interesting matters, we must complete the list of his publications: *An Idea of the Perfection of Painting*, a translation from R. Fréart, appeared in August 1668, and *The History of the Three Imposters* followed early in the following year.

The story—or rather some evidence—of his friendship with two Maids of Honour is continued in his manuscript *The Legend of the Pearle*.[2] From this we learn that he was perfectly contented with his wife; indeed she made 'the best wife in the world, sweet, and (though not charming) agreeable, and as she grew up, pious, loyal, and of so just a temper, obliging and withall discreet, as has made me very happy'. Perhaps to the reasons

---

[1] Letter, W. Glanville to Mrs. Evelyn, 23 Oct. 1671.
[2] Evelyn MS. 304.

already suggested for his quest of friendship, we may now add his wife's lack of charm—though doubtless her own admiring trio would not have accepted it. He says that she freely gave him the liberty to converse with other ladies and to make virtuous friendships with the sex. In this new sphere he was diffident: 'I was a man of the shade, and one who had conversed more amongst plants and books, than in the Circles: I had contracted a certain odd reservedness, which render'd me wholly unfit to converse among the Knights of the Carpet, and the refined things of the Antechamber: some said I was morose, and affected, others that I was plainly stupid and a fop.' But we cannot believe these depreciatory remarks: had he not been in and around Whitehall ever since the Restoration? Of course he disapproved of much he heard and saw; when he heard—in March 1671—Nell Gwyn hold 'a very familiar discourse' with the King—with whom he was walking—in St. James's Park he was 'heartily sorry'. But to call her 'an impudent comedian' was rude and inaccurate. (Pepys, it will be remembered, said on another occasion, that she looked pretty in her shift.) Besides, Evelyn should have left the King and walked on.

Evelyn was well-preserved, careful in his dress, of middle stature, with fine eyes set in a face not to be judged handsome —for his nose was a trifle too long. Formerly he despised a peruke; from the early 1670's he wore one to enhance his youthfulness. His success in the antechamber was at first somewhat slow; the Maids of Honour said he had 'a forbidding countenance', and took him for a schoolmaster. He believed they thought his wife the unhappiest woman in the world—a remark that Glanville would have undoubtedly described as hyperbole in Evelyn's own defence.

Anne Howard, and her sister Dorothy, first attracted him. They were the daughters of Mrs. William Howard, housekeeper to the Duchess of York. Dorothy was already a Maid of Honour, and her sister joined the ranks a little later. According to Evelyn, Anne, in her teens, full of vitality, and witty, was the centre of attraction with her 'thousand pretty impertinences'. He is careful to say that 'that which most deeply engaged' his peculiar esteem was 'a piece of solemn devotion she had composed for regulation of her own life' that he 'found by chance upon her table, and which, unheeded by her', he had perused.

Thus he assures us that this friendship was based on religious grounds; and after the seventeenth-century fashion, named her *Ornithia* (the bird-like), giving himself the name *Philaretes* (a lover of virtue).

However, Anne's name had soon to be changed to *Penthea* (the sad), when he transferred his affections to a friend of the Howards, another Maid of Honour, some time in or after 1669. She was Margaret Blagge, one of the four daughters of Colonel Thomas Blagge, and Mary, the daughter of Sir Francis North, both of ancient Suffolk families. In 1666 she became a Maid of Honour to the Duchess of York, and on the latter's death in 1671, transferred her services to the Queen.

At Court, Margaret Blagge had the reputation of a saint. She also composed a scheme of devotion, which put God before all else: it was headed, 'My life, by God's Grace, without which I can do nothing.' There were safeguards against the frailty of the Court: 'When I go into the withdrawing room, let me consider what my calling is: to entertain the Ladies, not to talk foolishly to men: more especially the King.' She possessed moral courage: 'Be sure never to talk to the King when they speak filthily, tho' I be laughed at.' If in a lax Court Anne Howard was a rarity, Margaret was a pearl. And Pearl was Evelyn's name for her—though sometimes he called her Electra (the bright). Between the summer of 1669 and the autumn of 1672 he sought her on every possible occasion, and in due time she afforded him opportunities to visit her in her chamber in Whitehall. All these things we find in *The Life of Mrs. Godolphin*[1] (which he left in manuscript); he also tells us therein that Margaret was elegant, charming, a beauty, and witty enough to reprove his moroseness, 'and greatly devout, which put me out of all fear of her raillery, and made me look upon her with extraordinary respect'.

Mrs. Evelyn was perhaps indifferent to her husband's new interest, or at least discerning Margaret's merit, assured herself that no harm could come of it; 'never were two people more alike in way and inclination', she said. On his visit to Margaret's chamber on 16 October 1672, Evelyn made a pact of friendship with her. She had told him that she had no friend in the world. Had she forgotten Sidney Godolphin to whom she had been engaged for six years? After his election as a member of Parlia-

[1] First printed in 1847; references are to the 1939 ed.

ment for Helston in 1668, he was nearly always abroad as a
special envoy in France or Flanders. Just now—at the age of
twenty-seven—he was following the French Court during the
campaign. So careful, calculating and unobtrusive was he at
Court, always waiting his chance to be useful, Charles II said of
him: 'He is never in the way, and he is never out of the way.'
He must have been rather like that in his association with
Margaret. According to the *Life*, when Evelyn asked her:
'What do you esteem a certain gentleman beyond the seas to
be?' she replied to the effect that Godolphin could not help her
in spiritual affairs, nor would she give him the trouble.

Evelyn then gave her, in characteristic wordiness, his definition of friendship, concluding, 'understand that friend in the
way you mean is the nearest relation in nature'. He then drew
something on a paper, like an altar, with a heart upon it
surrounded by a halo of stars, and wrote: 'Be this the symbol
of inviolable friendship.' Margaret, taking a pen, added: 'Be it
so: Margaret Blagge, 16 October, 1672.' To her it was serious,
to him sacred. To Evelyn it was a spiritual opportunity; to give
his soul and expect Margaret's reciprocation. He then said:
'Do you know what you have done?' and proceeded to talk
of bonds, the marriage of souls, and the virgin state being
happier than the conjugal. Each had obligations: to visit, write,
discourse, read, pray, admonish, 'in short, something of all
relations and practical duties, and something above them all:
these madam are the laws, and they are reciprocal and eternal'.[1]
It was a strange compact for a man of fifty-two to make with
a girl of twenty. She had apparently renounced her secular
engagement for a spiritual pact in which Evelyn desired to lose
himself in a greater reality.

Though Margaret could be soft and melting at her devotions
she probably showed in sexual matters, not frigidity, but some
physical aversion. Therefore the friendship was likely to remain
Platonic. Yet Evelyn could not refrain from warning her against
the exciting danger of physical attraction. At fifty-two he was,
of course, qualified to incite it, and to put it to the test. At least
he must have warned her that Agape might flare up into Eros.
This seems to be her reply: 'When cheap thoughts arise of you
I believe I shall pay dearly for it, for I must undervalue that

[1] Op. cit., p. 24.

which I have often upon my knees acknowledged as a blessing: but why will you say these things?'[1] Unsophisticated as she was, the risk had never occurred to her.

Between the signing of the pact and 21 December Evelyn spent fourteen days with his wife and forty-five in London. It is not at all unlikely that Mrs. Evelyn now regretted her acquiescence, at the outset, of his friendship; his absences from home were becoming more frequent and more extended in duration. On the 28 November he went to London and we might well be persuaded by the entries in the *Diary*, that he spent the time in a normal manner: he was chosen Secretary of the Royal Society, heard three sermons and received the Holy Communion once, solicited money at the Treasury for the sick prisoners, attended the Council of Plantations, supped with Lady Sunderland, and carried out some public business. There are, however, in the *Diary* several days in this period left blank. We can only guess that he was visiting Margaret.

Mrs. Evelyn, tired of stilling and preserving, and with no one more exciting to talk to than an occasional sailor from the dockyard (and Glanville's entertaining epistles just now were somewhat scarce), justifiably felt neglected—and it would be Christmas in five days. Exercising her ingenious way of using expressions very pleasing yet somewhat obscure, on 20 December she reminded Evelyn of the difference between his courtly life and that of his rustic *Hortensia*: 'Dear Philaretes, I hope you do not imagine though I live in the country and converse with sea nymphs, now and then with a tarpaulin hero, that I do not apprehend the difference between this kind of felicity and that which you possess in a glorious Court amongst great beauties and wits, and those so refined that the charms of that splendour has no influence on their spirits, persons whose ideas are of a higher nature, whose minds are pure and actions innocent; these if I could be capable of envy, I should make the subject; but I am so far failing in that kind that I rejoice in your happiness, I acknowledge you a better judge of such perfections, and to merit the honour of . . . the friendship of the sprightly saint, and to be allowed the liberty of a playfellow to Ornithia, whose excellencies unites admiration and esteem; since you have qualifications which entitle you to as much good fortune

[1] Letter, M. Blagge to J. Evelyn, n.d. [Jan. 1673].

as any man, if knowledge and discernment in curious and choice speculations, joined with virtues not common though desirable in your sex may obtain returns of friendship from persons who cannot be unjust and therefore must allow you a share of their esteem, you may pretend, but should I hope for a part, it must be upon no other account but as I have a little interest in you and possibly am kindly thought of by you, which happiness produces many advantages to Hortensia.'[1]

In response to this charming and touching appeal Philaretes (being a lover of virtue) returned home the next day. Before leaving London he gave Margaret an *Office for Nativity*[2] for her own use, based, in style, on Henry Vaughan's *The Mount of Olives*, 1652. This included a meditation to be read with him, which shows pretty plainly what form the friendship was to take: 'Hail, O Incarnate Word! I adore, I admire, I praise, I magnify Thee, yea I love thee, for thou hast loved me, when I loved thee not, when I loved the world, and the follies of it . . . come, take possession, dwell in me forever . . . let my ambition be to serve thee, my delight to obey thee, my glory to admire thee, and never to set my love upon any creature which may take it off from thee . . .' With these words, Evelyn makes clear his intention to deny Margaret the joy of human affection. She had become an instrument to his own purpose.

As soon as the Christmas festivity to his tenants at Deptford was over, he returned to London in readiness to wish Margaret a happy new year. But he did not forget the usual new year gifts of crowns or half-crowns to the various doorkeepers and porters in Whitehall, including a crown for Robin Ellis the doorkeeper of the Queen's withdrawing room, and one for Margaret's man.[3] For Margaret he brought another short devotional manuscript, entitled *Circumcision or New-years-Day Office*, the second incitement to sacred love: 'Lord: make me willing in this day of thy power . . . this very day, in which I hear thy Voice, let me no longer harden my heart . . . circumcise it from the flesh and cleanse it from its adherences; . . . wash it from wickedness, that I may be saved, and let vain thoughts lodge no longer within me . . . free me from all hypocrisy: the heart, O Lord, is deceitful above all things . . .

---

[1] Letter, Mrs. Evelyn to J. Evelyn, 20 Dec. 1672.
[2] Evelyn MS. 125.   [3] Evelyn MS. 64.

O sanctify my whole man, spirit, soul, and body, and let me never fall from my integrity.'[1] Evidently, despite the pact, Margaret was not yet able to satisfy Evelyn that her break with Godolphin was complete.

A few days later he presented her with a handsome turquoise locket set with sixteen diamonds costing eleven pounds—a pretty thought to remind her of the 16 October. The locket contained, or formed, a five-pointed star or pentacle, probably with the letters of the word *ΑΓΑΠΑ*[2] (spiritual love) between its five points. The pentacle, and the motto *Un Dieu un Amy*, now marked all things written for her, and the letters she wrote to Evelyn were also marked with the pentacle by him. (*Un Dieu un Amy* does not signify any fraternal generosity in Evelyn's Idea of God.)

In the first week of January Margaret obtained leave from the King and Queen to retire from her appointment as a Maid of Honour. Doubtless the friendship could not flourish if she remained at Whitehall; Godolphin had returned from the continent and, of course, both Evelyn and Margaret agreed with the appropriateness of the King's delineation of his character. Therefore we cannot altogether believe Evelyn, who said in the *Life* that she 'vacated entirely to religion and solitude'.

We have no evidence that Godolphin made any suggestion that she should stay at Berkeley House (the home of Lord Berkeley of Stratton), but as Lady Berkeley was related to Godolphin, this cunning choice of residence may well have come from him. The house and gardens covered a large part of what is now Mayfair between Berkeley Square and Devonshire House. Except when he was at Windsor with the King or racing at Newmarket, Godolphin was at Goring House, a stone's throw on the other side of Piccadilly. At Berkeley House Margaret's apartments were on the first floor, and on every possible Tuesday, Beck her maid showed Evelyn through the hall, where the story of Francis I was depicted in tapestry, up the cedar staircase to her room. Here the two friends prayed and read together, generally after having dined at midday with the Berkeleys.

For three years this happy Tuesday routine went on, broken only by their occasional visits—at Margaret's instigation—to

[1] Evelyn MS. 110.   [2] He never used the form *agape*.

84

sick and poor people, and by a country holiday in the summer months which Margaret spent with Lady Berkeley at Twickenham Park. Prayers and Offices for their joint use flowed from Evelyn's pen without cessation. Early in 1673 he wrote what is nothing less than an anti-Godolphin prayer: '. . . we seek no other satisfaction than that this love of ours may be totally immersed in the fruition, and Love of Thee: Ah, let that flaming Charity of Thine . . . born likewise in our hearts, to consume all that is earthy, and sensual, and repugnant to thy spirit of holiness . . . never oh never suffer us to depart from Thee O Lord, for the love of any creature or thing in this world . . .'[1]

By Margaret's letters to Evelyn in March we can see why he inserted these last words, for, despite the pact, she was, on occasion, visiting Godolphin at Goring House. She found that she could not live up to Evelyn's ideals; perhaps she was haunted by those terrible words, 'never to set my love upon any creature'. She was beginning to realise her inability to allow Evelyn to take more from her than he was giving her; that a spiritual pact could be one-sided. We have no letters of Godolphin's; however, through Margaret's evasion of Evelyn and her confession of the inability to satisfy his spiritual demands, we can sense Godolphin watching, and making arrangements to meet her at Goring House: he was always there in the background, pulling strings.

Yet Godolphin could not altogether reclaim Margaret. Evelyn strove hard to retain her as his spiritual toy. When she slipped away from him, he would say: 'Why was I so unhappy, or so foolish to imagine that because I thought Electra the creature in the world, whom I would wish and choose to be my friend, and the repository of my heart; she should have the same sentiments and opinion of me unless our perfections had been equal? This must needs be the cause, Electra, of my ill success . . . call me your friend for that's true, to death I'll be that; and be a little sorry, you can be no more mine— because I am imperfect.' Then skilfully skating over the borderline between love and devotion, he would go on: 'But stay, is there no punishment due to the little thieves who steal away our hearts, give me that back again if you can. Now would this look as like a love-letter as any thing in the world, to any body

[1] Evelyn MS. 120.

living, who should light upon it, but you and I: nor without reason; God Almighty knows my heart: I do love you; but it is because you love Him . . .'[1] Thus could Evelyn, for a while at least, restrain her visits to Godolphin, and demonstrate the immemorial delight of loving God and of loving one who also loves Him. Presumably Evelyn could say with Henry Vaughan,

> For I not for an houre did love
> Or for a day desire
> But with my soule had from above
> This endles holy fire,

and cast Godolphin for the role of the mighty Amorist.

After a visit to Goring House, the contrite Margaret, using a penitential office written by Evelyn, would say: 'I did deplore my horrid sins . . . tomorrow I shall not be at the first service but will call you as I said and when I said together we will pray: and when no longer you will permit me, asunder: for methinks if I am but with you I am safe.' In any spiritual attachment, the woman is the more tender. Margaret, unable to resist Evelyn's borderline, passionate protestation, replied: 'What mean you to make me weep and to break my heart by your love to me? take me and all I have, give me but your love, my dear friend Tuesday is longed for by me, and nights and days move a tedious pace till I am near you.'[2]

Yet to Evelyn the joy of reunion was a mixed one. He was always haunted by the question of her marriage. It seems, however, that his influence, his hold, was complete: 'as for my being married, you know you won't let me resolve', she said. His spiritual love therefore took on a quality of persecution, which was bound, sooner or later, to act against him. As we read Margaret's letters of 1673, we are moved by her struggle: her soul is Evelyn's and her loyalty to him unquestionable, but her heart, despite utterances to the contrary, is elsewhere.

It was about this time that Evelyn's daughter Elizabeth, being ill, his former 'playfellow' Ann Howard was invited to Sayes Court to nurse her. The boisterous charm that Evelyn rejected is seen in her delightful acceptance of his invitation—an honour which in fact surprised her, for she deemed that the

---

[1] Letter, J. Evelyn to M. Blagge, n.d. [1673].
[2] Letter, M. Blagge to J. Evelyn, *c.* 20 April 1673.

former happy times at Sayes Court which she enjoyed as 'Ranting Nanny', when they danced the Maypole to *Sellenger's Round,* had gone for ever: 'most constant and loving playfellow I was, I confess, in deep mortification having banished all thoughts of the past and present of the vanities of Sayes Court —absence and the mulligrubs beginning now to cure those feats of activity I once played there: but I find Morose is never to be forgotten, yet as soon as I perceived myself going to such maturity and wisdom, I thought it might be no small favour to give you the title of my friend instead of playfellow and ranting Nanny. Thus was I become a new creature and full of sobriety, when in comes the humble petition of John Evelyn esquire; which I had no sooner perused but all these good resolutions vanished, and vanity once more took possession— for which it had a large subject, together with hard words and superfine compliments, which you know gains much upon the weaker vessel, especially when told one by a man of con- science.' This invitation fills her 'as full of mischief as ever, therefore look to yourself playfellow, for I shall come like a lion broke loose from his den and play more tricks than Robin Goodfellow'. She then breaks into rhyme, having noted Evelyn's assurance

> that Little Blagge as bright as day
> nor all the rest of the Court splendour
> could make to playfellow your love less tender.

Therefore, none of the spoil-sports of Sayes Court, 'the sleepy wight' Sir Richard Browne,

> Who ere the day has done its dawn
> first stretches out a grievous yawn
> nor madam Evelyn's jealous eye
> who lives so circumspect and looks so shy
> nor Bohun that quintessence of sniff and spleen
> my foe so mortal and so keen[1]

shall have the power to part her from Evelyn during her return to this scene of former happiness. Alas, that *Ornithia*

---

[1] Letter, A. Howard to J. Evelyn, 20 Nov. 167- dated by Evelyn— wrongly.

was changed to *Penthea*: what an attractive creature she must have been.

At Whitsuntide, Evelyn administered to Margaret another rebuke in the *Office for Pentecost*: '. . . thither let the desire of my heart ascend, and never come down again to dwell upon anything here; for there is my Treasure', adding what seems an unnecessary corrective for the erstwhile accredited saint of the Court: 'Burn up, O divine Fire! all the dross, and refine the impurities of my corrupted nature.'[1]

In May, at Sayes Court, when the garden was in all the glory of its spring colour and a pink and white carpet lay over the orchard grass, Lord and Lady Berkeley, Margaret and Godolphin were entertained. That such a meeting could take place, is the measure of Godolphin's equanimity. Patient and inscrutable as ever, perhaps he strolled with Lady Berkeley down the long grass promenade to listen to the latest news of the friendship, while Evelyn and Margaret were happy together in the Grove. And doubtless the hearty Lord Berkeley found something amusing to say to Mrs. Evelyn over a glass of wine in the wooden parlour.

In June, Margaret's portrait was painted by Matthew Dixon, at Evelyn's request. It was a heavy sepulchral affair, with a tombstone for her seat and a funeral urn in the background: her hair tied back like a servant's, her face downcast—a setting and posture doubtless intended by Evelyn to suggest her spirituality. We note, however, that his own spirituality was not above 'tying her hair ribbon on his wrist in the studio and to his returning home so adorned.'[2]

For the greater part of July and August she stayed at Twickenham Park for the summer recess. Her intention of meeting Godolphin during this period is reflected in a letter written prior to her departure. Evelyn had praised her for all his spiritual benefits, but she tells him: '. . . You have endeavoured with all the sincerity imaginable to make me better, and as you have said to me the more good one does, the more tender one grows, and God is better pleased with us, and then we need not doubt but we are better: this is it and nothing else, therefore give God the praise that you have so much

[1] Evelyn MS. 126.
[2] Letter, J. Evelyn to M. Blagge, 18 June 1673.

grace: and for me I beg you will not yet so much praise God for me, as pray to him. This I beg for I am yet bad very bad: I know it and you shall too when we meet if ever we do.'

At Twickenham, Margaret must have pondered and realised how Godolphin's comforting equanimity contrasted strangely—but pleasurably—with Evelyn's possessiveness. She was happier with Godolphin under the widely spaced alder trees than in Evelyn's rather over-planted Grove. At a later date, Godolphin remarked that there was 'good air and harmless entertainment in the country', a sentiment to which Margaret would now agree. Yet she was not able to give him any hope or encouragement. Glanville's words to Mrs. Evelyn, at this moment, are coincidentally most apt: 'I wish I did know when and how I am in your thoughts, but that is a secret a woman's breast will never reveal, for commonly where she loves with passion, she thinks herself obliged never to discover it, and many times counterfeits kindness where she hath none at all.' Margaret revealed nothing with certainty to Godolphin, and continued to counterfeit her attachment to Evelyn.

Glanville goes on in his letter to Mrs. Evelyn to disparage spiritual love—and he gives us some news of the recent portrait: 'Were I in love with you I could not love you better than I do, and since I am so perfectly your friend, I hope you will value me no less than if I were a passionate lover; because there is no such thing upon earth as seraphick love . . . I dare not wish our friendship had begun when we first saw one another, for I am conscious I could not have trusted myself with loving you twenty years ago as well as I do now; you in those days might have been safe in your virtue, but I could not then be sure of my peace . . . But sister why may not you doat upon a diamond, as well as the philosopher doth upon Pearl. My picture drawn by Dixon might hang as well in the closet, as the lady's doth in the bed chamber, but I would presume, however, to fix mine eyes where I had bestow'd my heart, and not be drawn with dejected looks.'[1]

With September the normal tempo of Tuesdays at Berkeley House was resumed, and the *Meditation for Michaelmas Day* duly accented with such words for Margaret's utterance as 'teach me submission . . . humility . . . not to be high-minded . . .

[1] Letter, W. Glanville to Mrs. Evelyn, 21 Aug. 1673.

make me of an hospitable sweet and courteous disposition . . .
and above all so innocent and meek that I never offend any of
the least of thine'.[1] A few weeks at Twickenham obviously had
a humanising effect upon her. She complains to Evelyn that she
experiences 'a dullness in meditation, a scarcity of tears, and a
coldness in prayer and many imperfections', which being interpreted, means that she has enjoyed her holiday. But still she
gives Evelyn some hope: '. . . but I labour against my sins
and from my heart detest them . . . and I hope I shall improve'.

In October, on the anniversary of the pact, she again
acknowledged her shortcomings: 'I hope I shall improve, more
the next year than I have this, or you will rise up in judgment
against me: oh that I did love nothing but God and you.'
Of course, she loved Godolphin—and if Evelyn had been wise
he would have released her. In November his average of four
visits to Berkeley House a month increased to six—evidence as
good as letters (of which there are none) that Evelyn had
managed to purge the effects of Margaret's summer holiday.
At Twickenham Godolphin could recall the happy past, at
Berkeley House Evelyn pointed to the celestial future.

Mrs. Evelyn, in the meantime, continued to be entertained
by Glanville, who again provided some not altogether irrelevant
worldly wisdom: 'I am now perfectly convinced that all women
naturally take pride and content in seeing themselves adored,
and there is not any who hath not some tenderness for those
her charms have smitten.' He then has a dig at his rival Bohun,
the 'poor Heaven driver', who 'thinks as often on the comfortable importance of a good lady as of a good living; and
truly for my part, I see no reason why a mistress may not be
as well allowed to a mortified Divine, as to a Platonique
philosopher. Indeed I am now very sorry I did not yield to
your importunity for the sinecure, but doubtless your interest
with the plump prelate of Rochester or his lean Grace of
Canterbury may in some short time procure a dignity for your
reclaimed and regenerate Levite; and then, being a Dean,
Archdeacon, or a prebend, his picture drawn by a good hand,
may hang cheek by jowl with Pearl's in the parlour.'[2] (Had it
become embarrassing in the bed chamber—where we left it?)

[1] Evelyn MS. 72.
[2] Letter, W. Glanville to Mrs. Evelyn, 20 Oct. 1673.

CHAPTER VI

The Great Friendship

~~~~~~

I F we tried to discern any spiritual high-water mark in the
ebb and flow of this strange friendship we might choose one of
the occasions in January 1674 when Evelyn and Margaret
participated in the celebration of the Mental or Spiritual
Communion at Berkeley House: 'Did not our hearts burn within
yesterday', writes Margaret, 'and our very spirits glow whilst
we were in Communion with Christ: how delightful it is, what
relish it kept all the day, and even to this moment, and must
we not be very careful that we lose it not this week.' Evelyn
had also poured out his soul into an 'Ejaculation' to be used
by her before the Communion: 'I have letters of yours', she goes
on, 'which break my heart to pieces at any time . . . and that
divine ejaculation of yours: O how heavenly are they my dear
friend . . .'[1]

Mrs. Evelyn, mourning the death of Sir Samuel Tuke, sent
Bohun some lines that—had he seen them—might have warned
her husband: 'No felicity here has any duration; we are solicitous
to obtain, we fear whilst we possess and we are inconsolable
when we lose . . . we fall from life by degrees when our friends
go before us.'[2]

By April Margaret's felicity had dwindled, and in *An Office
for the Lord's Day*, Evelyn applied a scourge that seemed at
once better suited to the vilest reprobate of the Restoration

[1] Letter, M. Blagge to J. Evelyn, n.d. [Jan. 1674].
[2] Letter, Mrs. Evelyn to R. Bohun, 29 Jan. 1674.

scene and to possess all the authority of Holy Writ: 'I am toss'd with the tempest of my impetuous passions . . . rebuke the waves of my unruly affections . . . I am stung and bitten with the fiery serpent of my sensual appetite'; and urged her to present her heart to the Son of God: 'but thou wilt have us give it thee . . . take it, my sweet Jesus, take it: never will I require it of thee again, but to make a new oblation of it to thee . . . nothing [my Saviour] is there in this world, which so bitterly afflicts me, as that I had not presented it to thee sooner, and Thou hadst been my first Love, my only Love.'[1]

But, of course, it was one thing to be so inspired, the fulfilment was quite a different matter. By Easter she writes of her 'coldness in holy duties, and my being upon the least step into the world apt to be ensnared by its temptations, caught with its follies . . . on every side I am polluted and defiled'. Probably Godolphin tempted her to go to Twickenham; anyway, in the last week of May she was there.

A little later in the summer Godolphin precipitated a crisis by proposing marriage. The details of what followed are confused; some of Margaret's letters to Evelyn are missing (she retrieved six from him), she habitually destroyed all his, and the account of his part as given in the *Life* does not, in every aspect, carry conviction. A copy of a letter dated 27 February 1673 (it should be 1674), in which he advised Margaret to marry, savours of embellishment if not of fiction, and his subsequent conduct cancelled out any such advice. What is plain is Margaret's poor state of health; her gentle, susceptible nature was on the point of breakdown; she was pale and lean, and her surviving letters manifested something approaching mental instability. After rejecting Godolphin's offer, she considered the possibility of renouncing the world altogether, and living in retirement at Hereford: she wrote to Evelyn, 'I can't but think it most suitable to my humour and the nearest way to heaven, and you can't blame one so weak as I to choose that path that will bring me soonest to my Journey's end, but be assured I will observe your rules and take your counsel and will not leave until *he* give me free leave to do it.'[2]

From this we are pleased to note that Godolphin still had

[1] Evelyn MS. 90.
[2] Letter, M. Blagge to J. Evelyn, 26 June [1674].

some influence over her, though it seems of small account in comparison with the arduous day of prayer that Evelyn drew up, and inflicted upon her. . . . 'Then will I rise and till ten be at my private duties, then pray with my maids, then by eleven will I be dressed, then shall I have time before prayers to read a chapter with Diodati and write a prayer and collect out of it: and whilst I am dressing, Beck reads out of the Bible and other good things: at six at night I will for an hour be at my private duties, and after that for half an hour or an hour will learn such things by heart as I would gladly retain: at nine pray with my people, and by myself at eleven when I come up, when undressing, as in the morning, Beck reading to me and then with peace lay my self down to rest. This for ordinary days, not fridays, for on that day and please God I will not fail to fast and pray and on Sundays to be early up, and all the day well employed, but else on other days this is the rule I intend to set my self: if as I said before you like it . . .'[1] Thus, distraught, she aspired to reach the heights that Evelyn had set for her to climb.

Lady Berkeley—who throughout the friendship seems to have acted as a concierge for Godolphin—naturally opposed the flight to Hereford. Evelyn was in a fix: while calling Margaret a magnanimous virgin for sacrificing all her beauty to God, he is forced to lament, 'Why leave you one behind intangl'd in the world? Whilst you are in the light, I in darkness and a chaos.'[2] But at last he changes his mind, and gives her permission to go. He had breached Margaret's engagement, and now he had broken his own friendship. Margaret acknowledged his permission: 'Ten thousand thanks I give you for your kind letter, and take your resignation of me to our Lord better than anything you can do for me: for it shows you the best Christian and friend in the world.'[3]

Lady Berkeley (who was three times married) had strong views of spiritual friendship. She had watched the deterioration in Margaret's health as she ascended the spiritual heights; under her eyes a potential wife had become a nervous and fanatic celibate. Lady Berkeley's plan—probably suggested by Godolphin—was to keep Margaret at Berkeley House at all costs.

[1] Op. cit.   [2] *Life of Mrs. Godolphin*, 49.
[3] Letter, M. Blagge to J. Evelyn, n.d. [Summer, 1674].

Unfortunately Godolphin was constituted to give orders rather than to accept advice—though doubtless Lady Berkeley minced no words with him in her reports: he was as patient as she was exasperated. (We must understand, however, that neither of them knew anything of the nature of Evelyn's Offices and Meditations; they knew only their effect.) Lady Berkeley's success in persuading Margaret to stay with her was nothing compared with Evelyn's; his elation may be judged from Margaret's manner of telling him of Lady Berkeley's persuasion: 'Now for Tuesday I am still what I was, say what you will, hours and days move dully on.'[1]

'I am still what I was' signified a moral victory for Evelyn. Lady Berkeley, however, was content to hope that eventually Godolphin would bring Evelyn's weekly visits to an end. Doubtless Godolphin would prefer not to marry until he had purchased the office of Master of the Robes; as we shall discover he was forced to act before he had attained to that position.

Evelyn now suggested that Margaret should stay at Sayes Court, but the wise Lady Berkeley objected; perhaps she considered those delectable private walks and alleys to be unsuitable at such a juncture. Margaret's outburst to Evelyn illustrated my Lady's wisdom: 'My best friend, as to my being in your family, it was *almost*, and *ah!* that it had not been *almost*, but *altogether*'[2]—a revelation that well-nigh persuades us that Glanville was right in his disbelief of seraphic love. As a cooling diversion, Lady Berkeley took Margaret to drink the waters at Southborough. The frustrated Evelyn visited some friends in Kent and Sussex, and when homeward bound looked in at the wells—not to drink the waters—to pay Margaret a visit. But Lady Berkeley had arranged further diversion for her: to go on to Twickenham to meet Lady Fitzharding; and then to Moor Park to meet the Duchess of Monmouth. Evelyn found no consolation in Pepys's company at Windsor, where they watched a mock battle of the storming of Maestricht (just fallen to the French), nor in returning with him to London.

The wise Lady Berkeley extended Margaret's holiday until the middle of September—a round of social visits described by Margaret as 'these perpetual hurries'. At Twickenham she saw

---

[1] Letter, M. Blagge to J. Evelyn, n.d. [Summer, 1674].
[2] *Life*, 52.

Godolphin, whose sister's illness was causing anxiety; Margaret wrote to Evelyn, saying: 'I have been so sorry with him, and for him, that I can scarce see.' We may wonder, in this instance, if pity was akin to love. Yet, a fortnight previously had she reassured Evelyn—whose spirit was torn and twisted by her absence—of her loyalty: 'For you there is nothing that I know of I would not do; I would deny myself any pleasure without exception for you, and undergo all I am capable of enduring, for to my death I will love you . . . for all I have I would not lose you.'[1] But of what she had we are not certain.

On 15 September Margaret and Evelyn met again at Berkeley House after two months of cruel separation. To outwit Lady Berkeley, Margaret arranged that Evelyn should 'come at six o'clock directly up to my chamber and not dine here, but come then so we might pray together, for I would willingly have our first meeting consecrated with prayers and thanksgivings'.[2] Thus she escaped what might have been an embarrassing midday dinner with the Berkeleys, by contriving an evening of candlelight with her friend.

We have seen that the year 1669 brought Evelyn's main flow of publications to an end and the Maids of Honour into his society. It may be somewhat surprising that there was a little relief to the unending stream of Offices and Meditations which had flowed during the last two years. Since 1670 he had also been engaged upon a history of the Dutch War—an uncongenial subject undertaken only at the King's bidding. In May 1674 the introduction entitled *Navigation and Commerce* was published. With that obligation fulfilled, his pen was completely freed for further aids to spiritual progress. He began to write, for Margaret's edification, the story of the seven days of Creation. By July 1675 he had completed the story of four days' creation,[3] each day's part forming a meditation—interspersing the cosmogony—as necessary—with admonitions for use at Berkeley House.

Meantime, Margaret's second anniversary letter on the pact apparently precipitated the need for admonitions. The crisis was over, Hereford forgotten, and perhaps most important of

[1] Letter, M. Blagge to J. Evelyn, 12 Aug. 1674.
[2] Letter, M. Blagge to J. Evelyn, 9 Sept. 1674.
[3] Evelyn MSS. 73, 82, 84, 85.

all, Godolphin still avoided further foreign service. She begins by criticising Evelyn's pride in his efforts on her behalf: 'I fear that sometimes there may be self love in those things wherein we imagine we only intend God's glory.' Her mind is not at rest; she is 'cold and wandering' in her prayers, peevish to her servants, 'backward to holy duties, apt to relapse and grow worldly'.[1] In other words, she is again thinking of Godolphin.

Margaret's obedience and loyalty to Evelyn seemed now to be wavering, and any security that he enjoyed during the summer had vanished. There was a resounding crack of his confessional whip in the autumn—for did he not almost lose her in the summer?: 'But above all, the sins I have committed since I have tasted of thy love: in those I knew I had offended, but in these who it is I sinned against, even one, who by his many mercies has prevented my ruin, and drawn me from death forceably, yet gently, and with the cords of love; one that has not shown his angry, but inviting face and sweetly compelled me by abundant kindness . . . Lord, I will sin no more, I will be Thine; make me but partaken of Thyself, and I shall never abandon thee again.'[2] We have the task of reconciling this passage with the advice that she should marry—or do we now decide that he could never have so advised her?

In November she acknowledged the first instalment on the Creation, and opposed some criticism Evelyn had made of her conduct: 'I never was so reproached in all my life . . . truly I can not think my self guilty in any of the particulars you seem so bitterly to accuse me of.' She is beginning to see Evelyn in a new light, and declares, naïvely, 'I am so much your friend as ever I was and ever will be so if you continue good and I lover of goodness'[3]—qualifications not now so easy of realisation. She has become wary of what she puts in her letters, confessing that she does not 'affect writing upon all occasions'; and in fact, there is little of interest in the surviving letters written after November 1674 which is not used by Evelyn in the *Life*.

Lady Berkeley now arranged with Mary Beale (of the Lely School) to paint Margaret's portrait. We may reasonably suppose that her Ladyship disliked the Dixon portrait with its

---

[1] Letter, M. Blagge to J. Evelyn, 16 Oct. 1674.
[2] Evelyn MS. 97.
[3] Letter, M. Blagge to J. Evelyn, n.d. [Nov. 1674].

accent on death and funeral urn; she wanted something more attractive—perhaps a gesture to Evelyn—and decided on a portrait of a potential wife, complete in silks and curls—tokens of worldliness, with—to crown all—a Cupid! Perhaps that was the Godolphin touch. Evelyn must have shuddered. (At a later date, Godolphin demonstrated this delicate humour by presenting Evelyn with a Guido Reni, the subject of which was a sleeping Cupid!)[1]

In December Margaret returned to Court to act the part of Diana, goddess of chastity, in John Crowne's pastoral *Calisto*. Evelyn watched two rehearsals; the official first performance probably took place at Shrovetide in the new year, and there were repetitions, with new costumes, as late as in April. Mrs. Evelyn tells Bohun that 'the dances, scenes, music, singing are extraordinary and in their kind excel the poet's industry or genius'.[2] Here is a specimen of the poet's industry which may well have fallen upon Godolphin's ear—now somewhat more responsive:

> Kind lovers, love on,
> Lest the world be undone,
> And mankind be lost by degrees:
> For if all from their loves
> Should go wander in groves,
> There soon would be nothing but trees.

According to Evelyn in the *Life*, Margaret found no pleasure in acting; immediately after each performance, without complimenting anyone, or taking refreshment, she slipped away to Berkeley House 'and to her Oratory whither I waited on her and left her on her knees thanking God that she was delivered from this vanity . . .'[3] It is much more likely that she felt her ignominious position in having left the Court two years previously to reappear there still unmarried: it was an embarrassing situation for a retired Maid of Honour.

In the third day's Creation, Evelyn still shows himself concerned to keep Margaret from the world's contagion. We may suppose that, in acting in *Calisto*, she found opportunities for

[1] Inventory of Pictures; Evelyn MS. 53, leaf h.
[2] Letter, Mrs. Evelyn to R. Bohun, 24 Feb. 1675.
[3] *Life*, p. 55.

seeing Godolphin. Hence the leaven in the cosmogony: 'The person and interest of my only friend (who is as my own soul) let me look upon *as my soul*, and to whom nothing is more due than my fidelity, never let me fail to continue it by my prayers, my counsel, my avowed esteem, and all other offices of sincerity, and the most Christian endearments: so few are there whose friendships are combined in Thee, that 'tis no wonder to find that most blessed of relations on earth, so often violated and betrayed; preserve therefore to me my dear friend.'[1] Evelyn knew nothing of psychology.

Glanville—had he the opportunity—could have enlightened Margaret; just now he wrote to Mrs. Evelyn: 'I hope you fixed your respects upon me as much out of deliberate choice, as inclination; there are so many virtues necessary to make a person worthy of being a friend.[2]

In February and March Evelyn made a surprising variation in his Berkeley House routine; instead of dining with Margaret and the Berkeleys at midday, praying and reading in the afternoon and returning to Deptford in the early evening, on five occasions he had supper with her, before going alone to his lodgings in King Street, Westminster, for the night. Presumably Lady Berkeley informed Godolphin of these *soupers à deux*. Spring was in the air, but even if Godolphin were perturbed, he would exhibit what Evelyn admitted, later, his characteristic —'great prudence and dexterity'.[3] He would never force an issue; he would merely become—to Margaret—a little more accessible. The more Evelyn preached, the more approachable Godolphin became. As Sir Winston Churchill says of the latter, in his later years, 'he invariably declined with almost invincible obstinacy every post which was sure to be forced on him'. He would now wait for Margaret to ask him to marry her. Boyer has told us that Godolphin 'had a prying contemplative genius, a slow but unerring apprehension, an exquisite judgment'. This he now exercised.

By 13 March Godolphin's greater accessibility seems to have had some effect; on this day Margaret confessed to Evelyn, 'I have this week committed a fault which these two years I

[1] Evelyn MS. 84.
[2] Letter, W. Glanville to Mrs. Evelyn, 26 Jan. 1675.
[3] Letter, J. Evelyn to Godolphin, 16 June 1696.

have not done, I know it was a fault and yet I did it . . . I am in great affliction and do hate myself for this thing, and yet I hope God will pardon it . . . I could not help letting you know . . . chiefly that you might no longer set a value and esteem upon me, for I am not fit to live upon the earth. . . .'[1] There is little doubt that the 'fault' was the humanising physic of Godolphin's kiss—the seal of things to come. Further opportunities to indulge her latent liking for this physic which she had not taken for two years were apparently afforded during the following month—Evelyn's visits being then reduced to two. In two months' time—in June—Godolphin was going to The Hague: an absence that Margaret could not now bear to contemplate. She was in need of immunity, of protection. Godolphin's serenity seemed a haven. No word from him survives to tell us exactly why he ceased to be a passive spectator of Margaret's problem. Did he diagnose the struggle of the flesh against the spirit, and persuade her that neither must win, that the triumph of one was sterile? Whatever stung him into action, suppers, the spring, his impending absence from England, or a natural resurgence of love, he married her at the Temple Church on 16 May. The ceremony, conducted by one of the Duke's chaplains, was witnessed by Lady Berkeley and Beck. Evelyn was completely oblivious of what was happening; three days before the marriage he read the second part of his *Philosophical Discourse of Earth* to the Royal Society; in fact he was kept in the dark for nearly twelve months.

The couple went on exactly as before. Margaret contrived to receive Evelyn at Berkeley House. Godolphin re-adopted the role of spectator. Lady Berkeley and Beck became, at Berkeley House, an amused audience sharing a secret; Evelyn was a protagonist in ignorance of it.

It is highly significant that Margaret could keep Evelyn in ignorance. (His word that he advised her to marry is now seen for what it is worth.) She had revolted against Evelyn's pursuit of the spirit—nothing less. But she was unable—as yet—to confess to him—for she had also broken the pact. At the Altar of Friendship she had declared that, in the event of her marriage Evelyn should be a witness. Time alone could bring her to confess that violation.

[1] Letter, M. Blagge to J. Evelyn, 13 March 1675.

In June the artful, consistent Godolphin embarked for The Hague and returned without calling for any notice from Margaret. His friendliness to Evelyn was made possible by her staunch and continued loyalty—a loyalty so deep that all knowledge of Evelyn's aspirations and scourges was withheld from Godolphin's ears.

Arrangements for the Congress of Nimeguen were now in progress, and Lord Berkeley was appointed as Ambassador Extraordinary to France, and (with Sir William Temple and Sir Leoline Jenkins) plenipotentiary at the congress. Berkeley was to proceed to Paris, and Lady Berkeley would accompany him; later, they would move on to Holland. Lady Berkeley decided to take Margaret with her; possibly Godolphin made the suggestion in view of his present inability to set up house. Margaret, with too many calls upon her powers of acting, would be eager to escape the attentions of Evelyn. Mrs. Evelyn would doubtless welcome Margaret's departure—though refraining from any expression of her feelings. Everybody was pleased except Evelyn; some consolation, however, was afforded him by the arrangement that his son John, now twenty years old, should travel with the party, and reside with them in Paris. Margaret agreed to act as his governess.

John junior had improved since his Oxford days, though in his second year at the university he showed a disinclination for early rising, the attending of prayers, and the punctual delivery of written exercises—but these are failings common to all. Emulating his father, he began to read seriously after leaving Oxford. Glanville, who was most impressed with his studying every morning during a stay at Wotton in the autumn of 1671, said to his father, 'you have all the assurances imaginable that he will prove a great blessing to you'. This was excessive optimism, however. Two years later, Glanville told Mrs. Evelyn that her son was so very like her, and a better character than that could not be given him. She entrusted Glanville to instruct him in the way of the world, and she reciprocated, in some degree, with his son. Accordingly, Glanville endeavoured to protect John junior against the wiles of women, and caused him to make a collection of all that is said against them either in canonical or Apocryphal scripture and to learn it by heart; 'I know no better armour or antidote against the attacks and poison of the sex,' he said to Mrs. Evelyn. By October 1673, Glanville reported to her that 'her son had discovered that the finest women are indebted for the greatest part of their beauty to shoemakers, tailors, tyre women', and that he 'looks upon himself as a Monsieur now complete enough for the nicest damsel in nature if she does prefer making legs, dancing corants, and wearing pantaloons and a periwig *à la mode* before all other accomplishments'. This also was an exaggeration— as we shall discover; he was not at all a lady's man. Fortunately, he had overcome his former physical disability—at least, we hear no more of it.

Four months had passed since Lord Berkeley first received orders to sail. During this delay, Margaret's letters revealed the despondency into which she was thrown; to hide the truth of her state from Evelyn was a great burden: 'Never any body undertook a journey with less inclination, but you will say why do you go: why only because I think it is fit for me to do it, and for no other reason.' Again, 'God knows I am a wretched sinner and nothing but infinite mercy could pardon my innumerable faults . . . I wish from my soul you would not praise me: oh if you know me: but the less I seem to think myself, the greater I appear in your humble eye: therefore I am silent.'[1]

Evelyn evidently questioned her on the prospects of marriage —a question that she answered with a lie: 'I am not so near that state of life as you imagine, nor may be shall never venture. I have quite other thoughts, but I am God's, let but his will be done on me in me and by me: your friend will be happy howsoever or wheresoever I be disposed of.'[2] Perhaps she lied to cheer the disconsolate Evelyn, for her impending departure hung like a heavy cloud over him.

Godolphin remained as silent and inscrutable as ever; not a word remains. Margaret was at Twickenham in August and probably met him there and at other times as his Whitehall— Windsor—Newmarket circuit allowed.

Mrs. Evelyn offered her son's bedroom to Bohun in a manner showing her certainty of his acceptance, writing 'amid the groans of Sir Richard Browne with an attack of the gout (with an addition of pain which leaves us doubtful whether stone or

[1] Letter, Mrs. Godolphin to J. Evelyn, July 1675. [2] Op. cit.

wind) the interruptions of my daughters, the noise of a hammer in the next room and my father's complaints'. But there was enticement in her description of some recent hospitality; a 'hot venison pasty' when her 'success in the oven was not ill, so that we were very merry at the eating of it, two of the company soaked over a pipe and bottle till eleven at night with great contentment, your company being only wanting . . . I fancy you will be very commodiously lodged in Jack's absence'. There is no doubt that the menfolk were attracted by Mrs. Evelyn's excellent cooking; Glanville, at this time, recalled the delights of the skilful cooking of her 'own dinner and a bottle of Bar O Bar'[1]—perhaps her special brew of barley wine.

In addition to managing Margaret's finances, Evelyn was to undertake on this side of the water Lord Berkeley's affairs, both official and those of his Twickenham estate, perhaps as some return for his son's inclusion in the party. He informed his wife: 'I shall receive the odd hundred to put Jack in equipage . . . I am going this day to the exchange, by direction of Sir Stephen Fox to take order with a French merchant for the return of Mrs. Blagge's and Jack's money by bill of exchange . . . I am to receive all my Lord Ambassadors orders about his business, which he puts entirely into my hands and management, and I know not how to avoid or refuse it . . . he will trust no creature but me.'[2]

At last orders to sail were received. On 10 November Evelyn met Berkeley and his entourage at New Cross to accompany them to Dover. Margaret's state of mind may be imagined: although she had said that she 'may never venture marriage' she could not, of course, give him any encouragement. She was unable to restrain her tears as she declared that she was leaving England only for Lady Berkeley's sake: that was the ostensible reason. Two days' travelling brought them to Canterbury, another to Dover, where Margaret gave Evelyn her will. Prayers followed. The next morning was Sunday and the sun was shining when Evelyn 'waited on her again' as he says in the *Life*.[3] Fiction, alas, breaks into his account of their farewell: 'I know not how you part from your lover . . . go back, go back, then and be happy both, for this course will wear you

[1] Letter, W. Glanville to Mrs. Evelyn, 1 Oct. 1675.
[2] Letter, J. Evelyn to Mrs. Evelyn, 18 Oct. 1675.   [3] P. 62.

both out.' Being still in ignorance of her marriage, his knowledge of her emotions was imperfect. Margaret's tears were divided; tears of sympathy for her blind and punished friend, tears for Godolphin with whom she was in love, and some for her own miserable state: Evelyn remained on the beach until her boat was out of sight. All that day he heard—in the distance —the waves breaking on the shingle.

In Paris, Margaret received no letter from the perplexed and wounded Evelyn for six weeks, and she sent him no word of her arrival for three. His silence she excuses: 'I dare say you have a very good reason for it, as you have for most things you do.'[1] But by the end of January Evelyn had recovered from the shock of separation and had written seven letters to her three; and, of course, he wanted to know how his son was faring. Margaret criticised Evelyn's proposed course of study: 'I beg of you not to write to him to change his studies, nor to put so many things upon him at once, for it is impossible he can profit by that way; but let him be well versed in one thing first.' Evelyn's letters to Lord Berkeley were too long: 'I beg of you . . . make them as short as you can, for the poor man does fret at a long letter most wonderfully much.'[2] Margaret gives the very essence of Evelyn in 'too many' and 'too long'. Mrs. Evelyn took Margaret's common-sense direction for granted: 'I had rather follow your counsel than any person I know.'

Evelyn, anxious to discover her attitude towards Godolphin, referred to his virtues and suitability, but Margaret was wary in her answer: 'As for Sidney being good I doubt it not, as for his being worthy of me I believe him not only that, but worthy of anybody.'[3]

Margaret's eventual distaste for Lady Berkeley's social activities apparently gave Evelyn an opportunity to describe to Margaret the sense of his loss—and there was some ambiguity: 'What do you mean by doing extraordinary things?' she queries; 'I could content myself with any thing I think now so I were at home again, but I must do nothing rashly: I hope . . . to return as soon home as ever I can quickly to see you, and therefore leave wondering.'[4] He replied with something of his former

[1] Letter, Mrs. Godolphin to J. Evelyn, 13 Dec. 1675.
[2] Letter, Mrs. Godolphin to J. Evelyn, 28 Jan. 1676.
[3] Letter, Mrs. Godolphin to J. Evelyn, 4 Feb. 1676.   [4] Op. cit.

ecstasy: 'If my wishes to see you, my delight to hear from you, my continual thoughts of prayers for you be symptoms of Love, I cannot help it . . . You are the joy of my heart' . . . going on in this strain for two folios, making the old assertion that he still loves her because she loves God.[1]

Margaret must have been embarrassed, and seems to have treated it curtly: 'This post I have no manner of time, next Tuesday you shall have a particular account of all things . . . I can't say a word more, but that I am yours with all my heart.'[2]

What with Margaret's restricted letters and the Berkeleys' treatment of Evelyn's son, there was little pleasure in hearing from Paris. Young John was housed in a high cold garret without hangings or furnishings, next to the servants. Lord Berkeley, contemptuous of his social qualities, told his father that ' he will never dance, nor make a leg well, nor have his perriwig or cravat in good order, or be *à la mode*, but he will prove an honest, solid, and judicious man, and be very good company'.[3] Young Evelyn fell for Margaret's charm, and he was very sad when at the end of March, her return to England was arranged: 'Her conversation has been the only circumstance that has made my being here tolerable,' he writes to his father. 'She is now going from hence, which puts me into extreme melancholy . . . Pray, sir, consider that I am left here alone for now she is out of that family I cannot endure the thoughts of it, and if I should put myself into it again, I am sure I should die with melancholy in a little time: all that I have any value for in France goes away with her. All her virtues, all her charms, her piety and her goodness to me assault me all at once . . . I am become most desperately her humble servant.' He then hurt his father with, 'that man is too happy who is to be master of such a treasure', and implored: 'either let me come home and settle to the law or let me travel'.[4]

Three times a week Berkeley bombarded Evelyn with letters on money matters. At the Treasury he was brow-beaten by the

[1] Letter, J. Evelyn to Mrs. Godolphin, *c*. 14 Feb. 1676: copy on the back of Mrs. Godolphin's letter of that date.
[2] Letter, Mrs. Godolphin to J. Evelyn, 28 Feb. 1676.
[3] Letter, Lord Berkeley to J. Evelyn, 27 May 1676.
[4] Letter, J. Evelyn, jun., to J. Evelyn, 25 March 1676.

Earl of Danby, to be asked in reproach, whether he were my
Lord Berkeley's steward. These humilations he endured week
after week, winter and summer.[1] Lady Berkeley made use of
him, too, to supervise the fitting of some new wainscoting and
fireplaces at Berkeley House. Ah! Berkeley House—but alas,
the shutters were up.

[1] Letter Book, 4 Nov. 1688; Evelyn MS. 39.

CHAPTER VII

Mistress Godolphin

~~~~~~

WHEN Lord Berkeley received orders at the end of March to proceed to Nimeguen, Margaret left Paris for England, laden 'with a world of fine petticotes'.[1] Evelyn would have us believe that her departure was an escape from the 'interruption of her assiduous course and devotion'[2] and the Berkeley household. Her feelings were confused. She was eager to see Godolphin, but disturbed by the impending, inevitable confession to Evelyn of her marriage; in fact, she had brooded over it unceasingly since May. In Paris, she had been safe, if uneasy. In England, confession could not be avoided. In May, her heart would not allow her to confess. Now her head might enable her to do it. If Evelyn had only advised her to marry, how much easier it would be to confess. His last passionate letter increased her difficulty. She hardly dared to be alone with him.

She landed at Dover on 3 April, arrived in London three days later, and coolly arranged to meet him on 7 April. Lady Sunderland, Mrs. Graham, Mrs. Howard, and the Evelyns attended reunion dinners and suppers: Godolphin made no appearance. Temporarily, Margaret was lodging in Covent Garden, where, on 26 April, Evelyn dined with her and her sister, Lady Yarborough. Count Grammont has told us something of Lady Yarborough's fluffy, feckless character—and that she had long white eyelashes and small eyes. She was born to

[1] Letter, J. Evelyn, jun., to his sister Mary, 10 April 1676.
[2] *Life*, p. 66.

let the cat out of the bag. Unfortunately no details of the confession scene are known.

In the *Life*, Evelyn speaks only of 'friendly expostulations' between Margaret and himself 'for the unkindness of her so long and industriously concealing from me the circumstances of her marriage, because she had expressed her sorrow with such an asseveration, as in my life before, I never heard her utter—so as I could not but forgive her heartily . . . save that I took it a little to heart, she should so long conceal a thing from me, who had so earnestly advised her to marry'.[1]

We have seen that this alleged advice had given Margaret no urge to confess. His statement that he forgave her we shall presently be forced to doubt.

Her reply to Evelyn's 'Why didn't you tell me you were married?' could only have been something like this: 'Despite all your efforts to keep me celibate, I fell in love again with Godolphin. After all, he'd been expecting me, waiting for me, for nine years. Thus I failed you—a failure I could not bring myself to confess. And I had broken our pact. You know how weak a creature I am, how sensitive a regard I have for you: so I was forced into silence. My visit to Paris enabled me a breathing space: it was Godolphin's idea. I dearly hoped that you would hear of my marriage from other lips. I have no courage.'

Evelyn might have answered: 'My Saint! I tried to keep the love of Heaven in your heart: what more could I do?' But he also kept some anger in reserve. His greatest friendship had been lavished upon a woman who rejected it. He had tried to translate Margaret into a saint; but he had failed. She had cheered him for nearly twelve months with a lie. As we shall see he had not yet finished with chastisement. In the *Life*, however, he would have us believe that all was well, saying that Margaret desired that he 'would continue to assist her, with those little services she was pleased to accept'.[2]

There is, of course, no mention of these exciting episodes in the *Diary*. However, our knowledge of them enables a little light to be shed on some apparently normal entry. On 28 April Evelyn recorded: 'My wife entertained Her Majesty at Deptford for which the Queen gave me thanks in the withdrawing-

[1] *Life*, p. 67.   [2] *Life*, p. 68.

room at Whitehall.' Lord Ponsonby in his *John Evelyn*, p. 53, quite naturally comments: 'We should have expected to hear more about the Queen's visit, but the entry reads as if he himself was not present on the occasion.' He was not; it was the day after Margaret's confession—one of the blackest days in Evelyn's life. Even the prospect of a Queen's visit could do nothing to disperse the gloom.

By the end of June the married couple were living—temporarily—at Berkeley House, pending the completion of their apartment near the Thames by Scotland Yard in Whitehall. There was probably a period of anger and argument between the confession and 14 August, for Evelyn did not pray regularly with her until the latter date; then followed such piety that was paralleled only in the early months of 1674. We may well believe that by August the friendship reasserted itself and for the first time modulated into *Agape* and became perfectly disinterested.

Evelyn was willing to free Margaret of all obligations under the pact; to this offer she replied: 'As to your freeing me . . . I think myself much obliged to you for trusting me: be assured it shall not be done the less for my having liberty for so long as you love God I shall love you.'[1] Hence his disinterested love.

Her obligations under this new alignment appeared in a lengthy manuscript entitled *Œconomics to a newly married friend*.[2] Here he set down the obligations that still might lie upon her 'not to think any new condition or circumstance' of force to absolve her from their pact at the Altar of Friendship. He says that their friendship is where it was, and her marriage 'alters not the case'. It is indissoluble. He also included all the advice that a young married woman could possibly require—and a great deal more. (Several pages on sexual intercourse have been removed and lost.)

Glanville's pursuit of Lady Lewkenor seemed to be drawing to a close. On 19 August he told Mrs. Evelyn that he had visited her at Tunbridge, when the supper—perhaps intentionally—offered to him was like to knock the heart out of any worldly

---

[1] Letter, Mrs. Godolphin to J. Evelyn, n.d. [1676].
[2] Evelyn MS. 106; B.M. Add. MS. 15950 (2 pp.).

person like Glanville; it consisted of 'a platter of pitiful pottage, made of a piece of the crag end of a neck of mutton no bigger than an apple, and of a little musty minced rabbit, rank with butter boiled to oil'. He was happier in protesting to Mrs. Evelyn, 'were you not another man's wife, I could safely say you are my mistress, for never was any other in my thoughts or made thinking a greater pleasure or more sincere; I may flatter myself with an opinion that I am sometimes in your mind, for if our friendship be equal why should I not have as great an interest in your heart, as you have in mine'.

Godolphin's attachment to the Court and the King on the habitual Whitehall–Windsor–Newmarket circuit often left Margaret in Evelyn's company. Together they contrived the new apartment, when his architectural knowledge was allied to her taste in decoration. Robert Hooke was the surveyor. How delightful it was to go to Lambeth together to choose marble fireplaces or order looking-glasses at the Duke of Buckingham's glass-works. At the end of September Margaret came to Sayes Court while Godolphin was racing and hawking. What joy it was to be with her for three whole weeks; to spend one week with her in London and share her for a fortnight with Mrs. Evelyn, when the garden was in its autumn glory: never had the Grove seemed more beautiful.

Now that jealousy was impossible, an idealisation took place, Evelyn's spirit rapt in pure and exquisite passion. At last they were happy together. With her marriage Margaret acquired a new self-possession, and she could say—with no more naïve qualifications—'as long as you love God, I shall love you'—or could there still be a qualification? Was perfect *Agape* possible?

Margaret and Godolphin were a supremely happy couple when, hearing that Lord Berkeley was planning to return from Nimeguen, they moved to their new apartment on 31 March 1677. Godolphin possessed all the qualities that Margaret lacked. His love of gaming, his equanimity, his buoyancy were foils for her piety, her sweetness, her grace. In common with her he had none of the Court's failings. Mrs. Evelyn gave her written instructions in domestic art: 'As to our family,' Margaret told Evelyn, 'eight is the number we are to have nor more nor less, three dishes of meat at dinner we would willingly have, and no suppers at all, no coach do we intend to keep but he

[Godolphin] has always two riding horses.'[1] Thus, says Evelyn, she settled 'with that handsome and discreet economy so natural to her'.[2]

Margaret allowed Evelyn an average of four visits a month during her first three months at Scotland Yard: there was no limit to her loyalty, or any relaxation of Evelyn's claims upon her. We lose sight of her, however, between 3 July and 18 September, and doubtless she warned him of her intended absence. Godolphin was at Windsor with the Court in the middle of August, otherwise we have no knowledge of their whereabouts. The couple had lived more or less in retirement during the winter, and now, in the summer, there was an opportunity for a honeymoon. Lord Berkeley had relieved Evelyn of his 'intolerable servitude and correspondence', which is duly recorded in the *Diary*, 24 June 1677: 'I had leisure to be somewhat more at home, and to myself'—a note of sadness that seems to be reflected from his thoughts of her prospective honeymoon.

Evelyn appeared to be restless; after spending a fortnight at Sayes Court, he journeyed over the countryside calling on friends and relations at such places as Wotton, Albury, Abinger, Bury St. Edmunds, Thetford, Ipswich, Harwich, Newmarket, Audley End and Bishops Stortford; he was the guest of Lord Arlington at Euston (where the 'mutton is small but sweet') for seventeen days. Mrs. Evelyn sulked, and told Bohun where Evelyn had 'taken his pleasure', grumbling that she had not dined outside Deptford for months.[3]

By 18 September Margaret had returned home; Evelyn dined with her that day, and left with her a lengthy Office. Four days later she wrote to him—a well-poised, happy letter which we may regard as a thank-offering for her beneficial honeymoon: 'Lord, when this day I considered my happiness in having perfect health of body, cheerfulness of mind, no disturbance from without nor grief within, my time my own, my house quiet, sweet, and pretty, all manner of convenience for serving God in public and in private, how happy in my friends, husband, relations, servants, credit, and none to wait or attend upon, but my dear and blessed God from whom I receive this, what

[1] Letter, Mrs. Godolphin to J. Evelyn, 11 May 1677.   [2] *Life*, p. 69.
[3] Letter, Mrs. Evelyn to R. Bohun, 19 Nov. 1677.

a melting joy ran through me at the thought of all these mercies.'[1]

On the following day Evelyn visited her and prayed with her—for the last time. What happened we are not certain. Perhaps he wrote something for her reading of which she did not approve. On the 16 October—the anniversary of the pact —he dined with Godolphin alone. We cannot but be curious to know why Evelyn ceased to pray with Margaret, and why that sacred 16 October was commemorated so strangely: in her absence. In her anniversary letter she gives thanks to God for 'an husband, that above all men living, I value: in short, I have little to wish, but a child; and to contribute something to my friend's happiness (which I most impatiently desire) . . .' Does she not imply that now she is happily married, Evelyn is unhappy, or it may be, he is unhappy because he has prayed with her for the last time?

If Evelyn was tortured at the thought of Margaret on her honeymoon, we would expect to find some written chastisement —something that Margaret was now strong enough to resent. Perhaps in *An Office for the Lord's Day*[2] we have the clue to the cessation of prayers, and to Margaret's absence on 16 October: '. . . To the death then will I love Thee O my Saviour, who hast loved me when I hated Thee; and can I doubt thou wilt now disdain me coming with a broken and penitent heart, and with tears of love, to bathe my wounds and mingle them with thy blood? No, my Jesu, Thou hast given they self to be flesh of my flesh, and bone of my bone, God incarnate "Immanuel" God with us—O mysterious union! O Love unexpressible, and altogether astonishing! What shall be able to separate my heart from Thee—Love stronger than death—I am espoused to one Husband, and desire to present him a chaste Virgin; for I have vowed to be only Thine O blessed Bridegroom of my soul! To how many lovers have I yet been prostituted! To the world, the flesh, to Satan himself and shamefully departed from my first Love, ungrateful, disloyal wretch; and yet thou sentedest after me, offering me gracious conditions, and promised, that if I would return, thou wouldst receive me into thy bosom . . . Nothing is immaculate, nothing is pure, nothing worthy to

[1] Letter, Mrs. Godolphin to J. Evelyn, 22 Sept. 1677.
[2] Evelyn MS. 130.

approach thy Holiness, but what thou cleanest and purifiest and renewest . . .'

These angry words, this flagellation, this lapse of Evelyn's act of sublimation—probably written when Margaret was on her honeymoon—she would resent. In any case their praying together ceased, and so did her letters (except for two written a year later). If Margaret's absence on 16 October had been caused by some indisposition, Evelyn would almost certainly have recorded it; but by his omission of any explanation we may conjecture that she had not recovered from his anger. Godolphin acted as her deputy and—by Margaret's magnanimous loyalty to Evelyn—remained uninformed of the real reason for her absence. And he remained in ignorance. Thus was it made possible, throughout the autumn and winter, for Evelyn's prayerless visits to continue—as indeed they did.

In November, Sir Gabriel Sylvius, Hoffmaster to the Prince of Orange, married Evelyn's former 'playfellow' Anne Howard; he was over forty years old, Anne twenty-one. Mrs. Evelyn remarked that Mrs. Howard only parted with her daughter out of England because Sir Gabriel 'is in so good a station for honour and profit'. Mrs. Evelyn's sagacity—and that of others—was proved wrong; Lady Sylvius failed to obtain a post in the Princess's Court, and soon returned to England—and to the outskirts of the Evelyn circle—an unhappy, childless wife. Sir Gabriel died in 1697.

Margaret's wish for maternity, expressed in September, was soon to be fulfilled. In early January it was known that her child was expected in early September. Godolphin continued to journey between England and the continent, and in April 1678 instructed Henry Frederick Thynne, a secretary in Henry Coventry's office in Whitehall, to keep a protective eye on Margaret. We may ask why Evelyn's good offices were passed over. Godolphin also arranged with Thynne to deliver letters to her, or when stress of work prevented his writing, to inform her of this; in fact, Thynne was instructed to regard Margaret as his 'charge'.[1] In July, Godolphin purchased the office of Master of the King's Robes, a post which brought him more intimately into the Royal counsels.

[1] Coventry Papers, vol. xli, ff. 464, 487, 503.

In May, Evelyn wrote his last devotional work for Margaret, for *Trinity Sunday & Octaves after Pentecost*,[1] marked significantly, 'The end of the annual private offices'; it also bore the readopted sign *ΑΓΑΠΑ*, spiritual love, and contained only normal devotional matter; it completed his output of spiritual aid which was no less than fourteen hundred closely-written octavo pages. The friendship had come full circle.

Five weeks before her confinement Margaret saw Ashmole's library at Lambeth with Evelyn and his wife. Godolphin and Margaret gave a dinner party at Scotland Yard for them in August. Apart from these occasions, Evelyn saw little of Margaret during the summer, and it is apparent that the friendship was now a little out of joint. It was inevitable that his visits should be curtailed, but she had practically ceased to write to him. 'The end of the annual private offices' is itself a knell. In August she wrote to him in a changed manner: 'Pray do me the favour to call in £100 out of [Sir Robert] Clayton's hands for my use . . . I shall be very glad to see Mrs. Evelyn when she comes: and of my friendship you may always rest assured, let the appearances of the contrary be what they will . . . I am with all sincerity yours.' What of her obligations under the new *Œconomics for a newly married friend*? Any signs of them are non-existent, and we are bound to conclude that the theory had fallen into disuse, and that Margaret was too deeply involved with *Eros* to bother about *Agape*.

On the morning of Tuesday, 3 September, Margaret's child —a boy—was born. Evelyn had called to inquire after her health, and finding her in labour, stayed until the birth. (It is distressing to find that even on this occasion Evelyn should equivocate; in the *Diary* he says he went to dine according to his custom every Tuesday—but he had not dined with her for a month.) The child was christened Francis—after Godolphin's father. By Sunday Margaret had become very ill, and Godolphin had been recalled from Windsor. When Evelyn was attending the morning service at Deptford, he received this note from Godolphin: 'My poor wife is fallen very ill of a fever, with lightness in her head and ravings: you know who says the effectual fervent prayer of a righteous man availeth much and the prayer of faith shall save the sick: I humbly beg your

[1] Evelyn MS. 83.

charitable prayers for this poor creature and your distracted servant.'[1]

On arrival at Margaret's house, Evelyn and his wife found her suffering from what we would now call puerperal sepsis; she was delirious. Mrs. Evelyn stayed a little while and then returned home. Evelyn wrote[2] to her the next day. Four doctors were called, Richard Lower (the famous author of *De Corde*), Thomas Short (who attended Charles II during his last hours), Peter Chamberlain, and Gasper Needham. Chamberlain was 'fully persuaded the midwife (to whom I perceived he was no friend) had left something behind that might be the cause of these malignant vapours'. Both he and Needham were 'altogether averse from ordering any kind of thing, the malignancy of the distemper being so high and dangerous . . . both agreed there was no safe medling; whatever they should prescribe for one thing, being so repugnant to the other accidents'. When Lower and Short appeared they found 'not only all her back down to the waist, but all her breast to the navel exceedingly inflamed with those pimples, as thick and fiery as you can possibly imagine'; the pigeons—applied to the feet—were changed, and the blisters 'which run abundantly' dressed; otherwise nothing was done. Her heartrending delirium could be heard 'to the farther part of Whitehall . . . so as it grieves our very hearts to be near and yet without great strength and company there is no keeping her in the bed: when she is out of one of these, she sinks into profound silence and in one of these, I fear she will go away'.

Godolphin was 'almost dead with grief, and lying for the most part flat on the boards, which he drowns with his tears, begs of me to stay: for that he is not able to speak to the physicians, and is almost besides himself'.

Lady Mordaunt sent what we would describe as a quack medicine—the *Aurum potabile*,[3] 'but none of these Methodist Physicians value, nor will advise it'. Evelyn says, 'I have not been in bed at all since Saturday; but find myself very well in

[1] Letter, S. Godolphin to J. Evelyn, 8 Sept. 1678.
[2] Letter, J. Evelyn to Mrs. Evelyn, 9 Sept. 1678.
[3] Potable gold: it had cured dropsy, fevers, quotidiana, bloody flux, vomiting, scurvy, gripings, and looseness, White's and Fits of the Mother, and pleurisy.

health, I bless God: I am afraid I shall conclude this letter with
the saddest news, who write it by snatches, being continually
called away on some occasion or other; the rest being so tired
out . . . this tragedy teaches me how vain it is to set our hearts
on any thing in this world . . . they are very miserable who have
any friendships or attachments to which they cannot frame
themselves to part with, when God thinks fit to deprive them
of them.'

At last Margaret's raging reached 'that impetuosity' that
Godolphin was 'no longer able to hear or bear it: with the
silence, though I cannot say consent, of the doctors, gave way
that the famous (I must now call it something else) *Aurum
potabile* was given her . . . immediately she had taken two or
three spoonfuls of the Aurum, her raging and convulsion
abated; she wept abundantly, and thence falling into the
agonies of death, departed this miserable life, and is now an
angel in Heaven: my tears suffer me to say no more, you will
think it is because I truly cannot say enough to describe a loss,
that is not to be expressed: for I am in sorrow unspeakable'.

Evelyn then describes the disconsolate household, 'the
miserablest man in the world her husband with his brother and
sisters none of them able to bear up against this torrent . . .
no creature in the house who either goes about anything, or I
think minds what is necessary to be done, either with the corpse
or the poor child, or any thing else . . . I am for my own part
confounded also, and begin to be weary and to desire solitude
. . . The Lord Jesus bless us all, and ah that I were where my
friend is, for she is happy, her part is finished. At four in the
afternoon: she departed just at half an hour after one.' Thus
with a singular detachment did Evelyn complete his letter on
that unusually hot September afternoon.

Godolphin was completely overwhelmed with grief. Evelyn
went home to spend two days in solitude and sad reflections.
Mrs. Evelyn, practical and—his wife, consoled him: 'Remember
all are not gone that love you, and that you still have some who
require your care for them: they would be comforts to you
would you receive them so,' and with downrightness charged
the sluttish midwife with carelessness.

In her will, Margaret wrote of Godolphin: 'My dear, believe
me that of all earthly things, you were, and are the most dear

to me; and I am convinced that no body ever had a better, or half so good an husband.' Evelyn, after quoting this in the *Life*,[1] says that he himself was mentioned at the end of the will as 'the depository of her trust, as I was the distributor of her bounty'. To balance this small mention, he goes on to say that 'she knew nothing she had more to wish for in this world, but that she might do him some signal kindness' and that this wish of hers was made known to Godolphin, who observed it by 'allowing me the honour of his friendship and accepting my little services'. But we shall see presently that this friendship did not derive from Margaret's wish.

Evelyn undertook the funeral arrangements for the sorrowing Godolphin, who was unable to travel to Cornwall with the cortège. Surprisingly, Evelyn suddenly returned after seeing the hearse as far as Hounslow—'obliged to return upon some indispensable affairs' as he records in the *Diary*, 17 September. We may guess that these affairs were dealt with on the following day, when he and Godolphin looked over Margaret's papers; had she not retrieved six letters, and had he not written certain meditations? Godolphin (having concealed his surprise that Evelyn had avoided the journey to Cornwall) knew nothing of what he hoped to find. However, 'among the effects', Evelyn says, 'was a small packet sealed up, which she desired by the superscription, might be burnt, and not opened, as accordingly it was performed, and as I conceive, might contain the cipher, by which she used to correspond with the Dean of Hereford and some particulars which she would not trust her memory with, in case she had lived: for she kept a register of mercies, deliverances, successes and resolutions for the discussion of her conscience . . . but I enter no farther into this secret'.[2] We are not convinced by Evelyn's 'as I conceive'; we conceive that the burnt packet contained his retrieved letters. A month later his meditations were found and returned by Godolphin, and presumably unread by him.[3]

We may see by a letter which Godolphin wrote to Evelyn that the latter, and not Margaret, was the originator of the friendship which ensued between the two men: '. . . 'tis the greatest consolation my condition is capable of to see you so

---

[1] *Life*, pp. 79–82. [2] *Life*, p. 83.

[3] Letter, S. Godolphin to J. Evelyn, 27 Oct. 1678.

desirous of my friendship and so kind and good natured to promise me yours . . . I lay hold of it in the manner you offer it to me . . . I promise you mine most faithfully and inviolably as long as I live, and I will keep your letter for ever as the pledge of your constant friendship to me . . .'[1]

When offering his friendship, Evelyn informed Godolphin that he proposed writing the story of Margaret's life—a proposal that Godolphin approved, though he stipulated: 'By no means let it go farther I conjure you, at least for the present, you and I will debate the matter when we meet.'

This was the manuscript *The Life of Mrs. Godolphin*. As a friend Margaret had failed him; in death he would grant her success. In the glorious vista of the rising Godolphin's friendship and all that his patronage might bring, any sense of failure or frustration vanished. In a new spirit of sublimation he would make Margaret's sainthood a success. There could be no second failure; he would share her glory, and each would wear a halo.

Two months after Margaret's death Evelyn wrote to his friend Philip Packer of Groomsbridge: 'I confess this late loss has touched me nearly, and were it not for the consolation of that worthy person (her dear husband) I would not care at all to live: 'tis long that he has let me into his friendship and brotherly affection . . .'[2] Thus Godolphin's friendliness, so readily and generously reciprocated, seemed—in the circumstances—to be of much longer standing, such was its impact.

The writing of the *Life* demanded great skill; his Offices and Meditations could be ignored; her letters needed careful pruning; some portions would have to be destroyed. He was encouraged by the certain knowledge of Margaret's loyalty to himself—a loyalty that ensured Godolphin's ignorance. It was fortunate that she had destroyed his own letters, especially those which she had described as being 'a little too passionate'. The packet which was burnt after her death? Well—it was burnt.

After two years' hard work, he had made good progress: 'If God spare me one year more alive,' he wrote to Godolphin, 'I hope to render you a better testimony of which though it possibly may create you some tender resentments, will be composed again with the most happy transports that certainly can flow

---

[1] Letter, S. Godolphin to J. Evelyn, 22 Sept. 1678.
[2] Letter, J. Evelyn to P. Packer, 16 Dec. 1678.

from the contemplation of a person who arrived so near perfection: nor be afraid I should offend your modesty by publishing anything to the world though even that were to be one day wished (you are all the world to me). But if I show you the person you most esteemed in it, breathing, alive again and immortal, you will receive her and acknowledge that I am just to her dear memory and to you.'[1]

[1] Letter, J. Evelyn to S. Godolphin, 9 Sept. 1680. For a fuller exposition of the friendship, see the present writer's *John Evelyn and Mrs. Godolphin*, 1951. To the critics who said I had dealt somewhat harshly with Evelyn in that book, I would reply that now his confession has come to light (it was discovered after the book was in print—and is described in the following chapter) it is apparently unnecessary to change any part of my interpretation of the psychological aspects of the friendship.

CHAPTER VIII

Sorrow and Confession

Aᴘᴀʀᴛ from the writing of *The Life of Mrs. Godolphin*, Evelyn was now enabled—as far as his busy spirit allowed—to enjoy a more relaxed routine. His work for the prisoners of war had resolved itself into little more than a fight with the Treasury for his salary and expenses. However he was optimistic now that he was to enjoy the fruits of patronage; indeed his prospects brightened considerably when, in April 1679, Godolphin was appointed to the Treasury.

Evelyn was thinking of his son's prospects, too. Young John had returned from Paris in the summer of 1676 somewhat disappointed with his abortive visit and piqued at his father's refusal to allow him to travel farther on the continent. He settled down eventually to his books at home, published *The History of the Grand Visiers*, a translation, in 1677, and found diversion with his cousins at Wotton. But drink was the great temptation there. (At Sayes Court his father was too vigilant to allow any immoderation.) Fortunately the Wotton orgies were now less dangerous. On one occasion some years previously, his elder cousin (who died at the age of thirty-two in 1676) and four friends drank 'almost two dozen of claret' after dinner.[1] So far young John remained uncontaminated and still deserved the compliments that Glanville gave him in the early 1670's. Pepys was taken with him in 1677, called him 'the most hopeful gentleman', noting the 'early proofs of his ingenuity and style'.

[1] Letter, J. Evelyn, jun., to J. Evelyn, 18 Sept. 1671.

He was acquiring facility in the writing of verse, and Latin letters—at his father's instigation—to men who might remember him and be useful. When Evelyn sent five hundred trees to the Earl of Arlington for his Euston estate in 1677, John junior was brought to the Earl's notice by sending him a number of maps.

Moll was still single. Despite her lazy habits, she seems to have been often sought in marriage, but all attempts at settlement had so far come to nothing. Both she and her father were hard to please; if sometimes she was averse to marriage, her father was a good bargainer. When, in 1672, Sir R. Napier's son was proposed and £5000 portion demanded—which was £1000 more than Moll's father could provide—he said to her, 'so that is broken off; I hope now you have your desires', relief was doubtless felt by both of them. After his eldest son's death, a marriage portion or a jointure was still more difficult to find; £5,500 being charged upon his estate for the three fatherless daughters, though George was conservative in estimating his estate in 1679 at no more than £2000 per annum. But when Sir Robert Clayton the Lord Mayor proposed a young lady with a £10,000 portion for George's son in that year, George was willing to settle upon his son £1000 for present maintenance and a jointure of £700 or £800 per annum in addition; 'that is too great for my fortune, though not to the lady's portion, as jointures now are made'. However, George was sceptical: 'I find the citizens must have great jointures (which ruins all estates) and great settlements'. In fact nothing came of the proposal—and the Wotton estate was not endangered.[1]

George had a continual struggle to induce Moll to take any interest in household affairs. On the death of his housekeeper in 1672, he promised Moll the future proceeds of the dripping and tallow 'to encourage you to look after things'—a curious inducement for the daughter of a Knight of the Shire. A year later, Glanville puts the Wotton marriage prospects in his inimitable nutshell; to Mrs. Evelyn he wrote that 'the nymph is much tarnished and in general become a drag, the market extremely overcharged and charges very severe'. Three years later he says that Moll is now almost come to 'any husband Good Lord', adding his dash of philosophic wisdom by wishing

[1] Letter, G. Evelyn to J. Evelyn, 11 July 1679.

Mrs. Evelyn's 'leash of girls at seventeen just so much beauty as may make them happy and no more'. His own son was not without faults; 'I know you will give my son good counsel,' he said to her, 'but I had rather you could give him a good character.'

Six months passed by before Godolphin showed his readiness to do Evelyn some service: 'I have had Mr. Godolphin an hour in the chamber here,' he tells his wife, 'and walked alone with him two hours . . . in the park.' He was desirous of providing some employment for Evelyn or his son—'and that with so much affection'. But nothing was decided, though 'Mr. G. has hinted . . . an intention of re-establishing a Council of Plantations . . . he doubts not of bringing me in, and this is for the present the hopefullest prospect I can as yet have.' But despite his excellent qualifications he was passed over; many years later, he told Lady Sunderland the post was given to one who had seldom been out of the smoke of London, where though there was a great deal of timber, there were not many trees.[1] But it was no subject for wit now.

The somnolent Sir Richard Browne—who had completed his term of office as a Clerk of the Council in 1672—was still seeking a mitigation of his estate debts incurred during H.M.'s service, and Mrs. Evelyn had urged her husband to find him favour among the great ones—on which he now comments: 'As to the other Lords you speak of . . . I find nothing but fair words and of course obliging,' and he wishes that Sir Richard could 'renew his pretences vigourously' in person, 'but what to advise is beyond my skill, and if you expect that I should do wonders upon my own score of acquaintance (as you seem to do) farther than I have told you, you lay a thing on me which I cannot promise you to succeed in . . . I can not force great men to what we wish.'[2] As regards the prospects of employment for the Evelyns, the truth was that worthwhile offices were rarely vacant, though ill-paid ones often were.

Amid these anxieties Evelyn did not forget his friend Pepys, who since 20 May had been committed to the Tower on an alleged complicity in the Popish Plot. On 4 June Evelyn dined with him, and recorded in the *Diary* that he believed he had

---

[1] Letter, 4 Aug. 1690 (*Diary*, 1854, ed. III, 318).
[2] Letter, J. Evelyn to Mrs. Evelyn, 29 April 1679.

been imprisoned unjustly. A month later they dined together on some venison which Evelyn had sent him.

The first anniversary of Margaret's death was commemorated by Evelyn in these words to Godolphin: 'I place her in the Calendar of Saints and call this Her Day . . . I lost in that happy creature all relations: she was neither wife, mother, nor sister to me; but she was something to me which is above them all, but which has no name in this world.'[1] Whether Evelyn improved his or his son's prospects of employment by this kind of thing it is difficult to say. Certainly his son was not improving his own prospects just now; perhaps as a result of intemperance something was amiss, and Evelyn suggested that 'his melancholy and sickness are a chastisement for sin'. Evelyn himself was depressed: 'Something doubtless there is, and has been amiss, which has put our family of late into this retrograde condition and frustrates all our attempts. I pray God you and I and all that are concerned, finding out the plague of our own hearts, may seriously repent and amend.'[2]

In November we first hear of his son's proposed marriage to Martha Spencer, a daughter-in-law of Sir John Stonehouse of Radley. Evelyn at once recommended some preparatory reading 'that you may not lay any neglect to my charge'; this consisted of prayers of Dr. Simon Patrick's, the *Change of Condition* and *Deliberation about Marriage*;[3] he also gave some extensive advice regarding the nuptial bed: 'Take heed of those filthy lusts even with your own wife, nor delight to feed and satisfy your eyes or incite your fancy with nakedness, or unnatural figures and usages of yourselves, for they will breed impudence, loathing and contempt . . . be none of those who brag how frequently they can be brutes in one night, for that intemperance will exhaust you, and possibly create importunate expectations, when your inclinations are not so fierce. Such excesses do oft times dispose to involuntary issues and other noisome inconveniences, through the straining of nature and relaxation of the seminal vessels, which are sometimes incurable.

'The like caution I would give you to forbear when your wife is in her monthly purgations, not only for the indecency

---

[1] Letter, J. Evelyn to S. Godolphin, 9 Sept. 1679.
[2] Letter, J. Evelyn to J. Evelyn, jun., n.d. [1679].
[3] Letter, J. Evelyn to J. Evelyn, jun., n.d. [1679].

and pollution, but for that the conception (which yet frequently then happens) disposes of leprosy[1] and marks the children with evident signs of the parents' incontinency . . . It is likewise experimentally found that carnal caresses upon a full stomach, or in the day-time, or in excessive heat and cold of weather are very pernicious, and too much frequency of embraces dulls the sight, decays the memory, induces the gout, palsies, enervates and renders effeminate the whole body and shortens life.

'There should therefore repose succeed these wasting exercises, and therefore physicians permit it rather after the first concoction is made, namely the first sleep; but rarely in the morning, never totally fasting, as indisposing the body the whole day after.

'These particulars I only touch, knowing the young married people will hardly be reasoned into that temperance, and perhaps they are to be indulged some liberties for a time, especially at first; but it is profitable to know these things once, and much better to use moderation . . . I do not by these abridge you therefore any decent satisfaction; a man may eat . . . not only to satisfy hunger, but to cheer him, and if there were not some gratification of the inferior sense accompanying this and other natural action, the world would cease.'[2] (This passage may be acceptable because the *Instructions Œconomique*—written for his wife—is a faded manuscript, and the section on sexual intercourse in *Economics for a newly married friend* has been excised and lost.)

Young John's marriage took place in February 1680. His wife's portion was to be £5000, and Evelyn settled on his son an annual income of £500—saying that it was 'all we have in the world but one poor farm in Sussex'. This left him—rather illogically—'only a precarious and uncertain supply'[3] from Sir Richard.

There is no doubt that with the transference of the Sayes Court rents to his son, Evelyn was now in dire straits for money, while for the time being his son felt comparatively opulent—or exercised opulent tastes. At any rate, in 1680 he began to consume more wine than was good for him—and this at home. Evelyn came down sharply upon him at once . . . 'I am your

[1] There is no evidence that this is so.
[2] Letter, J. Evelyn to J. Evelyn, jun., n.d. [1680].   [3] Ibid.

father and that you are still as much subject to my reproofs as the sons of old Eli were', maintaining his 'right of animadverting whenever I find you offend and forget your duties, as too often I find you do . . . your consuming an whole night with an insipid sot, heat your blood and disorder your health, in the boast of being able to contain more drink than another, making your body a tun'. He had been drinking, too, after receiving Holy Communion. 'Are you not sensible of your own body's growing corpulent and unwieldly?' his father asked. He suggested the reading of good authors, or to translate some useful book, constant exercise, to walk, bowl, fish, to study plants, or play some instrument; 'Nor take it ill,' his father added, 'I advise you of that which in my own self I find would have the same effect, did I not labour to prevent it, whilst I am in as many unhappy circumstances for want of some more lucrative office than any I yet have prospect of: but whilst I have a soul to save, an infinity of passion to subdue, I find employments.'[1] . . . (Surely there was a complication in his present passion and employment in writing the *Life of Mrs. Godolphin*?) But never before had Evelyn so revealed himself. His son resolved to study the Law.

To this end, young John desired to live in London. Evelyn at once objected: 'Have you considered all the circumstances of house-rent, furniture, servants, parish-duties, housekeeping, not to add the temptations of as dissolute a town as is the Court in every degree?' Apparently young John had found little company to his liking at Sayes Court, or as his father put it, 'there's no ingenious diversion here'. The angry parent said, 'Pray God when you are fixed (as you call it) at London your company be no worse, your diversions more innocent.' In truth, his son—being now in debt—was extremely rash in entertaining this move; 'nothing but your frugality or industry or both during all your life will extricate you'. He must have been extravagant in matters other than drink, but the details are not known. Evelyn concluded his angry protest: 'In God's name, take your course. . . . You shall need write no more to me on this subject, but do as you think fit.'[2] The young man must have hesitated; we do not yet find him in London.

Evelyn's financial troubles now impelled him to write to

[1] Letter, J. Evelyn to J. Evelyn, jun., n.d. [1680].   [2] Ibid.

Godolphin in a style that a lover might use to solicit his mistress: it was the usual style for one's patron and one in which Evelyn was proficient. His thoughts on patronage were conveyed to Pepys some years later. 'Great Persons and such as are in place to do great and noble things . . . are to be panegyrized into the culture of those virtues, without which 'tis to be supposed they had never arrived to a power of being able to encourage them.'[1] Yet now in his velvet strain he levelled a pistol, reminding Godolphin of 'that generous concession of your friendship which stands recorded in my heart and under your hand'—and he quoted Godolphin's operative words. He then lamented Sir Richard Browne's debt that was contracted in His Majesty's service, through which he himself was forced to part with so considerable a share of his estate for his son's marriage portion, which left him 'as susceptible of all your good wishes and intention for me as ever: look upon me then as part of your care . . . being mindful of me, when opportunity presents itself.' He then suggested that 'if [for] any other Office or Commission I or my son might be named, Sir Richard would most readily discount of the debt according to the salary'. But, of course, these are mundane affairs; so he concludes: 'but why mention these sordid interests; I have enough and abound whilst I have you as my friend, and that you increase in power'—and in all holy things—'Oh, were it God's holy will, that all high places were filled with such as you are . . . some great and good issue I cannot yet but expect to be a result of your counsels and endeavours for the composing of this unsettled, wretched nation: you know the best time, the best expedients, and cease not to pray for the divine assistance to cooperate with you.'[2] We are almost persuaded that Evelyn's financial straits were of small account.

In fact he now prepared to qualify himself for divine assistance. He would deserve Ranting Nanny's phrase: a man of

[1] Letter, 12 Aug. 1689 (*Diary*, 1852 ed., III, 303).
[2] Letter, J. Evelyn to S. Godolphin, 9 Sept. 1680. In the Letter Book (Evelyn MS. 39, pp. 10–11) is a similar letter to Godolphin dated 13 Aug. 1680, in which Evelyn states Sir Richard Browne's case, and the debt he incurred during his service in France. It is a less fulsome letter than that of 9 Sept. 1680, makes no allusion to Godolphin's promise of friendship, though it ends: 'Remember I am your Friend, you mine, and now do like a Friend.' Presumably there was no reply; hence the letter of 9 Sept.

conscience. He resolved to confess his sins. Then could the uneasiness felt the year before—by the voice of conscience—be eradicated. He would obtain mercy and find grace by purgation and cleansing. He well knew the way; in Henry Hammond's *Practical Catechisme*, 1649, p. 54, he had noted that repentance meant a lasting durable state of new life, and that confession was acknowledgment of sin in prayer to God, and by enumeration of the particular sorts of sin of which he knew himself guilty. From the deepest recesses of his memory he made a list[1] of his sins (for the most part in contracted Latin difficult to decipher), spanning the years from schoolboy quarrels to recent filial anger—his memory as active as his conscience; vanity, hypocrisy, avarice in computing his Sick and Wounded Prisoners Account, ambition, perjury, taking the name of God in vain, neglect of public business during the Friendship, intemperance in the 1660's, excessive affection for Margaret Blagge, and many undecipherable failings; including—we must believe—the falsehood that he advised her to marry. Her initials P. B. (Pearl Blagge) occur several times. It was a birthday confession—on his sixtieth birthday, 31 October—'an accurate scrutiny of all my actions past', as he recorded in the *Diary*; 'and oh, how difficult and uncertain, yet most necessary work; the Lord be merciful to me and accept me'. Four days later he asked Thomas Tenison if he might wait upon him 'to receive more particularly the seal of remission' from his 'ministring and discerning spirit, and extraordinary power with God, full of holy compassion as you are'—having told him, in general terms, of his desire to review his life.[2] By this act of conscience he gives us a clearer image of himself than any we have had before; devout we knew him to be, now by these sincere aspirations, he comes fully to life.

Young John continued to idle. He had embarked upon the study of the Law—and dropped it. Evelyn encouraged his aptitude for modern languages, but these also had ceased to interest him. He was spending too much time with 'the young master'—his cousin John at Wotton. In fact he was suffering for the lack of a definite pursuit. In the spring of 1681 he suggested to his father that a Court appointment would be agreeable—a

[1] Evelyn MS. misc.
[2] Letter, J. Evelyn to T. Tenison, 4 Nov. 1680.

suggestion that Evelyn strongly opposed. 'Attendance at Court', he said, 'is most anxiously tedious . . . you will be paid at great leisure after you are perhaps exceedingly out of purse.' (This was common to all in the King's service.) 'They owe Sir Gabriel Sylvius now £1900. For a mere courtier there is not so much as eating . . . the young gallant must play deep and pay dear for his experience . . . I do not say but 'tis possible, by God's special grace, to emerge there: you know I have seen of both sexes without reproach but they were persons extraordinary . . .' There is no doubt that his son was not sufficiently *à la mode*, as Lord Berkeley noted—or likely to 'emerge'. Evelyn again endeavoured to persuade him to resume his study of the Law: 'O how would I make it my business to introduce and procure you an interest, where I am certain to succeed,' said his father. He would get him made one of His Majesty's Council. 'Might you not get a perfect interest in my Lord of Arundel?' The possibilities were great. 'You have seen enough of the young master, the drinking, racing, hunting conversation of the country and town: set down and cast up the whole account . . . three or four years seriously employed would bring you past all the difficulties. . . .'[1]

It was a blessing that a daughter could be more amenable. Mary, now sixteen years old, was charming, accomplished, and dutiful. At the age of eleven, when her brother described her as 'aery and charmant', she could sing in French or Italian. Apart from Mrs. Evelyn, she was the only female member of the Evelyn circle who could spell. And now, at sixteen, she could write a letter in a style of which her mother might be proud. Strange as it may seem, her father had suggested that she should undertake the religious education of her cousin Moll, now thirty-three years old. Mary reported her progress in a creditable seventeenth-century manner: 'Your instructions took not so slight an impression upon my thoughts as that I would suffer anything to divert my endeavours to perform them.' She goes on to say that in the course of their friendship she has 'introduced something of piety (without seeming too great an undertaker, that I might not shock her in the beginning)'. The measure of her success was that Moll received the Holy Communion on Easter Day. Actually Moll was unconfirmed, but

[1] Letter, J. Evelyn to J. Evelyn, jun., 17 March 1681.

Mary, having noticed that 'she had so earnest an impulse, thought it were better to maintain her zeal than lose the opportunity of so considerable a benefit to her'.[1] The Archbishop of Canterbury could not have written more stylistically.

But her letters were rare—and she tells her father why: 'The fear of your imputing my long silence to neglect and forgetfulness of my duty was the reason that I now venture to overcome a very just diffidence in my own strength, especially when one produces it to a parent that judges so exactly as yourself.'

We have learnt something of the daily devotional course devised by Evelyn for Margaret. He gave Mary similar directions, which she collected into a manuscript of her own entitled *Rules for spending my pretious tyme well*[2]—self-revealing in its title. These directions—for one of a weak and unsteady disposition (as she describes herself)—had to be modified. Fasting before the Holy Communion caused sickness and was abandoned. Like Margaret, she was melting and susceptible; 'when my temptations attack me,' she wrote in her *Rules*, 'be sure I run immediately to my book with black strings, not delaying and there consult the remedies'. Even a dance must not be too worldly: 'When I am dancing, come up and read between four dances and pray.'

In her later teens she spent part of the year at New Palace Yard, Westminster—and we learn something of her daily routine.[3] In Term time, she was up at six o'clock for prayers. This early start to her day was made solely to avoid the 'crowding through Westminster Hall among the lawyers and other inconveniences'—which occurred at ten o'clock. She also went to four o'clock prayers. She rises earlier in London than at Sayes Court because she has more pieces to play for her harpsichord master. In the London house there were no Family Prayers before dinner—as there were at home—so she says a prayer at twelve o'clock. At Sayes Court there were times set apart for walking in the garden; in London, she walks in St. James's Park 'in the mornings constantly', occasionally in Hyde Park. Before her private prayers in the morning and at night

[1] Letter, Mary Evelyn to J. Evelyn, 5 April 1681.
[2] Evelyn MS. 92.
[3] 'Necessary additions to those Directions of my Father when I was at Sayes Court' (Evelyn MS. misc.).

she reads Josephus and the *Whole Duty of Man*; after her morning prayers the *Traité de la Civilité*,[1] Galatians, or her own remarks. Every Saturday afternoon she attends to her linen and mending, and prepares her dress for Sunday.

In the summer of 1681 Mrs. Evelyn, Bohun, Mary, the younger daughter Elizabeth, and Moll took the waters at Tunbridge, when there was 'a great deal of company of a middling rank', wrote Mrs. Evelyn, 'none great besides the Duke of Monmouth and my Lord and Lady Arundel who are every day upon the walks, the entertainment of water drinking, raffling for any toy as at St. Germain's fair . . . for handfuls of guineas'. It must have proved to Mary a welcome break from her London regimen: the conversation, 'the music which plays all the morning to the company upon the walks, then divides in the afternoons to the greens of Southborough and Rusthall'. There they danced, 'and on Fridays and Tuesdays music and company all join at either green in their turns'. There was good preaching twice on Sunday at the new chapel; daily prayers at eleven, 'after which people return home to drink and eat'. At the Fair, Mary won a silver cup 'which made no small noise upon the Walks'.[2] Evelyn was left behind at Sayes Court with Sir Richard (who had 'a very painful wind-colic') and the youngest girl Susan, now twelve years old. Mary's 'just diffidence' seems reflected in Evelyn's grumble: 'I did think that she would have written to me some of her observations.' There was a very witty, perceptive streak in Mary, and Tunbridge would have made a good subject; but exacting parents have only themselves to blame. Moll returned to Wotton 'the same woman still', said her father; 'Tunbridge hath wrought no reformation as to her hours, though it might do her good as to her face, which is now tolerable if her ill habits do not return her pimples again.'

The terms Whig and Tory now began to be used with reference to the exclusion of James, Duke of York, the former party opposing his succession, the latter opposing his exclusion. Small landowners were usually Tories, but in Evelyn's case his choice of that party was probably made because it was Godolphin's. George and Glanville were still Whigs, 'as you are a Tory', said George to Evelyn on 23 September, 'and notwithstanding the Game is seemingly yours [the acceptance of James]

[1] By A. de Courtin.   [2] Letter, Mrs. Evelyn to J. Evelyn, 26 July 1681.

you will find the lands to alter and persuade you to be of our principles.'

At Christmas, 1681, Godolphin was again approached by Evelyn for some employment, calling upon him 'often to mind the inviolable terms of friendship, which entitle me to more than ever I will ask of you'. His reply was most disheartening: 'The post I am in may and does give me many opportunities of being able to recommend people to inferior employments, but of late especially, it seldom happens that any one that could be worth yours or your son's acceptance comes to be disposable, but it is disposed of, even before I know anything of it.'[1]

In the matter of Sir Richard Browne's grant, Evelyn had assumed that the reason for its refusal was Lord Hyde's 'severity'. Godolphin corrected him in his best diplomatic manner: 'In truth', he said, 'it was only to preserve a rule which hitherto has not been broken, and but for such rules, we ourselves must have been broken long ago, considering the daily hardships we are forced to suffer, if not to do.' However, there was hope—if Evelyn played his part: 'Let me therefore advise you,' continued Godolphin, 'if upon any occasion you see my Lord Hyde . . . let him see that you retain no resentments of that proceeding, which will make the way so much easier whenever any opportunity happens for Sir Stephen Fox or myself to propose anything in your favour.' Hope was the only consolation—and as Evelyn said, 'I find employments.' Pepys had said that Evelyn's industry and capacity was beyond any mortal man that he knew. He spent more time than ever in his study revising his *History of Religion*—begun as long ago as 1657 —and working on the *Life*; in August 1682 Mrs. Evelyn told Bohun that he 'lives most part of the night in his hole according to custom'. In the candlelight the old Sorbonne black cap possessed a curious trick of drawing one's attention to the length of the wearer's nose. Perhaps he declined the presidency of the Royal Society because he was so deeply involved with his pen.

Another year passed with no alteration in the family fortunes. Sir Richard had died in February 1683, at the age of seventy-seven—a happy release from gout and dropsy. There was joy,

[1] Letter, S. Godolphin to J. Evelyn, 24 Dec. 1681.

however, in Evelyn's friendship with Pepys which was growing with the years. How different they were; in character and temperament poles apart—a perfect example of the attraction of opposites. In August Pepys, just before embarking for Tangier, shows us in a letter to Evelyn, how firmly the friendship was established. He mentions some of his delightful shipboard companions, 'the additional pleasure of concerts (much above the ordinary) of voices, flutes, and violins; and to fill up all (if any thing can do it, where Mr. Evelyn is wanting) good humour, good cheer, some good books . . . But after all, Mr. Evelyn is not here, who alone would have been all this, and without whom all this would be much less than it is, were it not that leaving him behind I have something in reserve (and safe) to return to.'[1] It was the comradeship of two virtuosi. As the years passed they were to be still closer friends, when rarely a Saturday went by without their meeting at York Buildings; in fact, in those days, Evelyn would refer to his friend as 'my Saturday's mistress',[2] or as 'my ideal mistress'. There seems little doubt that Evelyn dwindled himself as a diarist.

There is a delicious scene depicted in the *Diary* on 4 October when Evelyn, at Charles's request, followed the King into the Duchess of Portsmouth's luxurious dressing-room when she happened to be 'in her morning loose garment, her maids combing her, newly out of her bed . . . but that which engaged my curiosity', says Evelyn, 'was the rich and splendid furniture of this woman's apartment.' What a superb self-portrait that is! Pepys would not have noticed the furniture; Evelyn would have us believe he noticed nothing else.

It was quite possible that Pepys found accommodation in Villiers Street, York Buildings, for Evelyn and his family (including young John and his wife) who resided there for the winter of 1683. Young John was still unable to please his father; now he displeased him by resuming his studies of the Law—'wholly without my approbation'. (What of Evelyn's recent plans to get him made one of His Majesty's Council?) Elizabeth, now sixteen years old—and Bohun's favourite—tells him, in November, that Mary now has a singing master, 'and we are all in the way of improvement and in great expectations

[1] Evelyn MS. 3; Vol. II, fol. 112.
[2] See Letter, J. Evelyn, jun., to J. Evelyn, 14 Jan. 1693.

of our winter's happiness'. In December, she tells Bohun of a wedding she has attended when the Lord Chief Justice, Sir George Jeffreys, 'made many jests upon the occasion and insisted on drinking the lady's health, drunk my brother's five times calling him John very familiarly, so that if it continues when he is sober you need not doubt but to see him a great man'.[1] But on the whole their stay furnished little social excitement: 'We have been at no plays yet, having no acquaintance of that nature to spend so much money upon us, so that I suppose we shan't see many.'

Mary—two years older than Elizabeth—found excitement enough, being sought in marriage by John Hussey of Sutton. These affairs of settling the heart and the purse generally demanded tender and skilful handling; they were often long drawn out. Hussey had only a moderate income. Mary was a most accomplished and charming girl. Evelyn had pre-conceived notions of a good match, and was ready—as usual—to give advice. But Mary was so different; if she discerned her parents' slightest disapproval of man or means, she would not be advised—she would please her parents: she says to her mother, 'I refer myself wholly to your self and my father whose commands I will obey by the grace of God all my life and in this concern. Pray do what you please with me and I shall think myself happy.' The affair lingered on throughout the year 1684. At times she encouraged Hussey and jested about their prospective coach, and lodgings in Pall Mall. Some little time after, Evelyn told his wife that Hussey had found a mistake in his income, a diminution of £80 or £100 which 'exceedingly alters the whole affair, for he will not have much above £400 per annum, which is no means fit for us to proceed upon . . . I only told him that I had not as yet leisure to consider what was fit to be done as to my daughter, and that these circumstances of estate and settlements would take up time and consult of friends . . . in the meantime while I should not discourage him . . . only reserving to myself the not compelling of my daughter in any case . . .'[2]

Mary's rejection of Hussey provoked a quarrel between Mrs. Evelyn and Glanville, for he had proposed the match. Her

[1] Letter, Elizabeth Evelyn to Bohun, 15 Dec. 1683.
[2] Letter, J. Evelyn to Mrs. Evelyn, 9 Dec. 1684.

rejection was communicated in a letter which was read to Glanville, of whose authorship he said: 'If she writ that letter without the dictates of a friend or help of a secretary, I believe there is not a woman in England of her years, and but one within my knowledge of greater age, that can write in such a style, in such proper and significant terms, with such nice distinctions, and dextrous evasions, with so much knowledge of the force of words and the difference of phrases, with so much coherence and so few grammatical faults, as it seems my cousin can.'[1] Unfortunately Mary's letter has not survived for us to exercise our judgment on its authorship, and we can only regret that—as we have already noticed—affairs of the heart were never fully recorded in the *Diary*. There we read that Evelyn was not averse to the match; yet—as we have learned—he told his wife that Hussey's income 'is no means fit for us to proceed upon'. Young John was asked by his father to 'let Mr. Hussey know, what I had rather signify by you than by giving him farther trouble'. The truth is rarely simple, and it is especially hard to find in this case. In asking his son to communicate with Hussey, Evelyn said, 'as to the gentleman's present fortune we have little to object (though we find it somewhat less in the particular than at first it seemed to be), we should not therefore in that regard discourage his addresses, were there any appearance of that mutual correspondence between the parties, which can only render that condition desirable and happy in the midst of the greatest affluence'.[2] What we do not know is how far the dutiful Mary's affections were swayed—after she had encouraged her suitor—by her perception of her parents' criticism of his financial position.

Meantime, in May, Evelyn suggested to his son that a grateful compliment in verse to the Duke of York would be acceptable on the latter's appointment to the Navy: 'by this you may make yourself known and be taken notice of amongst those who may do you kindness. I would not prevent your own invention (which is much better than mine).' Characteristically, Evelyn then proceeds to give his son half a page of suggestions: the Ship of State, the Hand at the Helm, the Arch Pilot, and hints 'against those unskilful late admirals, most of whom had hardly

[1] Letter, W. Glanville to Mrs. Evelyn, 3 Jan. 1684.
[2] Letter Book, p. 55 (Evelyn MS. 39).

ever seen the sea and knew not the name of a rope . . . and so I leave it to your better genius'.[1]

In early July there was bad news of Godolphin. He was in great pain with the stone, and told his sister Mrs. Jael Boscawen that he had made a will which lay in his cabinet at Whitehall; and instructed her to look over his papers alone, 'for that there were papers there which he would have nobody see but myself,' she says, 'and that I must see them because I might burn them'.[2] They were papers of Mrs. Godolphin, some of hers to him, and some of his to her. These instructions were made known by Mrs. Boscawen to Evelyn, who had just completed the *Life of Mrs. Godolphin*, long overdue. It will be remembered that Evelyn and Godolphin had together looked over Margaret's papers; these in Godolphin's keeping were, of course, unknown to Evelyn. What might they not contain on the subject of the Friendship? Evelyn pondered the matter for a month.

How difficult life could be! His income was dwindling, neither he nor his son had any employment. His patron had the stone. The Hussey affair was most vexing, and now after arduous labour he had completed the *Life* to hear that another batch of Margaret's letters had survived! Yet he felt convinced that Margaret's loyalty was unassailable—that her letters would reveal nothing. However, he decided that it would be prudent not to send the manuscript to Godolphin.

On 8 August he told him that it had been given to Lady Sylvius. (We may surmise that some time previously he had mentioned it to her, and that she had asked for a copy: hence the inscription 'Writen at the request of my Lady Sylvius' (which it bears) does not mean that she made the original suggestion; it was Evelyn's, formulated, as we learnt, when he offered his friendship to Godolphin). She was one of the *dramatis personæ*, but he ran a grave risk in submitting the story to her scrutiny: probably he obtained a promise of secrecy. It is significant that no acknowledgment or acclamation of the gift survives and—if we know Evelyn—any acclamation would certainly have been recorded. Was his pruning at fault after all? Well, faint praise, or silence, could be a warning: he wisely

---

[1] Letter, J. Evelyn to J. Evelyn, jun., 12 May 1684.
[2] Letter, Mrs. Boscawen to J. Evelyn, 6 July 1684.

refrained from sending a copy to Godolphin. There was plenty of time: he would make a few more adjustments.

It was a strange letter that he wrote to Godolphin on this occasion. After telling him of the disposal of the manuscript, he writes as if he were dying—as if he must make one last supreme effort to engage his patron's help and sympathy: 'And now would I beg some great and valuable thing of my friendship (with my dying breath) it should be the continuance of your friendship to my dear wife and children when I am gone . . . Dear friend, farewell, pardon all my confidences, all my imperfections: you had one who loved you as his soul, loved you entirely, but you knew it not and that did oft afflict him . . . I go in expectation and humble hope of seeing that blessed Saint in the arm of bliss and be with the Lord and her for ever.'[1] If there were any evidence of his ill-health at this time, we might excuse this fulsome outburst: but there is none. We do know, however, that Godolphin was seriously ill: perhaps Evelyn feared the worst, and hoped for a favourable codicil of patronage transferred.

Fortunately, by the end of the month the skies had cleared: Godolphin was given a barony. He was also made First Commissioner of the Treasury in the place of the Earl of Rochester (who became Lord President of the Council)— 'alterations', says Evelyn in the *Diary*, 'very unexpected and mysterious'. He congratulated him—not forgetting to appeal to those 'indelible lines' of Godolphin's acceptance of his friendship. But Godolphin's health was little improved; even as late as in November, Evelyn told his wife that 'he looks exceedingly ill, but goes about as he was wont'. However, he now began to take a personal interest in Evelyn's application for the Sayes Court grant, the suit being in progress. From November Evelyn was in constant attendance at the Court—and beginning to complain of the lawyer's fees: 'They had of me no less than 60 guineas for nothing, but what remedy?' he asks his wife. The case kept him in London for some weeks: 'Affairs go so cross that I know not when I shall be free of them.' He sent to his wife this month good news: 'I have taken my son by the hand and forgotten all that's past.' He also said that 'the greatest news I can tell you is that His Majesty lay with the

[1] Letter, J. Evelyn to Godolphin, 8 Aug. 1684.

Queen the night he arrived at Newmarket'.[1] Perhaps it was the last attempt to please that neglected woman: two months later Charles was dead.

In the first week of December, Godolphin tried to hasten Evelyn's case, but having some other affairs he could not be at the Treasury as he intended so as there was nothing done, he tells his wife; 'he excused it to me last night, and assured me he would despatch it on Saturday morning: so as you see, there's no remedy but patience. I could wish it were well over . . . there shall be no want of my industry and application, however I would be most glad to see our little home again, once in a month at least; but I am resolved not to stir from hence till I see what success we are like to have.'[2]

The year closed with Godolphin's 'despatch' still to come. The new year opened with Evelyn still in attendance. On 8 February the King died: Evelyn described the last scene to his wife, how after James's speech, Evelyn—as a gentleman of quality—was admitted—according to precedent—into the Council chamber, 'whilst they agreed upon a form how the King should be proclaimed', and after the Proclamation, 'we all returned to Whitehall: then I went to the King's bed-chamber', who was newly risen after his grief, 'and kissed his hand, and thence to the Queen's (who was in bed) whose hand I likewise kissed, and so you have the whole history of this dream'.[3]

A dream it might be—or even a nightmare. Would the new King mean a new patron? this was Evelyn's first thought. 'What will now be done with all the politicians and our friends, is variously reported . . . to what party of the present politicians the King will lean, is not known.' Of course Evelyn's case was shelved; 'nothing in my business will be done till things are more fully settled'. Apart from its being put into Rochester's hands, we hear no more of it for another twelve months: there was no change in the 'retrograde condition' of his family.

Greater blows were yet to fall. On 14 March, Mary died of smallpox. The loss of such a charming girl fell heavily upon every member of the family. Elizabeth wrote at once to her

[1] Letter, J. Evelyn to Mrs. Evelyn, ? Nov. 1684.
[2] Letter, J. Evelyn to Mrs. Evelyn, 9 Dec. 1684.
[3] Letter, J. Evelyn to Mrs. Evelyn, 8 Feb. 1685.

father: 'The best thing I can do now is to follow the good example of her who is gone.' Young John wrote to his mother: 'Considering her [Mary's] extraordinary virtues, I find myself incapable either of giving or receiving any consolation. Considering my own sinful, disobedient life and behaviour which reason, and the bitter experience of my folly have too late brought me to deplore, I looked on her as a blessing afforded you, to make full amends for my ingratitude . . . and should have been willing, had I been half so well prepared, to have died in her stead . . . I have had the same opportunities but have neglected them, and have nothing now but the remainder of a wretched life to offer to God, which I hope in his mercy he will accept . . . the falsehood of my heart is such, that I have need of more than ordinary caution against hypocrisy.' He went on to admit that he still found himself 'under an indispensable necessity of endeavouring to struggle with my entangled fortunes which I again own to be the effect of my vices and extravagance . . . of which I am ashamed'.[1]

He also wrote to Elizabeth: 'You would do well to write to my mother and comfort her, she is not able to write to you for grief. Pray have a care of your health and endeavour by your compliance and goodness to make up this loss; you have sense enough and ought now to have discretion to make the right use of it. Forbear trash and especially sweetmeats which have chiefly been the cause of Mary's death. She eat those filthy things so constantly at my Lady Faulkland's that it was impossible to overcome the tough phlegm they had bred in her.'[2]

This gifted child has left one poem—a token of the alliance of her heart and head. It is remarkable that she should anticipate Blake in the use of 'symmetry'.

> When I that well fram'd body see
> With all its perfect symmetry,
> How swiftly doth ye object dart
> Like lightning Love into my heart;
> And all ye humble homage that is due
> To so much Beauty that I pay to you.

[1] Letter, J. Evelyn, jun., to Mrs. Evelyn, 18 March 1685.
[2] Letter, J. Evelyn, jun., to Elizabeth Evelyn, 19 March 1685.

But when your tongue once charms my ear
With wit in every sound I hear,
A Goodness too that's all divine
And doth through all your actions shine;
That Love-sick fit with which before I burn'd
Is wholly now to mighty wonder turn'd.

Yet that which chiefly I admire
And raises my amazement higher,
Is that that creature so refin'd
With shape & soul for Love design'd,
Should yet to all a faith & love deny
And like a stubborn unbeliever, die.[1]

Evelyn could not help comparing his daughter's virtues with those of Margaret: he told both Mrs. Boscawen and Godolphin of his joy in finding that she had proposed Margaret's way of life for her imitation, and that Godolphin 'may haply call to mind how he himself was affected with me, upon the loss of one he loved, when he was pleased to require my assistance in looking over those holy collections'. We know what effect Margaret's daily devotions had upon her, and that Mary's had need to be relaxed—yet Evelyn goes on to Mrs. Boscawen: 'I am not for young women's surcharging themselves with wearisome and formal devotions to which their tender hearts dispose them . . . a thing which really I took some pains to persuade your sister from . . .'[2] Of course his head was full of his persuasion in the *Life*—recently completed. But one would have thought that this was not a time for equivocation. Godolphin—ominously—made no reply to Evelyn's gush; and Mrs. Boscawen, on being anxiously questioned, reassured him with 'you know the silent manner of his expressing himself to his best friends, which to those who don't know him very well may give just occasion to doubt of him'.[3] Godolphin's temper was always in subjection to his judgment; as Boyer says, 'His superior wisdom and spirit made him despise the low arts of vainglorious courtiers.'[4]

[1] Evelyn MS. misc.
[2] Letter, J. Evelyn to Mrs. Boscawen, 23 March 1685.
[3] Letter, Mrs. Boscawen to J. Evelyn, 28 March 1685.
[4] A. Boyer, *Hist. of the Life and Reign of Q. Anne*, p. 17.

Glanville sent a short letter to console Mrs. Evelyn for the loss of her 'deservedly beloved daughter, that flower of your family . . . from the very bottom of my sincere soul'. Six weeks afterwards, Mrs. Evelyn wrote most movingly to a relation in describing her loss as 'a trial that yet appears very severe, and though as a Christian I do submit and believe it is in mercy He has taken her, am apt to murmur at the decree when all her engaging ways return to my imagination . . .'[1]

[1] Letter, Mrs. Evelyn to ?, 25 April 1685.

CHAPTER IX

Rod and Revolution

〜〜〜〜〜〜〜〜〜〜〜〜〜〜〜〜〜〜〜〜〜〜〜〜〜

O<small>N</small> 27 July another blow fell. When all at Sayes Court were asleep, Elizabeth, now nearly eighteen, ran off to meet a nephew of Sir John Tippets, Surveyor of the Navy, and married him the following day. The young man's name was apparently unknown to any other member of the Evelyn family. It was both unexpected and distressing: 'We had never given this child the least cause to be thus disobedient,' said Evelyn . . . 'she of all our children had hitherto given us least cause of suspicion.' She was of 'a silent and particular humour,' he says, 'in no sort betraying the levity and inclination which is commonly apparent in children who fall into these snares'. Sometimes it is the silent ones that do such things. Perhaps Elizabeth had shared the secrets of Mary's heart, and felt the pangs of her sister's unhappiness. Elizabeth would take no risk; she would not allow love to wait upon money.

Three days later Evelyn made a will. It was a curious document, written in the form of a letter to his wife (as the sole executrix), and included some surprising advice for her spiritual welfare. He suggested that she read more of the New Testament with Hammond's Paraphrase, and 'Diodati's notes as you may find them in the large Italian Bible which language you understand. To this, if you join more frequent Communion . . . you will soon become a consummate and perfect Christian . . . and I am verily persuaded, more healthy in body.' To alleviate her sorrow and despair, he recommended Patrick's *Mensa Mystica* (she

was already using his *Christian Sacrifice*), 'for direction and incitement to free you from those embarrassments and confessions
which entangle and so discourage people'. He also wishes her to
'look into' Wilkins' *Account of Natural Religion*, Parker's *Demonstration of the Christian*, and Cave's *Primitive Christianity*. He then
says, unnecessarily, 'You have in . . . Fisher, Stillingfleet, Usher,
Chillingworth, Hooker and several others sufficient to guard
you from Popery or Fanaticism, neither of which I know can ever
make the least impression on you.' He suggested that a part of
the evening be given to serious and spiritual recollection, reading and prayer 'as you shall find yourself tender and disposed'.
Now for secular matters, his debts she 'will find pretty well
cleared considering how by living to this world's opinion they
have been contracted (though had your good father been either
more fortunate or rather more industrious in looking after his
arrear), I cannot so far blame ourselves'.

He then locks the stable after the horse has gone: 'you find
how necessary it is above all to have a vigilant eye upon
daughters', and recommends them 'to the inspection of some
discreet and pious divine, that they frequent the public
prayers of the Church and family, and often receive the
Holy Sacrament', an implication that Elizabeth was not so
well instructed.

Certain of his bequests signified how full his mind was of Mrs.
Godolphin. After his wife has extracted what she thinks fit for
her own use from his MS. Devotions, they are for his son,
though 'better fitted for the use of that dear Christian Mrs.
Godolphin, now with God, and since her death, for my daughter
Mary (now with that blessed Saint)'. Godolphin is to have
Dixon's portrait of Mrs. Godolphin; Francis Godolphin to have
the *Greek Testament* in marroquin, Mrs. Boscawen the pocket
Book of Common Prayer with silver gilt clasps, and Lady Sylvius
Lancelot Andrewes' *Devotions* 'which was Mrs. Godolphin's gift
to me'. The bodies of Richard (his infant prodigy) and Mary
'which the sexton of Deptford will find ready, wrapt in lead,
to be buried on each side of me at Wotton Church'.

'For the sake of that happy Saint whose memory I carry to
a better world . . . you would conserve a special regard to her
dear child, and have it as your own. Had I a granddaughter of
suitable age and had £100,000 to bestow with her, 'tis certain

I should seek to make an alliance in that family and with this sweet child . . . But how vain are our contrivances and thoughts at this distance and in our circumstances!' (We shall learn that, when the distance was covered the vanity had disappeared.) 'Pardon this excess of fondness to that excellent soul . . . I wish you to continue your great respect to the sisters of that most virtuous family, and particularly Mrs. Boscawen: they are sincere Christians and worthy of your confidence.' Two post-scripts were added: 'To Francis Godolphin, also two golden buckles that were given me by my Lady Sylvius in which is enclosed some of his dear mother's hair. To Lord Godolphin, the seal symbol *ΑΓΑΠΑ*.' There was still another addition, caused by his having already given the book mentioned for Mrs. Boscawen to his daughter Susan: 'You must exchange it for something else to my daughter and give that book as intended to Mrs. Boscawen.'[1]

In the *Diary* Evelyn tells us that Elizabeth's runaway marriage was the cause of the will, 'as was reasonable . . . I must let her see what her undutifulness deprives her of'. This is hard to believe, as Susan, now the only daughter, is mentioned but once: to have 'the picture of Mrs. Evelyn in the enamelled case'. Perhaps Elizabeth was deprived of a 'red silk network purse of old and other gold' which was to go to young John's daughter. No; the will arose out of the death of Mary, of the writing of *The Life of Mrs. Godolphin*, and of Evelyn's 'vain' hopes of an alliance with the Godolphin family. But we shall see that the family fortunes—now so low—were to improve, and to render the will obsolete and a mere mental reflection of the summer of 1685.

The improvement was not yet in sight. Three weeks after her marriage, Elizabeth—then in London—contracted smallpox. Mrs. Evelyn at once went up to visit her. Evelyn was torn between paternal, Christian compassion and a reluctance to meet the husband: 'Do not believe', he wrote to his wife, 'I abstain from seeing this unhappy child, either out of indifference or implacable displeasure: if my coming may signify any-thing besides trouble and confusion . . . I will to be sure to come . . . I confess I do not wish to see the injurious man, who has (in great part) been the occasion of this redoubled affliction,

[1] Letter, J. Evelyn to Mrs. Evelyn, 30 July 1685.

whether the poor creature live or die; and truly that has been the only cause of hindering me from being as often with her, as I was with one who had never brought this sorrow and reproach upon us. I have most earnestly besought Almighty God to be merciful to, and spare her life if He think fit; and in all events, to accept of this severe chastisement for all her errors, that she may be happy in another world . . . let me know what you would have me do.'[1]

Hearts were rent at the bedside. In her delirium she acknowledged that she had 'undone herself, that she should never obtain her parents' pardon nor God's blessing, without which she should be miserable live or die'. At this tearful outburst, 'good people that were with her importuned us earnestly', wrote Mrs. Evelyn to Bohun, 'to forgive her, which I was prevailed upon to do—and never mentioned one unkind word to her'. Her mother's forgiveness appeased her, but she wished also to see her father, and the Rev. Mr. Holden of Deptford. Both came; Evelyn gave her his blessing and the other administered the Sacrament. Subsequently her fever returned; 'and her thoughts still so disturbed that she talked idly very often upon her own misfortune'.[2] Evelyn recorded in the *Diary* that before she received the Holy Communion (and therefore prepared) she was 'very sensible and penitent for her fault'. But first love clings to the first love. Mrs. Evelyn had told Bohun: 'Love is so powerful she cannot repent as to the man.' Elizabeth was penitent for her disobedience but not for her young love. Both Bohun and Glanville were kept informed of Elizabeth's illness, and their sympathetic letters to Mrs. Evelyn survive. The letters which must have been written by them after Elizabeth's death are missing from the series. There is little doubt that some expressions would be too critical for survival.

At last the tide of fortune turned in early September, when Evelyn was made one of the Commissioners of the Privy Seal. He told his wife that the happy event took place at Windsor, where he was presented to King James by Clarendon, and congratulated afterwards by Godolphin, Peterborough, and Sunderland 'and some who used never so much as to take the least notice of me'. Public payments must have improved with

[1] Letter, J. Evelyn to Mrs. Evelyn, — Aug. 1685.
[2] Letter, Mrs. Evelyn to Bohun, 27 Aug. 1685.

the new reign, for he says 'the salary is £500 per annum punctually paid within a fortnight after each quarter'. He understood his duties to be 'a great trust and power to stop or hasten most business', to acquaint the King 'of what we think fit or unfit for H.M. to grant . . . as pardons, benefices, pensions, promotion of clergymen, estates granted, and all manner of patents and whatever is to pass the Chancery seal, all monies for the Army, Navy'. These impressive duties, however, are 'very easy and cannot take up above half a morning in a week', he tells his wife; adding, 'God is pleased after all our sadnesses and great affliction to refresh us a little, and that all our friends have not abandoned us.'[1] His friends Godolphin, Clarendon, and Sunderland had placed him in the appropriate office where the Sayes Court grant could be successfully dealt with. But he took his duties seriously, and in at least one instance exercised his power to stop the printing of Popish service-books.[2]

Young John, staying at Drayton in Buckinghamshire in September, sought recuperation under a quiet country regimen: 'We live here', he writes to his mother, 'in profound ignorance, see no body, nor hear a word how the world goes, we eat and drink, sometimes go a setting or hawking and in the evening the Squire summons us to Beast' (a card game resembling Nap). 'I am now entering into asses milk which with the air and moderate exercise I hope in a fortnight or three weeks may alter my ill habits and do me good.' There is hope in his contrition; 'it is perfectly my own fault that I have forfeited all the happiness of life'.[3] In the following months his health denied him the company of young Glanville and the young 'Squire' of Wotton when this 'brace of idle gentlemen'—as Glanville called them—went hawking at Nether Wallop; 'they have only wanted you', said Glanville to young John cheeringly, 'to make up three as merry boys as ever did sing three parts in a string'.[4] But he had renounced such merry company. This year his name was again in print; as a translator of one of Plutarch's *Lives* and as a contributor to Tate's *Poems by Several Hands*, 1685. A month later Bohun noted young John's repentance and told

[1] Letter, J. Evelyn to Mrs. Evelyn, 8 Sept. 1685.
[2] *Diary*, 12 March 1686.
[3] Letter, J. Evelyn, jun., to Mrs. Evelyn, 19 Sept. 1685.
[4] Letter, W. Glanville to J. Evelyn, jun., 20 Oct. 1685.

Mrs. Evelyn that 'he seems to be another person in all respects
. . . God may be pleased to fix him in the right way at last'.
Perhaps he had felt the Rod.

This question of the Rod exercised the mind of William
Glanville. We have seen that he could offer a commentary—
sometimes coincidentally—on the absorbing interests of love
and friendship. We surmise that his commentary on Elizabeth's
death would be a criticism of her parents. On the year's
accidents he was downright, not to say devastating. In
November he sent the following observations to Evelyn:
'Christian charity teacheth us to distinguish between common
calamities and divine judgments: there is as much difference
between God's punishing and his chastising dispensations, as
there is between the Axe and the Rod; with the one he cuts off
his incorrigible enemies, and with the other he only corrects
his faulty children. I doubt not but you, brother, have heark-
ened to the Rod.'[1] As far as can be discovered, Evelyn neither
wrote to nor received any subsequent letter from Glanville for
more than five years, so deeply did his thrust strike home. As
Evelyn says, Glanville 'was a great friend where he took a fancy
and as great an enemy when he took displeasure: subject to
great passions'.[2]

After the storm come the quieter seas. What of the crew, the
survivors? In every corner of the house Mrs. Evelyn could still
hear the voices of the lost. What of Susan, solitary, sixteen?
What does she do, or see, or cease to hear? Two empty chairs.
The playing-green is hushed. The children's banqueting-house
at the end of the long grass promenade is deserted. Two ribbons
hang limp on the Maypole. It's no fun to row alone on the moat.
The lonely child paints a picture. She was learning to draw.

Young John is 'almost always indisposed' wrote his mother to
Bohun in November: 'He is temperate and careful of himself,
yet cannot be delivered from ill effect or other of the piles
which is the sole cause of his illness; it either torments him in
the common place or flies to his head or appears in rheums,
coughs, or fever . . . and yet he is affected with as constant a
pain in the fore part of his head every night so violent he cannot
sleep.' (Perhaps it was a sinus.) The well-known physician Dr.

[1] Letter, W. Glanville to J. Evelyn, 3 Nov. 1685.
[2] *Diary*, de Beer's ed., 12 April 1702.

Ridgeley was treating him with 'little benefit'. As Evelyn's new duties or his suit kept him at Whitehall, Bohun is invited to Sayes Court: 'If you will be so kind to venture upon these uncertainties . . . you will find the same method in the family but less happiness; a perfect satisfaction will never inhabit there in my time . . . I am persuaded you will bear with infirmities as much as any friend can,' and she asks him to send 'a thin Yarnton cheese such as are eaten in the colleges'.[1]

If relations between Evelyn and Glanville were strained, the witty widower was still on good terms with Mrs. Evelyn. Glanville had a niece, whose husband, Captain Fowler, had been dismissed his ship for some discourteous treatment of a Court lady on a voyage from Constantinople. Mrs. Evelyn persuaded Pepys to give the Captain another command, so Glanville, of course, was grateful to her: 'I love and honour you as much as ever I did, but to tell you how much that is, would look like courtship . . . I write now to let you know how sensible I am of your kindness to my niece in employing your power with Mr. Pepys to procure for her husband a voyage.' The flatterer concludes 'with what may look like a compliment but is none because what I say is from my heart; I have found so little merit in most women, and so much in you, that I think you one of the best of those few who have kept me from despising your whole sex'.[2]

In April 1686, young John, being still without employment, tried his luck with Pepys. But he was not so fortunate as his mother: 'I was this morning with Mr. Pepys who tells me the employment of being Councillor to the Admiralty was disposed of . . . and when he had told me that he knew of nothing in the Navy fit for me so I had no more to say upon that subject.'[3] Disconsolate, he returned to Sayes Court to continue the heavy task of helping his father to re-catalogue the books, now numbering nearly five thousand. This uncongenial task completed, he spent the autumn in Devon on a Commission from the Treasury, making an investigation into an alleged concealment of land: Godolphin could not yet offer him any better employment.

[1] Letter, Mrs. Evelyn to Bohun, 7 Nov. 1685.
[2] Letter, W. Glanville to Mrs. Evelyn, 14 Dec. 1685.
[3] Letter, J. Evelyn, jun., to J. Evelyn, 7 April 1686.

In October, George paid one of his rare visits to Sayes Court, staying a week. Despite his sixty-nine years, 'he is hearty well and brisk as ever I knew him,' Mrs. Evelyn told Bohun; 'and was as merry as could be expected, Mr. Evelyn giving his whole time towards the entertaining him and allowing the Bottle with more freedom than ordinary.' (Another £500 a year—about £5000 of our money—was bound to make a difference.) Perhaps they spoke of family affairs, and of the deplorable state of the health of George's son, who was drinking himself to death —a debauched man of thirty-three who would never make old bones. Young John, too, was a doctor's problem. They were all getting old, or nearing the grave. In the *Diary*, following the text of a sermon heard, Evelyn now occasionally recorded, 'Drowsiness surprised me: the Lord be gracious.' He was sixty-six. What of the inheritance of Wotton and the beautiful woods? It was impossible to say who would succeed to them. Evelyn could never hope to have them for his own. He was resigned to end his days at Sayes Court. The garden had almost reached perfection. At this time he wrote 'Directions for the Gardiner at Says-Court',[1] a charming manuscript containing, in simple gardening language, the essentials of the art. It was a gesture towards keeping his garden in everlasting perfection.

For the loss of his children resignation must be sought—as Mrs. Evelyn was resigned: 'I would say something comfortable in my own behalf, but it can never be; past ideas return and I wear out time, images are ever present; yet I acknowledge God's mercy for what remains.'[2]

Evelyn's commission of the Privy Seal came to an end in the spring of the new year, and the Sayes Court suit came on—at the Chancery in Westminster Hall, when Evelyn employed 'seven of the most learned council'. Success was imperative. Later, it was heard by Godolphin and the other Lords of the Treasury. Optimism reigned, and a hogshead of claret was ordered by George, in readiness for the brothers, Mrs. Evelyn, young John, and Glanville 'to sing requiem'. On 2 June the King's consent was obtained to the Privy Seal for £6000. This meant that it was in Evelyn's power to discharge Prettyman— as Remembrancer—of £5000 arrear upon the First Fruit and

[1] Evelyn MS. 136.
[2] Letter, Mrs. Evelyn to Bohun, 21 Oct. 1686.

Tenths Office as soon as the latter re-conveyed the land, 'gave releases and good security to pay Evelyn £1000 in two years time' as young John told Glanville;[1] Mrs. Evelyn said: 'My father's integrity and credit vindicated to the full which is more valuable to me than any thing.' It was the first fruit from Godolphin. After the Wotton claret was drunk, Evelyn and his wife, with young John and his wife, 'rambled' for five weeks (a welcome respite from the lawyers) to Windsor, Bagshot, Cranborne, and Swallowfield: 'We have been very well treated,' said Mrs. Evelyn, 'according to the usual way of England, great plenty and in some places great exactness and neatness.'[2]

In May, the crafty Sunderland's rise to favouritism as Secretary of State kept Glanville 'upon the tenters of expectation'. Evelyn wisely made no comment; he was particularly friendly with Lady Sunderland, indeed the association was a second string of patronage—though Sunderland himself rarely, if ever, corresponded with Evelyn. Yet he had chosen well; Sunderland and Godolphin were James's most trusted ministers. But whatever possibilities lay with the Sunderlands, all were dashed in the following year. His Lordship's renunciation of the Protestant religion pleased the King (though it is said that the new convert only went to Mass privately) but unfortunately it barely preceded by a few weeks the news that William, Prince of Orange, was about to invade England and restore the Protestants. Accordingly, Sunderland advised James to refuse the naval help of Louis. He also advocated the restoration of the Protestant Fellows of Magdalen College, Oxford, and the lifting of the King's other popish measures. His aim was conciliation, but the endeavour aroused the fury of the Catholic party. The King dismissed him.

Evelyn says, in the *Diary*, that he did not know the cause of Sunderland's dismissal: 'There was doubtless some secret betrayed which time may discover.'[3] Sunderland obtained his pardon on 27 October. 'You have your pardon,' said the King, 'much good may it do you. I hope you will be more faithful to your next master than you have been to me.' Dressed as a woman, Sunderland escaped to Rotterdam, later moving to Amsterdam and Utrecht.

[1] Letter, J. Evelyn, jun., to W. Glanville, 7 June 1687.
[2] Letter, Mrs. Evelyn to Bohun, 24 Aug. 1687.   [3] *Diary*, 29 Oct. 1688.

William of Orange landed at Torbay on 5 November 1688. Desertions from James's forces and the disposition of the country for William made his progress certain. On 7 December Evelyn advised Lady Sunderland that her Lord should acknowledge his error. As the reasons for his dismissal have hitherto been little more than conjecture, Evelyn's advice is of particular value, and must be given in full: 'Let his Majesty and all the world understand that his confidence in the security of those who have deceived him (by their hypocrisy and wicked insinuations) has made him see the mistake he was led into, and to detest as well their religion as their politics: that nothing which has happened as to his secular concerns, is of so great affliction to him, as that to comply with H.M's continual importunity and the opinion he had of (at least) a tolerable profession of that Church, reconciliable with Christian truth (and indeed common humanity) he had from other human frailties, resigned to their persuasions, without that mature and just consideration, which so weighty a concern required, and for which he implores God Almighty's pardon. That this is sincere and from his heart, he gives the world leave to judge, by the favour and advantages he has sacrificed for the advice he gave his Majesty to undo what their pernicious counsel had extorted from him (naming the particulars: Ecclesiastical Commission, Restoring the Fellows of Magdalen College, Bishops Charge, Opposing the offer of French forces &c.) so soon as he discovered the violent and illegal courses they took, to enslave the nation, and ruin both Church and State ... And that the experience his Majesty now has, that the counsels which he gave him were the most salutary and only best expedient for reconciling the public misunderstanding and the calamities they have brought upon him, will at least extenuate what is past and obtain his gracious pardon.

'This is, Madame, what I had in my thoughts, presuming to take upon me to be his Lordship's Apologist: for I have the vanity sometimes to think what I would say and do if I were a great man: but at this your Ladyship smiles, and I am content so you'll forgive me.'[1]

When news came that William would pass through Oxford, Evelyn sent young John to join him. From Oxford the young

[1] Letter Book, pp. 108–9: Evelyn MS. 39.

149

man sent home the sort of news that soon became pretty general; that Lord Cornbury, 'having made a speech to his Troop that he would not fight for Popery is certainly gone over to the Prince, and two troops of the Duke of Berwick's Regiment of Horse are also gone over with my Lord of Oxford and Sir F. Compton'.[1]

The Prince, hearing of the King's flight, made straight for London. He did not therefore pass through Oxford; though he stayed at Abingdon at Mr. Medlicott's the Recorder's house, where young John and Sir John Stonehouse were presented; 'Lord Lovelace secured Oxford for the Prince,' wrote John from Radley on 15 December, 'with a garrison of gentlemen volunteers on horseback and the townsmen on foot who unanimously rose in his behalf, though at first but coldly seconded by the Passive Obedience men, who trembled for the plate and libraries, part of the King's army lying no farther off than Little Wycombe, Henley, and Reading, and none of the Prince's forces so near to cover them. Of this small garrison in defence of our English Athens, I had the honour to make one in my Lord Lovelace's troop, not without alarms, and some small bloodshed, till his Highness, when he lay at Henley, sent us order to disband, having no further occasion for our service. Having thus finished my five days Rebellion in very good company, if being in arms for the Nassovian Hero, the Primitive Religion, and the liberty of my country, deserves not a more honourable title . . . The Prince seems to be very grave, and deliberate in his speech and motion, and even while he eats not unthoughtful. Tranquility, order, and silence reign among his attendants. Dr. Burnet said Grace: I found time to salute him and present your service to him, which he received kindly enough.'[2] Evelyn made some use of his son's observations; in the *Diary* for 18 December we read that the Prince is 'stately, serious and reserved'.

Young John wrote also of 'the deluded flock, who here in the country, are not satisfied to disarm all the Papists, but abuse and pillage them of their reliques and altar baubles, all which if of any value the Prince has strictly commanded to be restored: so just are his Arms, and so well guided his zeal'. Bohun

[1] Letter, J. Evelyn, jun., to J. Evelyn, 12 Dec. 1688.
[2] Letter, J. Evelyn, jun., to J. Evelyn, 15 Dec. 1688.

entertained young John and Sir John Stonehouse at New
College; their womenfolk stayed two days in Oxford, but 'were
defeated in their hopes of seeing the Prince, who had nobler
ends to pursue than being gazed at by Topknots from the
windows'.

The Revolution gave young John renewed hope of employment; and he turned to his father for guidance: 'You . . . will
soon be able to discern which way things will settle, through
what channels performance is like to pass, whether friendship
alone or quickened with gold will most readily help one to
employment, whose distress you cannot be ignorant of. It is,
I confess, God's infinite mercy that I have subsisted without
much disgrace to see this miraculous Turn. But if I have not
some small share of temporal as well as spiritual advantages
that will attend Protestants in the Revolution, I must be content
to praise God in some private corner.'[1] This proved somewhat
prophetic—though it would be some time before he would have
employment and a private corner.

Evelyn watched the exciting London scene from a window of
the New Buildings in Whitehall. He was a trifle sceptical:
'A Parliament of brave and worthy patriots, not influenced by
faction, nor terrified with power, may produce a kind of new
Creation amongst us; but it will grow old and dissolve to Chaos
again, unless . . . Providence . . . dispose them also to use their
Empire with moderation, justice and piety, and for the public
good.'[2]

George's son, now thirty-five years old, celebrated the
Revolution in his usual, excessive, bibulous manner—though
Evelyn called it an apoplectical fit. Every such debauch brought
the inheritance of Wotton nearer to Sayes Court. Solely to
divert his son from the bottle, George frequently invited young
John and Glanville's son to Wotton for hawking and 'the game
of poults'. But there was no improvement. In December another
blow struck the Wotton line when George's grandson died.
Sooner or later George would be without a son.

Meantime, young John spent Christmas with Sir John Stonehouse at Radley, where the ripple of war soon died away: 'We
are here very quiet and ignorant and pass the time as usual in
the country at Christmas among clowns and tenants: sometimes

[1] Op. cit.   [2] Letter, J. Evelyn to J. Evelyn, jun., 18 Dec. 1688.

relieved with the Council of Trent among Sir John's old books, and find in it that Popery was as full of legerdemain 100 years ago as is like to be proved in this day of its (I hope) final doom . . . we feed on nothing here but the letter of the next market town.'[1]

With the new regime, one of the new 'channels', as he called them, was soon explored. On 9 February of the new year his father was informed that he had visited Admiral Herbert 'who came over with the Prince and is as well with him as any Englishman, who received me very kindly'. The young man was becoming desperate; his ability to 'subsist in the face of the world', he says, 'I do not promise myself for much time'.[2] But Herbert did nothing for him.

Evelyn was also looking to the future. Lady Sunderland, writing from Rotterdam in February, gave him an indication that her Lord was now using a Protestant compass to steer himself back to England and into a favourable harbour—but we think that the needle of his compass sadly lacked magnetism. Her Ladyship wrote: 'I bless God he is a new creature; you know I always bewailed his weakness, but still said I was sure he had too much sense to be a papist, and I thank God I am more and more convinced of it and that he thinks it as foolish a religion as I do . . . I think this one argument may not be improper for such a friend as you to urge when you think fit.' Her choice of Evelyn for this advocacy is significant. But one has confidence who knows the ability of another to sail close to the wind without his being taken aback. She also told him that Dr. Tenison would show him 'a paper that you advised the writing. I have ordered it to be printed'.[3] This was the well-known *Letter to a Friend*,[4] Sunderland's inept apologia, published at the end of March. On 22 February Evelyn reported to Lady Sunderland: 'I have made some considerable converts to declare in my Lord's behalf when it shall be seasonable.' But an exploratory voyage by the pilot was desirable: it was 'the opinion of friends here that your Ladyship should take the first

[1] Letter, J. Evelyn, jun., to J. Evelyn, 29 Dec. 1688.
[2] Letter, J. Evelyn, jun., to J. Evelyn, 9 Feb. 1689.
[3] Letter, Lady Sunderland to J. Evelyn, — Feb. 1689.
[4] There is an unrecorded 4to edition, dated 29 Jan. 1689, in Christ Church Library.

opportunity of coming over'.[1] She came over in June, and had several meetings with Evelyn, Sir William Godolphin, Tenison and Mrs. Boscawen. On 22 August she returned to Holland. In the following April, Sunderland returned, professing the Protestant religion.

[1] Letter, J. Evelyn to Lady Sunderland, 22 Feb. 1689.

CHAPTER X

Filial and Financial Troubles

~~~~~~

Young John, his wife and children, and his sister Susan
spent a few days at Tunbridge in August 1689, when there was
'a great deal of middling company', and 'no news but at second
hand and that so disguised and mutilated'. Although the waters
agreed with him, the place had no real attraction for one of his
health and temperament; in fact, he admitted that only Susan's
company rendered 'the repeated circle of diversion much less
tedious'. She was now an eligible twenty and undoubtedly a
social asset on the walks and at the dances. But we hear no
stories.

Evelyn was in a critical mood and disapproved of the place,
and sent his son a medical diatribe on taking the waters. 'I
cannot but believe it much better never to have used them';
health comes of temperance; he believed that 'by so consistently
ingurgitating the waters which might (though not cause) pre-
cipitate the calculous matter mixed in our juices through the
ureteries into the bladder to the engendering the stone; the
much taking of pretended remedies does frequently stir up and
awaken the seeds and principles of such diseases, as else never
would have appeared, or been subdued by the strength and
vigour of nature; *obsta principiis* is a general and excellent advice,
both for body and soul; all immoderate and periodic drinking
of accidulous or calybiate liquours (farther than necessary for
the due cooling of the body) makes the body spongy and opens
passages nature would have closed'. He says that forty years ago

young persons hardly used them and were in better health; only 'two or three ancient gentlemen in a whole county going to them and they such as were in a deplorable state, abandoned by physicians'. Furthermore 'the place is grown (I hear) an Emporium of all kinds of diversions, a mart of vanity, a formal Town, where you have fiddlers, dancers, gamesters, auction for both sexes and varieties innumerable and very grateful to men of pleasure'.[1]

Evelyn, of course, was thinking of the future, of Wotton, and of the young people. He hopes that Susan is not neglecting her pencil for delights unnecessary for one of her age. More important is his concern for his grandson Jack—though he was but seven years old. Fair hopes were qualified by embarrassing warnings. At present he saw nothing but good in him, yet 'these seeds and inclinations', he tells his son, 'will require your special care and culture, and you have experience how highly necessary it is in this abandoned age'. If young Jack was ill, Evelyn felt the shock of possible loss. In December scarlet fever caused deep anxiety for a few days.

Four years previously, Evelyn's portrait had been painted by Kneller. No contemporary comment on it has come down to us. Perhaps it did not please the sitter. In 1689 Kneller tried again —a portrait to be presented to Pepys: it shows us Evelyn looking somewhat apprehensive, and holding a copy of his *Sylva*.[2] It was eminently satisfactory to Evelyn: 'Kneller', says he, 'never painted in a more masterly manner.'[3] Pepys said that he had 'forty other reasons (founded upon gratitude, affection and esteem) to covet that in effigy which I most truly value in the original'.[4] But he does not say it was a good likeness. (T. Bragge's engraving of it is flattering—used in the first edition of the *Diary*; Bartolozzi's engraving, used in Hunter's edition of *Sylva*, pure idealism. The Royal Society's portrait is by John Bugdane after the 1689 Kneller and presented by Mrs. Evelyn. Ann Jackson sold the 1689 Kneller to Wotton for twelve guineas on 24 April 1724.)

In the new year, Evelyn published Mary's skit, in verse, on fashion, called *Mundus Muliebris: or, The Ladies dressing-room*

---

[1] Letter, J. Evelyn to J. Evelyn, jun., 13 Aug. 1689.
[2] Now in Christ Church.　　　[3] *Diary*, 8 July 1689.
[4] *Diary*, 1854 ed., III, 312.

unlock'd, and her toilette spread, for which he wrote the preface. The
rhyme of one of her couplets is of a kind often seen now in
Punch:

> One black gown of rich silk, which odd is
> Without one colour'd embroider'd boddice.

The problem of his son was still unsolved. Unfortunately, for
the greater part of 1690, Godolphin was out of office. In March
he retired—probably on account of the stone. In November the
King persuaded him to return reluctantly, as head of the
Treasury—an employment 'he was not sure . . . could be
avoided'. Despite Godolphin's absence from Whitehall in
August, Evelyn asked him to recommend young John for the
Sheriffdom of Jamaica—a post worth little more than £200 per
annum: no reply survives. Five weeks later, having heard that
Lord Sidney was Lord Lieutenant of Ireland, Evelyn turned to
his second string, Lady Sunderland (who was Sidney's alleged
mistress), for her 'favourable representation' of his son for 'any
station' there. Furthermore, the annual commemoration of
Margaret's death was delivered by young John—perhaps to
remind Godolphin of the Sheriffdom of Jamaica. How useful
these annual commemorations were!

In the autumn the news from Wotton took a more serious
turn. George's son was drinking larger quantities of claret than
ever; 'it is a wonder to me he is alive', said his father. Evelyn,
in December, declined—for the second time—to be President
of the Royal Society; of course he visualised that the affairs of
Wotton would soon demand his undivided attention. Indeed,
in the new year George's own health was deteriorating on
account of the stone. But the condition of his son was more
desperate. He had taken so much liquor, his stomach would
take no food nor 'the spaw waters'. He was in constant pain, and
averse to all physick. 'Nothing remains now', wrote George to
Evelyn, 'but my hearty prayers for the prosperity of you and my
cousins, who are the next to succeed in this place when I am
in the grave.'[1]

In the circumstances, it was time that Evelyn paid his brother
a visit. Yet the conditions in the Wotton household were not
propitious. Glanville was there—at the express wish of George

[1] Letter, G. Evelyn to J. Evelyn, 27 Feb. 1691.

—and advised Evelyn in March 'not to come now; when I myself am sick of being here, among so many hangers on, who have for several weeks pestered my brother's house . . . to stay under no better pretence than that of being with my cousin, though they cannot but know their company is troublesome'. The unwanted guests probably included the Wotton circle of relations and friends to whom the survival of George's son was of supreme interest. 'Whether you come or come not to Wotton,' continued Glanville, 'they that hear your brother's estate, if your nephew die, falls to you and yours, will upon that subject think and say what they please and measure your corn by their bushel.' There is no doubt that Glanville was on more intimate terms with George than Evelyn, and there is a hint that the latter somewhat resented Glanville's presence at Wotton at this juncture. 'I know nothing of my coming hither', he assures Evelyn, 'till my brother's coach came for me.' The same antipathy was expressed by young John when Glanville's son 'did not desire him to come down with him'. Evelyn, after all, was a brother, Glanville a brother-in-law. But Glanville was easier to get on with.

The inevitable happened: George's son died in May. In sending his condolences, Evelyn declared that his own family losses 'mortify all other low self-interests and concerns, which standers-by (who measure all things by their own sordid inclinations) fancy one should have in my possible circumstances by this mournful accident'. Young John wrote to George: '. . . you must give me leave to be as sensibly afflicted as it is possible to be for my nearest kinsman, my companion, the best, and almost only friend I had in the world. The future advantages that I may receive may perhaps incline some to think all this dissimulation, but I assure you those expectations are much outweighed by the just grief which has filled my heart.' In his acknowledgment to Evelyn, George included these words: "tis my comfort that you and my nephew are *in vivis*, to succeed me in the enjoyment of the estate our father left us'.[1] These are but words—and there were difficulties ahead; George had spoken of a necessary settlement, that 'all the encumbrances upon the estate and all my other debts may be satisfied'. It was by no means a case of waiting for George to die to enjoy the

[1] Letter, G. Evelyn to J. Evelyn, 26 May 1691.

woods of Wotton; the 'encumbrances'—George's female off-spring (one daughter-in-law and three grand-daughters) were entitled to their 'portions'.

Meantime, Susan had fallen in love—apparently unrequited love—in February, and her health had suffered. A change of scene was desirable. In June Mrs. Evelyn took her to Bath. The long coach journey tired Mrs. Evelyn: moreover, it was 'the middle season which invites more to the waters of Adstrop and Tonbridge, but since health is our chief end, we will dispense with diversions', she wrote from Calne, in Wiltshire, where they stayed en route with Aunt Hungerford. Perhaps here Mrs. Evelyn had witnessed some squire's treat to the villagers: 'I find discreet hospitality assists very much towards governing the nation, for common people are led by the mouth with moderate management, and without a little popularity they are perfect mules and ungovernable.' How wise was Mrs. Evelyn. Susan was still suffering from the dart and looked ill, though her mother hoped that 'Bath and the waters will dispel love and vapours; she is infinitely thoughtful notwithstanding all that is done to divert her: time may work a cure'.[1]

At Bath 'we know not one person', wrote Mrs. Evelyn; 'Sue and I sit in our chamber, either read or work, so that Deptford was never so great a solitude.' She tried to persuade Evelyn to join them—'the flying coach brings you directly hither in two days'.[2] A fortnight later, she dispensed more wisdom: she thought it desirable that Evelyn should visit his brother. 'It may be of consequence as to the knowledge of his affairs, and putting things in such a method as may make us all easy and for remaining with him.' This is the first news of the suggested arrangement that they should leave Sayes Court to reside with George at Wotton. How delightful it would be—with Evelyn as 'head Gardener'! Pepys is suggested as a tenant for Sayes Court: 'I wish he had occasion for a country house,' Mrs. Evelyn said; 'he should be preferred to any other for his neatness and friend-ship.'[3] As we shall discover, these were but castles in the air.

Susan, 'after hearing so much of the dull cittuation, heat and ill smells' of Bath, eventually found the place tolerable; and she

[1] Letter, Mrs. Evelyn to J. Evelyn, 10 July 1691.
[2] Letter, Mrs. Evelyn to J. Evelyn, 14 July 1691.
[3] Letter, Mrs. Evelyn to J. Evelyn, 25 July 1691.

gives us the only known scrap about her love affair, saying, 'I believe I shall return with the same inclinations towards marrying a conterry esquire as when I left London'—which seems to imply that there had been some parental opposition. In the first week of August—towards the end of their stay— young John joined them. By this time they had made a few acquaintances—and the company had become less middling; Lady Littleton was there, living 'as elegantly as my lady Sunderland herself'.[1]

During the summer there were rumours that Godolphin had married again; in fact during the last few years there had been much talk of romantic attachments. In the previous autumn, on hearing such a report, Evelyn—despite his annual eulogies of Margaret—was ready to approve: 'For whilst I understand you made choice of a lady so transcendently like her predecessor: accomplished in all the virtues and ornaments she was possessed of, not only my consent must be included in it, but my highest approbation: there's one thing yet to render your happy lady, not only the resemblance, but the very prototype, of that incomparable Saint, but her very self, remaining: that she accept of my humble service and regard me with some distinguishing grace for the sincere honour and affection, I have ever borne to him, on whom she has placed hers so worthily—which is all the merit I plead; and so God Almighty give ye both joy.'[2] Despite all rumours, Godolphin never married again, and his comment on Evelyn's anticipated approbation has not survived.

Now, in the summer of 1691, Evelyn showed more discretion in displaying his sense of proprietorship: 'I shall rejoice to hear', he wrote to Mrs. Boscawen, 'whether my Lord be married, for before you assure it me I'd suspend my congratulations, and perhaps say nothing to one who will not thank me.'[3]

George lost little time in drawing up a provisional settlement of his estate, to which the Evelyns and Glanville agreed—in the late summer. Evelyn had had no desire to go to Wotton while the widow was preparing an inventory—to create the usual embarrassing situation between unequal beneficiaries. He had

---

[1] Letter, Mrs. Evelyn to J. Evelyn, 3 Aug. 1691.
[2] Letter Book, pp. 140–1: Evelyn MS. 39.
[3] Letter, J. Evelyn to Mrs. Boscawen, 29 June 1691.

been forewarned by Glanville as to the burden: the portions
for the three grand-daughters, an addition to Moll's portion,
and a sum of money to be raised to pay George's debts. In
October the first knell rang in Evelyn's ears when his brother
wrote: 'I am now viewing my woods, those that are to be felled
for the raising of the £6000 for my own occasions and payment
of my debts.' The note became sweeter: 'and those trees that
are to remain for the ornament of the seat'. The provisional
agreement, drawn into Articles, George now expected John to
sign: there was nothing in them he said, 'but what must enable
me to pay off my debts, to make an addition to my daughter's
portion . . . and for the woods, after I have cut down £6000
[worth], there will remain the value of £6000 more to the heirs
and the ornament of the place: and what you, or others think
of the estate, that will come to you after my decease: I do
assure you, that if you will part with it, there be those that will
give you £50,000: and I hope that will be a good addition to
you and my cousin's fortune: and I must tell you I could have
given all the estate away from you for it was not entailed till the
settlement I made upon my son George's marriage'. He concluded by saying that until Evelyn had signed he could not
make any sale of his woods nor make his will.[1]

This letter was exceedingly distasteful, even cruel, to Evelyn.
'Consider the circumstance', he replied, 'in which the estate is
left; so great a share of it not likely to be of any advantage to
me, or mine in many years.' He was thinking of the desolation
of the woods, the acres of beheaded trunks, his birth-place, the
home of the author of *Sylva, or A discourse of forest trees*. He had
nursed Sayes Court from a field into a perfect garden; young
seedlings planted by him thirty-eight years ago were now
beautiful trees. Was life to begin again at Wotton—at eighty
(for George might live another ten years)? Yet his brother's
valuation of the estate was no incentive to part with it. This
valuation was indeed fantastic, and he ridiculed it: 'You cannot
reasonably imagine the land or place should raise £50,000,
unless they weigh the Air.' Evelyn felt that his brother had been
influenced by the envious and lesser beneficiaries of Wotton:
'These suggestions then (dear brother) do not sound like your
own; nor indeed like one who does not regret that the succession

[1] Letter, G. Evelyn to J. Evelyn, 10 Nov. 1691.

falls to so near a relation, who never gave cause to repent of the transferring a paternal estate to a brother, in failure of male-issue as some unkindly (but for most part, unprosperously) have done.' It was agreed that the interest on the £6000—which would be £300—should be shared by the brothers. But Evelyn's income was strained already. He therefore suggested that £150 worth more be yearly felled of the woods to enable him to pay his share.[1]

Nothing further passed between the two brothers until 1 January of the new year, when Evelyn pointed out 'that there was in that Agreement we made at Wotton that the woods for ornament and shelter about the seat were to be left entire, of which there was not one word in the Articles, nor of my receiving any assistance to enable me to discharge my part of the interest'. George must have taken Evelyn's previous criticisms as a refusal to sign the Articles, for Evelyn now sought to calm him by saying, 'if I had said that until I was satisfied therein I should not sign, you might have taken it ill . . . my speaking of the air, was far from raillery, but a serious belief . . . one should for all that hardly find so liberal a purchaser in all England upon that account. That passage therefore does by no means intimate my least undervaluing of Wotton, but the contrary . . . I conjure you therefore my dear brother, let none of these little accidental encounters and frailties (most innocently meant) lessen the mutual charity and brotherly correspondence which has hitherto been so long between us.' In all events, Evelyn puts the onus on his brother: 'I submit it absolutely to you . . . it shall be therefore your fault if anything interrupt the amiable conclusion of what you desire one moment, whether you gratify my so reasonable hopes or not.'[2]

Three weeks later the Articles were still unsigned, and Evelyn, unable to tolerate the transformation of Wotton woods into a wilderness, insisted that it was necessary to insert a safeguard that no more trees than the sum expressed be cut down, and that sufficient be left for the shelter and ornament of the seat. The Wotton beneficiaries now made a nasty accusation. They said that by Evelyn's refusal to sign, or by his procrastination (if George should have died during the interval), he hoped to

[1] Letter, J. Evelyn to G. Evelyn, 13 Nov. 1691.
[2] Letter, J. Evelyn to G. Evelyn, 1 Jan. 1692.

elude George's desires for the advancement of Moll's portion and the discharge of his obligations; to which Evelyn said 'this I again and again solemnly protest: one half hour's discourse between you and I with my brother Glanville I am most certain would have ended all these difficulties and misunderstandings'.[1]

At the end of January, Evelyn again insisted—backed up this time by Glanville—that it was necessary to express plainly the limit of the value of the woods to be cut down, mentioning particularly what were for shelter and ornament. He explains that he has no fears that George would exceed the Fell, but it was necessary 'to secure and prevent your executors' from doing so, 'should it please God to take any of us away before the £6000 worth were cut down'.[2] The executors would doubtless be led by Moll.

By the end of February all was settled and signed for £6500 worth of woods, leaving those adjacent to the house. Now could Evelyn unbend and avow his love for his brother: 'I am not now in an age becoming compliments, no interests to serve by flattering and servile arts, and if I have pleaded for the standing of some wood or should yet wish that some few timber trees fit for building might be left growing . . . some not yet of full growth but which after few years would be fit for building . . . without you being necessitated to cut down all those growing and yet thriving oaks,' it is no selfish plea, but 'for the sake of those that come after'. Evelyn was now in his seventy-second year, and all that he seeks and has to wish for in the meantime is that he and George 'may continue to live in all brotherly affection and confidence'. By another assurance in the summer, we see Evelyn at peace with his brother. In fact having got his way he is—we may think—too generous towards him: 'Most sorry and afflicted should I be', he says, 'that ever you should have the least cause to repent of what you have done so generously, naturally, and affectionately.'

This expansion of Evelyn's spirit resulted from other benefits about to be received—and from the vision of others on the distant horizon. In March his son had at last found employment as a Commissioner of the Revenue in Ireland—thanks to

---

[1] Letter, J. Evelyn to G. Evelyn, 25 Jan. 1692.
[2] Letter, J. Evelyn to G. Evelyn, 30 Jan. 1692.

Lady Sunderland and Godolphin—and to purchase his equipment and facilitate his journey George had opened his heart and lent him £4000. Evelyn was now convinced of his son's conversion to temperance: 'I have not only all his promises, but very good assurance,' he says to George, 'such as will become the exceeding obligations he has to his uncle.' He assures him that he will be a blessing to the family. But Evelyn was looking still further ahead—to his grandson Jack—saying: '. . . that what you leave to your family and name may not be diverted . . . my greater care shall be that your godson may be religiously educated and brought up in such principles as may render him a useful man and an ornament to your name.'[1]

Although the trees surrounding the house at Wotton had been made secure in the Articles, it was not a sufficient safeguard for Evelyn. He wanted to be there—to direct the felling. He concludes his letter by inviting himself: 'I again beseech you, dear brother, to believe and to repose yourself in the assurance of it, that I love you, pray for your health and life: and if I have fondly wished that seeing myself very aged, and however in health at present (by the course of nature, near my period, as well as you) I might hereafter pass some remainder of my few days, in the place where I was born, and that you have so kindly designed me: it is not (I protest most solemnly) to disturb the economy of your family in the least, but that you will admit a sojourner, and give him leave to cultivate your garden, refresh himself with books, and devote the rest of his time to his prayers for you, and be ready to do such services and assistances as becomes one whom you have so signally and everlastingly obliged.' This supreme example of the gentle Evelyn's epistolary art bears the tender postscript: 'I pray, brother, spare the aged beech tree, on White-deane as a mark of your clemency: I will ever call it by your name.'[2]

Meantime, in May, Moll had secured a husband. It must have seemed a miracle. He was Sir Cyril Wyche, the newly-appointed Secretary to Lord Sidney (an appointment made two months before young John's). There may, of course, have been a few mental reservations; he had been married twice before, no details of the financial settlement survive, and—strangest fact of all—Moll continued to live at Wotton while

[1] Letter, J. Evelyn to G. Evelyn, 24 June 1692.   [2] Ibid.

her husband was in Ireland. Certainly young John wrote with reservation, when in a farewell letter to George, he finds himself saying: 'My humble service to my Lady Wyche, who I hope will recommend me to her excellent husband.' Times had indeed changed. How important it was in their small world to be (like Godolphin) on good terms with everybody; an enemy one day might be a friend on the morrow.

Leaving his son at Eton, young John with his wife and daughter sailed for Dublin on 24 August, embarking in the *James* yacht at Chester, under convoy—for pirates or French men-of-war were still likely to be encountered. (Liverpool was growing, but Chester still held its own as the port of embarkation for Ireland.) All went well: the ship made a quick, safe, and pleasant passage.

Ireland was settling down: and young John tells George: 'We have here few Tories among the Protestants; their sufferings have given them a quick sense of their true interest, which is to be true to their heroical deliverer King William.'[1] Formerly, of course, most Tories in Ireland were for James.

Young John's work cannot have been particularly interesting: 'We live so divided from the rest of the world, and are indeed so insignificant to it, that little notice is taken of us.' The inland excise upon drink was the chief source of the Revenue, 'the Customs and Excise inwards holds up pretty well, but Customs outwards yield little, there being yet nothing considerable of their growth or manufacture to export'. At first, most of young John's time was taken up in letting the forfeited lands for short leases 'till we know his Majesty's pleasure, how they will be further disposed of'.[2]

For the first four months of his service his health varied with the weather; in bright and buoyant air he could enjoy his morning rides in Dublin Park; a moist close atmosphere proved a trial. He always went riding with a mounted groom, for fear of sudden illness; thus he kept two saddle horses. He says that there were times when he could hardly stand, was short of breath in the mornings 'which goes off about noon, and after eating am something brisker, till night returns with giddiness upon me'. Later on he underwent a 'steel course'.

[1] Letter, J. Evelyn, jun., to G. Evelyn, 3 Sept. 1692.
[2] Letter, J. Evelyn, jun., to J. Evelyn, 19 Sept. 1692.

His resolutions against the bottle prejudiced his social sucess, and probably prevented any real familiarity with Lord Sidney and Sir Cyril Wyche—though good terms were established with the latter. On one occasion in October he and his wife contributed to His Excellency's entertainment 'by bringing Mrs. Vincent to sing, which she did very well, considering her want of the late new airs which generally please those best who have no extraordinary skill'.[1] Modern songs rather than classical did always please most in unmusical circles.

On visiting Sir John Temple's fine garden two miles from Dublin, he found the gardener well learned in *Sylva* and the *Kalendarium Hortense*, 'which made our acquaintance not difficult, and will procure me very good winter fruit to roast', he said.

The news from home included some reference to Lady Wyche's attitude to young John; perhaps she felt that he was entirely to blame for his poverty, and that George had been unnecessarily generous in fitting him out for Ireland. 'I cannot call to mind', he writes to his father, 'that I have any ways offended or given just cause of resentment by any late expressions that could be carried to her. There are, I believe, never wanting some false friends, that constantly suggest to her what may feed her aversion to her father's relations.' Perhaps she feared further inroads on her father's new and rather surprising generosity. Young John assured Evelyn: 'I resolve to be content with my pay, and thank God for so honourable and comfortable a support as this, if my good friends Lord Godolphin and Sir Stephen Fox are pleased to continue and protect me in it.' But even now there was no real peace or security for him; time and again there were reports of Treasury retrenchment, against which Godolphin's friendship 'constantly solicited may be at last effectual'.[2] Fate, as yet, showed him no consistent encouragement.

Evelyn still awaited an invitation to Wotton, and although there is no evidence that the trees had yet begun to crash, he was anxious to save the younger oaks. In the autumn this anxiety manifested itself in a sudden beneficent gesture; he sent some evergreens—with directions for their planting—to Abraham, George's gardener. (Such things were sent by 'the

---

[1] Letter, J. Evelyn, jun., to J. Evelyn, 26 Oct. 1692.
[2] Letter, J. Evelyn, jun., to J. Evelyn, 19 Sept. 1692.

orange man',[1] presumably a carrier.) Furthermore, Evelyn promised to send seeds in the spring, 'to supply defects and support the plantation. I would also add a Conservatory for orange, lemon, and other rare and choice shrubs,' he says, 'could I hope for the happiness, you were once pleased to grant me, of a Retreat (with my sole companion) in the place that gave me birth, and must shortly, burial.' He again protests that 'the mutual enjoyment of those innocent and primitive refreshments (with books and such a friend) is the utmost and ardent desire of my cohabitation with you'. He had gone so far as to tell his Deptford neighbours that he would end his days at Wotton—which now caused him some embarrassment.

Yet he cannot refrain from expressing his disappointment, and asserting that if he had been allowed to come, it would have been 'in as silent, harmless, and humble a manner, as becomes one who has (by much and long experience) learned not to be so very fond of this world or any mention in it, as solicitous of that world to come, and of habitations not made with hands, but eternal in the Heavens'.[2] Why, then, did he allow his presumption to over-rule these noble thoughts? The reason for the lack of an invitation was a practical one: so long as Lady Wyche resided with her father she would object to Evelyn's self-appointed role of head gardener—not, of course, to be so crudely expressed. She also said that Wotton House was now the home of Sir Cyril. This gave Evelyn an opportunity he could not resist to express his scornful surprise. 'I humbly ask my lady's pardon', he wrote to his brother, 'for a presumption which your former kindness and my need of your charity misled me into; far from imagining that the character, public affairs, and other ample circumstances of Sir Cyril would be consistent with a private country sojourning for any considerable time: but he is prudent and times are hard.' Evelyn told his brother that he would 'be no more troublesome on this subject', resigning himself to the providence of God for the shelter he will shortly need.[3] However, he continued to live at Sayes Court.

Nor was any consolation forthcoming from young John on

---

[1] Not in *O.E.D.*

[2] Letter, J. Evelyn to G. Evelyn, 21 Nov. 1692.

[3] Letter, J. Evelyn to G. Evelyn, 7 Dec. 1692.

the subject: 'Whatever destruction of woods is on my uncle's estate I shall not be surprised at it, but think every stick that is left more than we were to expect.' He would be content with riding space to aid his health and his thoughts: 'you will smile and say that I labour mightily to be thought a philosopher on paper at least, but I resolve and endeavour to be a good Christian which is the true and most refined Philosophy', a remark which may imply that he disapproved of his father's concern for the woods. But Evelyn could forget trees and intractable relations at York Buildings when Pepys invited him to eat a dish of warm broth:[1] it was a case of thanking God for Pepys.

In the new year of 1693, both Evelyn and his son received a shock by being called upon for their share of the marriage portion of one of George's daughters. Evelyn declared that it was impossible to raise his share of interest on the Deptford property, encumbered as it was by two existing jointures, and he reminds his brother that this obligation depended 'upon your putting me into a capacity of doing it, by admitting me to sojourn with you'.[2] He always put himself in the right. However, the lawyers advised the raising of £5500—the entire sum necessary for all the portions. Young John also countered his uncle's demand by sending a full statement of his financial position which 'will much diminish his expectations'.

Young John also suffered domestic troubles. For his first six months he and his family had resided in a boarding house. In February he says he will be forced to keep house; as boarders they were 'coarsely treated and indeed pryed upon'.

His father, already thinking of the transfer of the Sayes Court library and of the necessity to reduce its size to the restricted shelf-accommodation at Wotton, suggested that his son's French and Law books be sold. Young John resisted, and showed himself a greater lover of books than his father. He protests that his Law books were well chosen, and 'not improper for a country gentleman's library; sometimes a family produces a genius for the Gown, and then a set of tools at hand, without charge, is no small encouragement to a young beginner'. Evelyn had no taste for French books either: his son defended

---

[1] Christ Church MS. 2: Letter, 29 Nov. 1692.
[2] Letter, J. Evelyn to G. Evelyn, 10 Feb. 1693.

them: '. . . though I have, as an Englishman ought, an aversion to the people, I always delighted in their language, and loved to read good sense clothed in it.' His collection contained scores of French translations of the classics: 'I do extremely value them,' he says, 'and should be very uneasy to let them go, unless great distress, which I continually expect, and am prepared for, obliges me.' He was in a sad plight, continually harassed by the interest due on his borrowings. If he is forced to sell his books, he says, 'I fear they will more need Millington's[1] eloquence when the inexorable £6 per cent brings them, and the rest of my poor movables *sub hasta*. If it must be so, the Bible and the world are a better library and much more worth studying.'[2] It was a brave utterance for one so unfit for this world. A month later he made another pathetic entreaty for his books: 'I would not but have it in my power to read sometimes. I was ever guilty of loading myself with books, and you will easily conjecture from whom I derive this laudable infirmity, if it be one—which I can hardly allow.'[3] Pepys knew of his love for books and gave him a copy of his own *Memoirs of the Navy*.

In March, a translation of de la Quintinye's *Instruction pour les jardin fruitiers et potagers*, appeared as *The Compleat Gardner, made English by John Evelyn*. In sending George a copy, Evelyn says, 'I do not attribute the whole to my self; the toil of mere translating would have been very ungrateful to one who had not so much time to spend in thrashing: but as a considerable part of it has, and the rest under my care, the publishers and printers will have it go under my name, altogether against my intentions.'[4] The translation, as a whole—hitherto accepted as Evelyn's—was undoubtedly the work of the King's gardener George London; with Evelyn's name on the title-page the publishers hoped for better sales than could have been expected —in those undemocratic days—from London's name. In fact London was an excellent French scholar who had lived and studied in Paris. Evelyn could have done little more than read the translation before publication—and lend his name—for when this folio of nearly 500 pages was reduced, in 1699, to an

---

[1] Gilbert Millington, regicide.
[2] Letter, J. Evelyn, jun., to J. Evelyn, 25 Feb. 1693.
[3] Letter, J. Evelyn, jun., to J. Evelyn, 29 March 1693.
[4] Letter, J. Evelyn to G. Evelyn, 24 March 1693.

octavo of little more than 300 pages, London felt under no obligation to ask his permission. We fear that the circumstances of the publication of the 1693 folio is yet another instance of Evelyn's inborn habit of equivocation.

CHAPTER XI

Unsettled Outlook

～～～～～～～～～～～～～～～～～～～～～～～～～～

I N the spring of 1693 a marriage was proposed between the 'exquisitely shaped' Susan and William Draper, a nephew of Sir Thomas Draper of Sunninghill, Berkshire. She was nearly twenty-four and he was twenty-eight. The proposal pleased everyone. Young John sent the first description—presumably given by Susan herself—of Draper to Evelyn: 'he has avoided the vices and tricks of the Age and Town, worth £6000 per annum, well humoured, seeming a little high till known, and then not at all so'.[1] It was a relief to himself in his sinking condition, to see his sister approaching firm ground. He was anxious for the settlement, to see the match 'out of danger of malicious old lovers and the spitefulness of tattling Jills about Town, who too often frustrate good matches'. Of the malicious old lovers we know nothing beyond the fact that there were two of them, and that on account of the unsuitability of one Susan sought diversion at Bath. Evelyn told George of her good fortune, and of Draper's having two rich uncles, 'from whom (having no heirs male) he has fair expectations'; he 'has £1000 a year at present, and will have £600 a year more after his mother: he makes my daughter £500 a year joynture; is to leave £1000 a year to his eldest son (if any) if daughters only her mother's portion, which is £4000—too much for me to part with (my condition considered) but it being left so by her grandfather [Sir Richard Browne] I can do no other'.[2] In the *Diary*, the

---

[1] Letter, J. Evelyn, jun., to J. Evelyn, 29 March 1693.
[2] Letter, J. Evelyn to G. Evelyn, 21 April 1693.

source of her portion is not stated, Evelyn merely records, 'I gave her in portion 4000 pounds', at once giving posterity an erroneous idea of his magnanimity and of his financial position.

The couple were married on 27 April by the Bishop of Lincoln at the chapel in Ely House. Curiously and belatedly George wrote the same day, advising Evelyn to make no delays in concluding the settlement: apparently George was not informed of the wedding day. However, after the ceremony, Evelyn told him of 'the congratulation of all that know us in this town and of the best quality in it'. In the *Diary* this news becomes 'came to visit my newly married daughter divers Countesses and other Ladies of quality, and gentlemen'. We cannot but reflect that in the matter of marriages the outlook of the most devout persons became excessively materialistic. It is also apparent that in this third attempt of marrying Susan, Evelyn's choice fortunately coincided with her own: 'I am indeed', he tells George, 'abundantly confirmed in the agreeableness of the choice we have made.'

Young John's problems continued to be as insoluble as ever. Out of an income of £1100, he was paying £50 rent for his Dover Street house, and £450 to maintain young Jack at Eton. (The £200 or £300 due as interest to his uncle probably came out of his Deptford rents.) And he was 'eaten up with interest' of his own. He had no credit to borrow in Ireland or any capacity to pay the five or six per cent off any principal to his uncle. On occasion he took up his salary before it was due. In his work there were no perquisites: 'there is not one farthing to be got beyond salary, with honour or safety, which I will never hazard'. His health prevented any gain through social avenues: 'I have too little time already for my health to desire a feather in my cap, which requires attendance without profit, and in my case one mouthful of fresh air is more valuable than all the foolish honour and formal debates, even Cabinet ones, in Christendom.'[1]

But he must have broken out sometimes from the daily round, when, for instance, with Wyche and another colleague, he was entertained by the Mayor of Drogheda, and at the Earl of Drogheda's place, where there was 'continual eating, in which they exceed England both for plenty and with drinking

[1] Letter, J. Evelyn, jun., to J. Evelyn, 29 May 1693.

too much wine'. At this time he gives us a thoughtful observa-
tion on his superiors—which perhaps has universal application: 'It is difficult to find the true value of men in their life
time; many times their reputation and way of living conceals it.'[1]

At Trinity College, Dublin, he attended the weekly meetings
of the Society of Virtuosi, to which entrance costs ten shillings
and contributions sixpence a week. 'If this colony of the Royal
Society and indeed the University of Dublin flourishes, it is all
to be attributed to the care, virtue, and example of the witty
Provost, Dr. George Ashe, who is a most polite, learned, and
ingenious man, a great encourager of the studious, communica-
tive, well-bred, well-fashioned and travelled, has all books that
come out worth reading with some of which he often obliges
me, understands most of the modern languages.'[2] Young John's
weakness for books was further indulged by his friend Edward
Philips, the nephew of Milton, who sent him lists of newly-
published French and English books.

His letters home never omitted enquiries and 'services' for
his friends, Lord Clarendon, Pepys, and Mrs. Boscawen. He
would send details of estates for Pepys, who never failed to be
grateful to him. He would say to his father, 'Your mistress's
good thoughts of me are superabundant recompense for all the
poor service I can do him.'[3] His 'services' to Mrs. Boscawen
were allied to thoughts for the future—to the friendship of
young Jack and Francis Godolphin, his son's fast friend and
pattern.

Since Evelyn's hopes of living at Wotton had been dashed
by Lady Wyche, he had ceased to send plants or to show any
interest in the garden. The reason for this cessation George
learnt from his gardner Abraham. George then wrote to
Evelyn, saying that the discouragement he had taken not to
proceed in his planting upon occasion of some idle impertinent
words 'said by I know not whom', extremely surprised him.
'Let this assure you,' he continued, 'never any such words was
said by me or my daughter (as she tells me) for she desires you
may go on with your plantation . . . dear brother, this is not
a time to conceive ill suspicions of one another and especially
brothers and dear relations: and therefore harbour no such hard

[1] Op. cit.   [2] Letter, J. Evelyn, jun., to J. Evelyn, 5 May 1694.
[3] Letter, J. Evelyn, jun., to J. Evelyn, 27 June 1693.

imaginations upon what hath been suggested, but go on to plant what you designed which my cousin your grandson may live to enjoy. I rejoice to hear that my cousin John is in such good graces with Sir Cyril [Wyche].'[1]

It was fortunate that Wyche showed none of his wife's antipathy to young John. Presumably Lady Wyche did not display, in her letters to her husband, her hatred of the Deptford Evelyns, and particularly of young John. In October some former utterances of his had thoroughly aroused her anger, and of this Evelyn informed his son. In reply young John let himself go: 'I will not deny my having often discoursed of her and her peculiar method of life with much freedom' with his uncle, his son, and Glanville's son. From these conversations he had 'received the character of her pride, vanity, trifling her time, covetousness, want of housewifery, the plague she has been to my uncle, her inveterate hatred to our family, and design on the whole estate, with all other ridiculous circumstances, of her frequent marriage proposals'. He goes on to recommend Tillotson's *Sermon before the Queen, 8 March 1689*, 'to cure her of all such venomous hatred and deliberate, diabolical implacability. I have done her many good offices here to her Lord by palliating some things he has inquired after, in which he will find himself miserably deceived, if ever he cohabits, which a certain sharp discursive lady here says he never cared to do with any of his other ladies.' (Sir Cyril must have been a true son of the Restoration.) 'I am sure he designs not her coming hither. I am sorry her predominancy obstructs your going into Surrey, but it is Interest (which never gives itself the lie) that frustrates your desires, and not her overacted malice to me. I look on her as a weak, foolish, if not half crazed woman, and defy her doing me any prejudice with all her spite and necromancy.'[2]

In response to his brother's appeal, Evelyn quickly resumed his consignments of plants and young trees to Wotton. At the end of the month he sent, by the Dorking carrier, a number of White Scio fig-trees 'of a very rare kind' and 'the best Frontiniac' grape vines. We must allow that by trial and experiment (since he first read Parkinson) he now knew the very best varieties.

[1] Letter, G. Evelyn to J. Evelyn, 3 Oct. 1693.
[2] Letter, J. Evelyn, jun., to J. Evelyn, 23 Oct. 1693.

The new year brought him the happy news which he had so long awaited: his brother invited him to Wotton. George's worsening attacks of the stone (despite the addition of rosemary flowers to his mead), his family's acceptance of the inevitable inheritance, and Lady Wyche's hopes of joining her husband in Ireland, all contributed to the invitation. But her Ladyship was still in residence. Evelyn embraced the offer on 3 January 'as a most brotherly and seasonable kindness . . . though it will require some time', he says, 'to dispose of my small affairs'.

March came with Evelyn still at Sayes Court. He sends word that Lady Wyche is to 'take her own time to remove what she thinks fit . . . we intending to send not only beds but hangings also, and all other furniture for those rooms, that nothing of her ladyship's may be impaired or suffer by their using'. He wishes to bring some cabinets, pictures, and maps for the dining-room—and expects to arrive after Easter. George asked particularly for a picture to hang over the chimney in the room allotted to his brother—'for we have none here'[1]—and tried to persuade him not to bring hangings, beds, or bolsters. Financial matters were now settled amicably, both for the payment of Evelyn's board, and of the interest due to George.

Young John shared the family's satisfaction at the thought of his father's returning to Wotton. He knew the Dorking road and the half-mile long track to the south which led to the house —the track which suddenly rewards the eye: 'I was always touched with delight', he says, 'when I came in view of Wotton.' His father, of course, now thought of his birthplace as the family estate; young John regarded it—or would like to regard it—merely as a personal haven. 'I suppose,' he says, 'besides the great Portion which the Lady carries with her, she is still a charge on my uncle, and so makes the Axe range further than at first designed.' All he requires is shade in which to read and meditate. His idea of happiness lies in good health, freedom from care, debt, and company; to breathe in the fresh air and preserve the sight for reading: 'These things I dream of here in the desert, where without God's mercy I may fall short, and never reach the promised land.'[2]

On 4 May Evelyn, his wife, and four servants, with two cart-

[1] Letter, G. Evelyn to J. Evelyn, 29 March 1694.
[2] Letter, J. Evelyn, jun., to J. Evelyn, 26 March 1694.

loads of books, left Sayes Court for Wotton. In the end it proved a difficult business to part from the place where he had lived for forty-two years. Of course, certain furniture had to be left behind—but he was leaving his own creation from which he could never make a complete break. Young John (writing the day after the family had left) was surprised at the delay; yet he knew how tempting Deptford or any place is 'that is neatly and carefully kept'; though the expense of upkeep and its proximity to London 'which in fair weather pours out its inhabitants into the neighbouring fields and gardens',[1] rendered it almost impossible for the Evelyns to continue to live there. It is true and surprising—as Lord Ponsonby pointed out—that no note of regret or lamentation occurs either in his *Diary* or in his then published letters at abandoning this beautiful home. But he was abandoning his own child (as it were) which had grown up with an increasingly predatory dockyard; there were also the financial reasons: such things were not for the *Diary*. None the less Sayes Court was worth preserving, and it is in no spirit of lightheartedness to say that probably the first requisite in any tenant would be a capacity for weeding. What a responsibility lay upon Draper, his mother, and Susan—who became the caretakers! But Draper was a conscientious person.

It was strange that Lady Wyche should have displayed her impatience for Evelyn's arrival; every week he delayed had been a disappointment to her. As soon as he, or rather as soon as Mrs. Evelyn was at Wotton to take care of George, Lady Wyche would be free to visit her husband. That was the reason for this reversal of feeling. As it turned out, her Ladyship was frustrated in her plan; 'no fatigue of journey or danger of the ocean shall keep me from coming over', she wrote to Wyche; but as young John handed back her letter (which he had been allowed to read) Wyche said, 'It must not be.' Obviously he was still in no mind to cohabit, or willing to allow her to run the risks of the journey. Therefore on settling at Wotton Evelyn and his wife became acquainted with the strange nocturnal habits of her Ladyship; for she seldom appeared on their horizon by day.

Perhaps it was as well. Evelyn had work enough on hand, arranging with Benjamin Tooke the printer, for the engravings

[1] Letter, J. Evelyn, jun., to J. Evelyn, 5 May 1694.

of the medals for his new book *Numismata*; and the completion of the manuscript. Nor could Sayes Court be forgotten; he instructed Susan to see that the servants look to the shutters of the windows, especially in the lower rooms, and the door of the Myrtil greenhouse, which had, on occasion, been left open all night after strangers have been to visit the gardens. Susan's skill in painting had progressed so well that Evelyn suggested that she could copy Dixon's portrait of Margaret, which he described as 'the likest' to her: "tis all I will impose upon you for this summer of that kind, my intention being to make a present of it to my Lord [Godolphin], being unwilling to part with the original unless it be for another of your hand, because I know you will equal, if not exceed it.'[1] Her baby was expected the following month; 'we long to know', he concludes, 'what the Goships think of the time you have to go; young married women often making great mistakes in their reckonings'.

The birth of Susan's child—a boy—brought Evelyn and his wife back to Sayes Court in the middle of September. As so often happened, there was a most anxious period after the birth when Susan's life was almost despaired of. Evelyn told Mrs. Boscawen that 'this month and our present circumstances often recalls sad thoughts'. Yes, September—and Margaret, the everlasting memorial.

There were other affairs that prevented an early return to Wotton. The provision of interest, and the insecurity—financial and otherwise—of young John. In fact these two were related. As young John got in arrears with his payments to George, the latter appealed to Evelyn—but in vain: 'It is beyond all my possibility,' he wrote to George, 'who know not where to have credit for £500. I am indeed infinitely obliged to you for your signal kindness to my unhappy son, for keeping him from an inevitable ruin and shame: but as I contributed nothing to his folly and prodigality and am so much the worse for it, so I know no reason why he should not himself bear that part of the interest which you require of me, who have no sort of benefit by it . . . however what I have promised you, I will punctually perform, though I am forced to borrow every farthing of it, as I do indeed. My poor fortune, with the grevious taxes, ill-paid rents, repairs of rotten tenements,

[1] Letter Book, Evelyn MS. 39, p. 182.

expense of this marriage and portion, which sinks me £200 a year, and has put me into considerable debt, should in all justice and reason excuse me . . . all my poor estate being so in joyntures, and bare of all things by which to raise money for the discharge of my debts and necessary subsistence, that without your charity to me in giving me a Retreat, I should yet have been put to the utmost exigencies.'[1]

A little financial relief could be expected by letting young John's house in Dover Street: a drop in the ocean. There was encouraging news of Jack's progress at Eton, engendering hope —though in the distant future: 'a good match for him may in due time do something when we are gone, and by God's blessing and your kindness, the name and family flourish'. In fact from now onwards young Jack and 'a good match' were never from Evelyn's thoughts. All things were to be directed to this end.

In the autumn we hear that young John's commission has become insecure; he spoke of slander, and of Lord Capel's opposition to him and his colleagues. An appeal to Godolphin was imperative. (What time was this for Evelyn to think of retiring to Wotton, when he could still be useful in Whitehall?) In November his son thought it not amiss for him 'to prepare my Lord Godolphin by letting fall some of these particulars'. Young John would make a fight for Godolphin's interest: 'When my patron', he said, 'told me I was a Commissioner of the Revenue . . . he himself added I should tell a fair lady that now he took himself to be absolved from all other promises, having made good his word to her, but I never expressed one syllable to that purpose and do not intend to release his lordship so easily.'[2] (The fair lady is, of course, Lady Sunderland.)

Would life never go smoothly? Such a question Evelyn must have asked, in November, when, added to his paternal and financial troubles, were the first proofs of *Numismata* to be corrected—with his books divided between Wotton and Sayes Court. How thankful he was that Richard Bentley, the famous classical scholar and the King's Librarian at St. James's, would 'reform' them. Yet in this Evelyn had misgivings; after the two first sheets had been 'reformed', he felt it only safe and prudent

[1] Letter, J. Evelyn to G. Evelyn, 2 Nov. 1694.
[2] Letter, J. Evelyn, jun., to J. Evelyn, 15 Nov. 1694.

to leave the rest to be revised and wholly disposed of by Bentley.[1] Two months later this great, obliging scholar reported that he had made scores of corrections of matter, of printing, and in the 'mending of points'. It turned out—and as we shall see—that Evelyn expected too much of Bentley.

In December, Susan's copy of Dixon's portrait of Margaret was presented by Evelyn to Godolphin. Is not his appreciation of it somewhat cool and ambiguous?—'I am to thank you for a great present you have made me, not so much in the value of the picture itself, as coming from you, and to me; I have received so many marks of your kindness and favourable opinion, that I had no need at all of this new one to lay an obligation upon me of being, sir, yours . . .'[2] Perhaps he preferred Mary Beale's portrait of Margaret as a potential wife.

Christmas drew near, and Evelyn and his wife prepared to return to Wotton, thankful for things accomplished. Susan had completely recovered her health, Evelyn had been elected to the Council of the Royal Society—an election flattering to himself rather than beneficial to the Society in view of his country residence—and arrangements for the laying down of the Wotton portions—whenever called for—satisfactorily negotiated. To further the association of grandfather and grandson it was decided that young Jack—now nearly thirteen years old—should accompany the old people to Wotton—which necessitated his leaving Eton a week earlier than usual. But Evelyn impresses upon Mrs. Boscawen that any lack of scholarship will be made good: 'Jack (who is an humble servant to his schoolfellow Francis Godolphin) has lost an entire week from his book by our sending for him that he might accompany us to Surrey: but he tells us he will endeavour to recover his loss with double diligence.'[3] Evelyn, thinking of 'the match', thus plants the good qualities of his grandson in the mind of Mrs. Boscawen, Godolphin's sister, who had a daughter Anne, nine years old. As things turned out, opportunity was found for the boy to sit for his portrait to be painted by Klosterman, the journey to Wotton being delayed three weeks until Mrs. Evelyn had

[1] Letter, J. Evelyn to R. Bentley, 22 Nov. 1694; Christ Church MS. 2, Vol. I, fol. 8.
[2] Letter, S. Godolphin to J. Evelyn, 13 Dec. 1694.
[3] Letter, J. Evelyn to Mrs. Boscawen, 9 Dec. 1694.

sufficiently recovered from a cold. They set out at last on 29 December, when the days were short and travelling bad: George suggested that Draper's coach could take them to Sutton, where his coach would meet them and continue the journey to Wotton—thus avoiding overnight stabling. Evelyn was awaiting a new coach—now being built. His last horse with 'the unsightly hoof' used the previous winter between Deptford and London was now 'abandoned to poor pasture at Wotton —otherwise', he said, 'there is not a more sightly, better mettled and good-natured poor creature'. (It will be remembered that in *Rambling Round Evelyn* Virginia Woolf was sure that the hens at Sayes Court laid the very best eggs in England.)

As we have seen, the idea of a hospital for seamen had long been dear to Evelyn's heart, and first suggested by him after the second Dutch War, and so well endorsed to receive the plaudits of Pepys, Albemarle, and Arlington. During the last few years the scheme had been subjected to two or three resurrections—but with no lasting sign of life. In October 1694 it was decided to convert existing buildings at Greenwich into a hospital. Evelyn and Sir Stephen Fox discussed the financial implications with Pepys who seems to have taken—on the basis of Wren's plans—a larger view of the project. When Pepys declared to Evelyn 'that no fond or method of settlement other than Parliamentary will (I doubt) be found of sufficiency for this undertaking',[1] Evelyn at once submitted this new cooperative conception to Godolphin. In the new year the idea— and his patronage—was successful; he was appointed by Godolphin Treasurer of Greenwich Hospital at a salary of £300 per annum.

Whether Evelyn was pleased it is difficult to say. Certainly it was not a very great salary; certainly not large enough for the news of it to be communicated by young Glanville—now a clerk to the Treasury—whom Evelyn did not particularly esteem. He made Evelyn's world seem very small. But any other person would have received only £200—so Godolphin instructed Glanville to say.[2] Such a salary seemed strangely out of proportion to Godolphin's power at the Treasury, and a

[1] Letter, Pepys to J. Evelyn, 7 Nov. 1694: Christ Church MS. 3, Vol. II, fol. 122.

[2] Letter, W. Glanville, jun., to J. Evelyn, 12 Feb. 1695.

poor inducement for one in his seventy-fifth year to break away from a dearly loved country seat. Furthermore, for nearly two years—as it turned out—the builders' demands left nothing for his salary. Young John considered the post neither equal to his father's merit nor answerable to his occasions; though he thought it might allow him to continue to live at Sayes Court.

By midsummer the prospects of young John's commission were desperate, despite the Treasury's approbation of the increased Irish revenue. For the year 1694 management charges were £30,000, leaving £190,000 for the Treasury. In the present year, however, he says 'the country becomes every day so much poorer for want of trade to export her own growth'. Owing to the value of guineas being raised in England, little ready money other than copper halfpence was available: 'already payments are made and received of them to £100 and more in a sum'.[1] Although congratulatory letters to Lord Capel from Evelyn and Wyche were suggested by young John, by midsummer he writes to say that the Commission is broken, and that all the probable successors are of Irish breeding and interest, 'which is called putting the Geese into the Foxes' keeping . . . to trust the natives with the Revenue will hardly improve it, nor was ever practised before under a Protestant government'. There is still some small hope in Godolphin: 'Might not the Pope of our other world, . . . and now Principal Statesman at the helm, contribute to keeping me above water?'[2] he asks his father. But alas, for the present, the only pleasures for young John and his wife were delighting in the grace of their daughter, now receiving 'a little finishing stroke of the Kitt and coupé' for her dancing, and contemplating Klosterman's newly-arrived portrait of their son: 'he has a thoughtful look and as if he were, and would be, master of a well furnished head'. Mrs. Evelyn remarked that all who see it believe the artist 'never painted any better'.[3]

Doubtless the portrait would also please grandfather who was just now thinking of the young man and of his going up to the University of Oxford. He was also thinking that if his grandson's school-fellow Francis Godolphin were at Oxford at the

---

[1] Letter, J. Evelyn, jun., to J. Evelyn, 26 Feb. 1695.
[2] Letter, J. Evelyn, jun., to J. Evelyn, 18 June 1695.
[3] Letter, Mrs. Evelyn to J. Evelyn, 26 May 1695.

same time their future friendship would be assured. Godolphin
had already decided to send Francis to Oxford. Then Evelyn
received the news that Godolphin had changed his mind. And
how humiliating it was for him to be told so coldly and
officiously by young Glanville: 'My lord Godolphin thanks you
for your kind concern and care of his son but says he has
changed his resolution and intends now to place him at Cambridge.'[1] Was there a limit to what even a patron could tolerate
in another's care and concern for his own son? Perhaps Godolphin remembered that when considering sending Francis to
Eton in 1690, Evelyn—bearing in mind the slight juniority
of his grandson—had suggested to him that the eleven-year-
old boy was rather young to be admitted. Evelyn's disappointment might have been more supportable had it been written
in Godolphin's own hand, and if young Glanville's appointment
to the Treasury had come from some interest other than his
own.

Young John was in a worse position; to find himself writing
to young Glanville (whom he never liked) in these terms: 'You
that are near the helm, are able to give us who are only towed
by your great vessel, now and then an hint how things go in
the steerage, so far that we might have a little warning before
cutting off and being turned adrift.' His 'duty' to Godolphin
and Sir Stephen Fox could only be conveyed when Glanville
thought it *à propos*.[2]

Domestic trouble in July intensified the patronal depression;
Susan's child dying of convulsions. After the event young John
proffered the Dublin 'godwomen's' treatment for such cases: 'to
cut the gums more than once if they should close together again
... it hath saved many children's lives'.[3] In July Evelyn returned
to Wotton, tired of wasting time attending meetings of the
Greenwich Commissioners when it was impossible to obtain a
quorum. In September he was slightly indisposed. He had now
arrived at an age when he felt that the third, or perhaps the
second, glass of wine must be refused; he was abstaining from
breakfast and supper—an abstention which Mrs. Evelyn divined
as the cause of his trouble (she was staying in London for the

[1] Letter, W. Glanville, jun., to J. Evelyn, 18 May 1695.
[2] Letter, J. Evelyn, jun., to W. Glanville, jun., 9 July 1695.
[3] Letter, J. Evelyn, jun., to J. Evelyn, 6 Aug. 1695.

birth of Susan's second child). She suggested 'some liquid suppings of gruel or milk, tea, or syrup of violets with water, and some drops of sulphur might help in the morning . . . as long before dinner as you can'. She had found that method a great help on the same account.

On 30 September she sent him good news of the new baby which did nothing but suck and sleep; there were 'no thoughts of a milch nurse . . . I wish you were here to rejoice in a cup of hippocras', and suggested that George's coach could connect with the Leatherhead coach—which would convey him to London Bridge—and a Hackney could bring him to Surrey Street (just east of Somerset House) where the Drapers were staying: 'it is pretty chargeable to keep four horses in town above a night', she said.[1] Evelyn's new coach—a country chariot with his crest behind and before and on both doors—was not yet ready for the road.

We have seen that young John had no intention of 'releasing' Godolphin. In September, fearful of being unemployed, he puts himself in his patron's hands; saying that he is perfectly resigned to his consummate prudence and sagacity, and whatever breaches others may apprehend in his Commission, he is by experience so assured of his Lordship's firm adherence to those he honours with his friendship that he is in no manner of pain for his fortune 'under so inviolable a protection'. Not content with this, in the following month he asks Evelyn 'to visit both my patrons, in the park, and the square, and so endeavour with them I may not suffer in case of a change'. His hopes of remaining in Ireland were blighted by rising taxes. Formerly, after payment of rent and school fees, he had some £600 a year remaining. Now—in October—he says 'our salaries here are taxed towards the discharge of arrears due on the Civil and Military List, my quota for being an esquire, my coach, and three shillings per pound will come to £129'.[2] Such tidings increased the weight on Evelyn's mind—and no respite could yet be effected by drawing on the salary of his new post.

Financial worries, however, did nothing to impair his epistolary output. On 18 October, Mrs. Evelyn answered a letter of the widowed Lady Tuke's in which she raised some

---

[1] Letter, Mrs. Evelyn to J. Evelyn, 30 Sept. 1695.
[2] Letter, J. Evelyn, jun., to J. Evelyn, 10 Oct. 1695.

question of the Roman Catholic religion. Mrs. Evelyn's copy of her reply is endorsed by Evelyn: 'After your compliments and the secular concerns of your letter in answer to her Ladyship, you may proceed as follows.' Then follows in Evelyn's hand no less than three thousand words on a comparison between the Church of England and the Church of Rome.[1] What a task of transcription for her!

Mrs. Evelyn, now back at Wotton, found it necessary in early November to cheer her husband who had returned to Surrey Street ostensibly for meetings of the Greenwich Commission. His financial troubles still possessed him; she tried to assure him that he had done all that was required of him, and that he should not give so much way to afflictions, but leave the rest to providence. Then, having tried to soothe him, undoes her good work by adding, 'I do believe the Glanvilles take as many advantages of my brother's necessities as they can with decency, which will fall on you and your son at last.' Young Glanville acted as George's accountant. Furthermore, he had increased the interest on money that Evelyn owed him from £5 to £6 per cent, 'and thinks he favours me in it', he remarked to his wife: 'How little real kindness there is among the nearest relations,' he observed.

He went on to give his wife all the news of the town: 'Of the knights of the Shire and drunken elections we every day hear, and expect a Parliament accordingly. I hear nothing of my cousin George Evelyn's being chosen but the contrary; so as there is not like to be an Evelyn in the House this session.' He is thinking of delegating his treasurership of Greenwich Hospital to Draper, and with this in view will introduce him to Godolphin. 'Sir William Halford's lewd lady has lately been surprised in bed with a gallant . . . found in the embraces of her paramour' . . . the cabinet that his wife and Mrs. Draper recommended has been 'sold to Mrs. Skinner (Mr. Pepys' inclination)'. Mary Skinner, concerned in Pepys's domestic arrangements at York Buildings, appears, by Evelyn's euphemistic 'inclination', to have been on somewhat more intimate terms with Pepys than those of a housekeeper; moreover, he was exceedingly generous to her in his will.[2] The meetings of the Greenwich Commissioners are 'put off from week to week . . .

[1] Letter, J. Evelyn to Lady Tuke, 18 Oct. 1695.   [2] *R.E.S.*, VII, 257.

money melts away' and Evelyn is ashamed of being so long a guest with Draper. Godolphin[1] has 'very readily given leave' that Susan shall have Morelli's picture of the Boys to copy— a picture which he had recently bought at auction for £80. Susan's baby 'is, I think the loveliest infant I ever saw'. He himself is in reasonable health 'but still digest my meat very ill'. He now assures her that he is endeavouring to take her good counsel 'as far as I am able amidst so many perplexities in this my great age', and then adds, endearingly, 'one who entirely loves you'. There is news, too, of 'the match'; he had had a letter from young Jack, who says there is but twenty-six above him in the fourth form, and that the boy had been at Godolphin's house where he saw Francis, Mrs. Boscawen, and her daughter Anne.[2]

The year closes with a letter from young John. There is little change for the better. As usual he attacks the Glanvilles: 'I am sure they yet never did kindness without prospect, from him [young Glanville] I never expect any. I am very sorry they have such hold upon the estate, which I believe is like to increase as more money is wanted for portions, for they must needs get and lay by considerably every year . . . Without the seasonable falling in of one of the jointures the mortgages are in a fair way of swallowing that seat, and part of the estate about it . . . I am neither greater nor richer than I was five months ago, and yet my mind forebodes nothing but good to come . . . I am healthier . . .' He enjoys a tranquillity of mind that till of late he has wholly been a stranger to. He deplores to see the name of Evelyn 'worked out of the list of Surrey senators', and should be glad either there or in Kent if he could hit on an opportunity to get into a borough . . . 'it makes a man weigh much more'.[3]

[1] Murillo, Bartolomé Esteban.
[2] Letter, J. Evelyn to Mrs. Evelyn, 11 Nov. 1695.
[3] Letter, J. Evelyn, jun., to J. Evelyn, 30 Dec. 1695.

CHAPTER XII

Still No Respite

∽∽∽∽∽∽∽∽∽∽∽∽∽∽∽∽∽∽∽∽∽∽∽∽∽∽∽∽∽

YOUNG John, to his chagrin, could never ignore or avoid young Glanville; a Treasury communication from him has to be acknowledged even though he is 'crazy in body' and 'uneasy in mind'. He has been granted leave to come to England for his health: he wants to know whether he is one of the Commissioners to be dropped; if so, he would bring his family and save a journey. If this were not humiliation enough, he has just received young Glanville's translation of *The Life of J. B. Colbert*, 1695, dedicated to Godolphin, if you please. To the uncertainty of receiving his salary in London was added the shortage of silver arising out of the recent re-coinage—difficulties as great though dissimilar to those he had experienced in Ireland: 'I shall be glad', he writes, 'when I come over to find coin of any denomination, allay, or weight to pay doctor's fees'; in Ireland 'by the assistance of a small pair of scales, money of all sizes, shapes, and nations passes current'.[1] He was at least prepared for the coinage troubles; Susan had told him that 'we have no silver at all, old or new, and gold is so unsettled that nobody cares to part with or receive it for it falls every day'.

But young John would return to a London that bore its troubles lightly: 'One would think', continues Susan, 'we had all the plenty and prosperity in the world, for never was more new plays, nor fuller houses than now'; the two playhouses, the Theatre Royal in Drury Lane, and the Queen's Theatre in

[1] Letter, J. Evelyn, jun., to W. Glanville, jun., 27 March 1696.

Dorset Garden, 'endeavour to ruin each other'. Young John (who was now forty-one, and apparently out of touch with London fashion) had bought a beaver—a purchase on which Susan comments: 'I am sorry to hear you are grown a Beaver, for it proves a scandalous thing here to be one, and we have a famous new play to ridicule them and they say he apes my Lord Beaver, who is one of our top ones.'[1]

Early in May young John left Ireland against Godolphin's advice. In the middle of April Evelyn had suggested to his patron that an equivalent post for his son might be found in London, but there was nothing available. Dispirited with ill-health and uncertainty, young John probably made the decision to return in the hope of obtaining better medical treatment in London. In addition to his sinus symptoms, he was now suffering from sores in his throat and on his neck and jaws.

While his son was on his way south from Chester, Evelyn made merry at a dinner party given by Archbishop Tenison and his wife at Lambeth. Included in the company were a number of Ladies, who arrived, as did Evelyn, by water from Whitehall; on landing they all went 'marching to the Bishop's palace', he tells his wife the next day; Tenison 'stood ready in the court and conducted us to his wife's apartments . . . very handsomely furnished . . . we dined most sumptuously . . . drunk your health, and with the best dexterity I could, hardly acquitted myself from an assignation they would gladly have made me hearken to of coming all to Sayes Court whilst they were in their cups: but this passed off, and so we parted about 7 oclock';[2] a seven-hour session of food, drink, and conversation, for a man of seventy-five.

It is a great pity that, on principle, none of his merry dinings are described in the *Diary*. We have missed so much, too, considering that he spent half his life dining out. Having protested at such protracted afternoons—when the cloth is removed —in *A Character of England*, perhaps he felt enforced to remain silent. On this occasion he merely records where he dined, adding 'and stayed late, yet I returned to Deptford that night'.

In the same letter, he goes on to tell his wife that he has

[1] Letter, S. Draper to J. Evelyn, jun., 25 Feb. 1696.
[2] Letter, J. Evelyn to Mrs. Evelyn, 7 May 1696.

been slightly indisposed again, 'though drinking whey and
spirit of violets, chocolate and other things' that were wont to
cure him; 'for the rest, I am pretty well, only more heavy and
clouded than usually'. Perhaps seven hours was too much for
him after all. But it was doubtless a welcome diversion, for
there was little to cheer him throughout the summer, beyond
the prospect of letting Sayes Court to Captain Benbow which
would add more than a welcome £100 a year to Evelyn's
income. In June, Mrs. Evelyn came to interview Benbow's wife
for this purpose—though the family's financial depression prevented her coming with a good grace: 'If I receive Mrs. Benbow
whilst I am here,' she writes to Evelyn, 'it will oblige me to
treat her, which will be a charge upon all accounts: I wish it
were well over.' Terms were agreed upon, and the Benbows,
in due time, took up their residence.

'We have many things before us not very pleasing,' Mrs.
Evelyn goes on; 'my son gives me many melancholy hours: I
pray God he may find a right cure and get out of the dangerous
way he is now in. I do not question your concern; you are
generally apprehensive of the worst. When all is done, we must
submit and acquiesce in what Almighty God determines
for us.'

Back at Wotton with George and Lady Wyche, Mrs. Evelyn
tells her husband something of the antagonistic atmosphere:
'I have been in a continual catechism and hope I shall hold
out till their curiosity is over. My brother is very brisk, walks
up the Mount, looks well, and shows the strength of the [Wyche]
jointure by his calling for things more freely than he had done
of late. I gave him your letter [probably on Evelyn's inability
to pay any more interest]: what his thoughts are he keeps to
himself, but in appearance he is kind and drinks your health
. . . the good entertainment is what I value infinitely.' Mrs.
Evelyn must have made a cake during her Sayes Court visit,
which Lady Wyche now declared to be 'the best she ever eat'.
(It was probably one containing about sixteen Sayes Court
eggs and plenty of butter.) There was more furniture—now
arriving from Sayes Court—than could be disposed of usefully;
her Japan cabinets 'are much admired'; Evelyn's weather glass
'has been of great use to their haymaking . . . cousin Glanville
is always begging one good thing or other'.

We learn, too, from this letter that young John had borrowed money from two friends of George's circle; it is no surprise to learn that the interest was not paid regularly. But the plight of the lenders must, at times, have been pitiable, 'having nothing else to live on'.[1] No wonder Mrs. Evelyn said that her son gave her 'many melancholy hours'.

He was prevented from making an appearance at Wotton this summer by undergoing a new treatment at the hands of the celebrated Dr. John Radcliffe and a surgeon. He tells his uncle 'I am falling into great straits', but there is no 'unwillingness to serve you, or ingratitude'. In July—an unusually cold month this year—the weather worsened his health and even hindered him from waiting on Godolphin. He reiterated his need of employment in London equivalent to his Irish post; if nothing is forthcoming—for he fears many competitors—he will return to Ireland. In his enforced confinement to London this summer he made up his arrears of reading—about ninety works of French and English history, literature, novels, plays, and classical authors. In his list[2] of the books he adds a few critical remarks; on *Othello* he says 'many fine sallies of natural fancy are improved by learning or art; wants unity of time and place'. On Etherege's *The Comical Revenge* he says 'very good, all but the love and honour part in rhyme, which would make a dog vomit'.

Evelyn—still with the Drapers at Surrey Street—expressed regret for his absence, to his brother, 'my best of friends', and describes Mrs. Evelyn—on whom he seems more dependent than ever—as 'absolutely the best and most sincere, innocent, well-tempered discreet affectionate and faithful wife in the world'. He then gives his brother the London news, that the shortage of money is still acute: 'There is not a penny stirring here; I had a Bill from my Lord Godolphin for £200 payable by the National Bank and they offer me £5: the goldsmiths part not with a groat, and tenants are more behindhand than ever, so as really the lawyers, physicians, Hackney-coach and watermen only are paid in ready money, the rest live on credit, nor is the scarcity to be imagined, unless you were here to see it: and now whilst the Land-Bankers offer yet to supply the

[1] Letter, Mrs. Evelyn to J. Evelyn, 11 July 1696.
[2] In Gassarus' *Epitome hist. & chron. mundi*, Lugd. n.d. (Press-mark f. 134).

public exigence upon such reasonable advantage as the Lords of the Treasury think very moderate, and willing to close with them, they have no security to give them, being so bound-up by parliament not to touch any of the pre-engaged Funds, or dispose of what is weekly coined and brought into the Chequer; one half of it being immediately swept away for loans upon tallies by the goldsmiths, who hoard it up (though it be the product and principal of monies concredited to them from others, and lent the King upon unreasonable interest) and the other half sent over into Flanders to maintain the Armies. Between these two unsatiable gulfs what can be expected by particulars, but the utter exhaustion of the very vitals of the nation in a short time, unless a sudden peace put a stop to this monstrous expense, and a wiser session of Parliament order matters with more prudence for the future.'[1]

Later he writes: 'Whatever you are made believe in the country, it looks like another plague in this town; people seem afraid of meeting one another for fear of being asked money . . . I sold this day a small Bank Bill at £11 loss the hundred to pay poor men'[2] working on Greenwich Hospital.

Thus Evelyn killed two birds with one stone: he flattered George—who was generally behindhand with the news—with this excellent digest of the monetary situation, and indirectly mitigated his own financial failings.

In gardening matters at Wotton there seems to have been a curious lack of co-operation between George's gardeners or servants and Evelyn's man Tom who was apparently practising the more accomplished gardening technique of Sayes Court. Mrs. Evelyn reported to Evelyn that 'Tom has mowed the grass walks and employed a weeder to clear the beds which were covered with weeds. He wants a new spade, and with some difficulty obtained a scythe; he wants a roller which I will try to get off my brother: whether the difficulty proceeds from the want of good will of the servants or that they have no tools to spare, but they part with none is certain.' Such a report must have disheartened Evelyn who wished so earnestly to improve the neglected garden. Nor would he find any pleasure in the news that young Glanville 'seems to visit for his health by

---

[1] Letter, J. Evelyn to G. Evelyn, 13 July 1696.
[2] Letter, J. Evelyn to G. Evelyn, 31 July 1696.

riding and taking the air, but what is besides does not appear'.[1] Obviously he was a 'snooper'.

But there was a pleasant side to Mrs. Evelyn's stay at Wotton; in acting as governess for her grand-daughter Betty and George's grand-daughter—in teaching them to draw—she was rather like a hen with her chicks: 'I have all my scholars about me,' she writes; and she touches our hearts with 'Betty is a very sweet natured good child as I ever knew . . . wishes daily for her Papa and maman to be truly happy.'[2] Poor child, she knew that her father, finding no relief from Dr. Radcliffe's treatment, had now made arrangements to go to Bath.

Three weeks later Evelyn appealed to Godolphin on his son's behalf. We may pardon Evelyn for telling him that his son 'wants strength rather than health at present, which he finds greatly improved since his being in England', as his appeal was for some employment in London. But surely Godolphin—if there were any truth in the reports of his romantic attachments —had not only tired of being approached for 'her sake, for whom alone you have been and still continue so kind to me', but was quite unable to agree when Evelyn said: 'I always come with confidence but not with boldness.'[3]

In August young John gave young Glanville all the news of Bath, which place he did not like half so well as Tunbridge. The company and the quality included the Duke of Devonshire, Lord Sussex, the Earl of Kingston, Lord Clifford 'the ladies' favourite', and Lord Winchelsea. 'Every other night a Ball at the Town Hall; Lady Wharton plays violently at ninepins, Mrs. Long and my Lady Earnly (Brigadier Earl's daughter) the beauties of the season; Lord Clifford and Mrs. Pierrepont the best dancers. There is Hazard every day after dinner at my Lord Kingston's, but the cash begins to run low, and chalk much used to keep reckoning: Colonel Henry Luttrell and Colonel Mordaunt are constant attendants and I believe, by degrees sink most of the ready.' The waters—as we should expect —had no good effect on his sinus; 'they are pleasant to take, just like warm milk from the cow, and when they pass, will give a keen appetite'. He goes on to say: 'this is a confounded

---

[1] Letter, Mrs. Evelyn to J. Evelyn, 16 July 1696.
[2] Letter, Mrs. Evelyn to J. Evelyn, 24 July 1696.
[3] Letter, J. Evelyn to S. Godolphin, 12 Aug. 1696.

Jacobite town, and one can hear of nothing but that we are making an disadvantageous peace, and that our Hero is going to marry a lean, crooked, red-haired squinting lady'.[1] During a stay of five weeks he wrote but once to Evelyn, excusing himself thus: 'Writing as well as reading to my great sorrow is inconsistent with the rule of water drinking.'[2] We can only hope that the sick man found some fun in going the social round. In due course he returned; on 23 October he saw Godolphin, who sensing his own anxious days to come, received him with less courtesy than usual—'as graciously as I think he is capable', said young John to his father.

On 31 October Godolphin resigned. Evelyn back at Wotton and out of touch with everything except the shortage of money for Greenwich Hospital—he had still received no salary—allowed a month to pass before realising the seriousness of Godolphin's absence. Late in November he wrote to William Draper: 'What becomes of my Lord Godolphin? I would be glad you enquire what the meaning of this recess of his is, and whether he be out of the Council and comes to Parliament, because they are particulars I cannot so easily ask of his relations, and I forbear writing to him till I know.'[3]

His withdrawal arose from his alleged connection with the Jacobite plot of the previous February to kill King William at Turnham Green. The main plotter Sir John Fenwick in a subsequent confession implicated Marlborough, Russell, Shrewsbury and Godolphin, charging them with acting in concert with Saint-Germains. Historians have dealt with their respective reactions to this accusation; how Fenwick came before the Lords, and regarding Godolphin's defence, generally quote Wharton's letter[4] to Shrewsbury in which Godolphin admitted that 'he was one of those that had, to the last, continued in King James's service, and he did not know, but from that, King James and his friends might imagine him to continue in that interest', but 'there was nothing in the world so false' as that he had entered into any negotiation, 'as was expressed in the paper'. Macaulay (and others) say that his resignation was

---

[1] Letter, J. Evelyn, jun., to W. Glanville, jun., 29 Aug. 1696.
[2] Letter, J. Evelyn, jun., to J. Evelyn, 12 Sept. 1696.
[3] Letter, J. Evelyn to W. Draper, 29 Nov. 1696.
[4] Shrewsbury Correspondence, p. 428.

brought about by the machinations of Sunderland—although there is no real evidence of it. Dr. Feiling in his *History of the Tory Party* says that by supreme management, and this the Whigs rather improbably attributed to Sunderland, Godolphin was persuaded to offer his resignation.

To this uncertain testimony we can now add Draper's reply to Evelyn: 'As to the reasons which made my Lord Godolphin quit the Treasury, 'tis said that when the Duke of Devon by the King's command had prevailed on Sir John Fenwick to send the King an account . . . of what he could say relating to the Plot, among others my Lord was named as a person who might be prevailed on to befriend King James in his restitution in case he landed. My Lord, apprehensive of the ill consequences that might happen from such a paper, which no doubt he foresaw would be laid before the Parliament, and displeased that, what David Floyd, one of King James's bedchamber had sometimes since in consult with Sir John Fenwick, told him as his opinion only, without the least pretence of any such hope given him by my Lord, should be suffered to appear as an information and be so far countenanced as to become public and be left to the censure and interpretation of the world, he desired Sir William Trumball to ask leave of the King to quit the Treasury, which the King but unwillingly, assented to; my Lord immediately left the Town, and went to my Lord Marlborough's, and from there to Windsor, not intending to return to London for some time, but the Lords having summoned all their members to attend Sir John Fenwick's trial upon failure to be sent for in custody, my Lord is come to town, and attends the House.'[1]

Godolphin voted against the execution of Fenwick—a typical manœuvre manifesting not compassion but insouciance, thus easing the weight of the charges against himself. He did not retire immediately—as is generally believed—though he handed over to Sir Stephen Fox; and not until the end of April did Montagu succeed as First Lord of the Treasury.

Therefore in the new year Godolphin was still accessible, and in fact visited by young John (now living in Berkeley Street 'in the way to Hide Park for the goodness of the air'). Young John also saw Lord Sidney who advised him to return to

[1] Letter, W. Draper to J. Evelyn, 4 Dec. 1696.

Ireland by Easter at the latest—which he promised to do if the spring dealt favourably with him. To add to his present embarrassments, he was offered £800 by 'a gentleman of quality' to surrender his commission, an offer which he indignantly refused. He was conscious that his long indisposition and stay in London gave people to think that he would not return, but he stoutly asserts, 'I could not have the face to apply for other employment if I had trafficed for this.'

With Godolphin in temporary shadow, Sunderland came into the sunlight; 'though he has no outward marks of favour . . . is in full power with the King', said young John, who now entertained thoughts of his help; Lady Sunderland must therefore be approached. Yet there were difficulties in extracting favours from her Ladyship. 'How to come at him [Sunderland] I know not, for the private merit which gives him so great an interest, is what I believe my Lady hardly owns to any but those from whom she may propose some advantage by the bargain, if she does them service; and that is a tender point to be touched.' He adds an early illustration of Sunderland's regained influence: by his intercession on the death of Sir Gabriel Sylvius, our Tory 'ranting Nanny' obtained the continuance of her husband's pension 'which is something extraordinary for the King to grant, considering she alienated him from his service and is openly addicted to the contrary party'.[1]

Early in April young John informed his father that he cannot defer his return to Ireland much longer than Whitsuntide—not that his health had improved; in fact, he says, 'the course I am in at present is asses' milk, frequent bathing and fuming my head with gums burnt on a hot iron'.

It was still possible to see Godolphin, who told him there was little prospect of any equivalent employment on this side and that he would do well to return. Young John reminded him of 'a promise that upon the reduction of Ireland and the recovery of the Revenue, our salaries be made up to £1000 per annum—as they were before the war'. Godolphin then asked him to 'take what he says for oracular truth; it would be delayed till Lord Galway's departure at which time all affairs would be despatched together'.[2] Therefore six months after his

---

[1] Letter, J. Evelyn, jun., to J. Evelyn, 23 Jan. 1697.
[2] Letter, J. Evelyn, jun., to J. Evelyn, 2 April 1697.

'resignation' Godolphin had not parted from the Treasury stage—or at least from the scenes. We are reminded of Burnet's words: 'He had a clear apprehension and despatched business with great method and with so much temper that he had no personal enemies.' Perhaps the friendliness and talents of this centre Tory quickly lived down any Jacobite charge; certainly he must have handed over the details of his office in a leisurely manner to Fox and Montagu.

By the 21 April, Sunderland was made Lord Chamberlain and Lord Justice. Nine days later Godolphin left the Treasury. Young John felt the flurry of these changes; he begged his father to write to Lord Galway, for 'there is nobody better with the King . . . or more likely to protect me . . . Courts are full of falsehood and secret misrepresentations which destroy a man without warning'. He felt, too, the pang of leaving young Jack behind: 'it is no small addition to the rest of my misfortunes that even for his sake, I lie under a necessity of parting not only from him, but from all my friends and relations for many years. I could otherwise be content with very small matters in this world for the little time I am like to stay in it, being rather fit for an hospital, than any employment that requires health and vigour.'[1]

Evelyn wrote to Galway congratulating him—in the usual manner—on his appointment as a Lord Justice of Ireland, which was due not only to his merits but 'to H.M.'s great discernment', and recommending his son 'who is shortly returning to his employment . . . with addition of alacrity since he is to be under your excellency's protection'.[2] It would have been of no use to have written more truthfully.

After Galway, young John's thoughts turned to the resurrected Sunderland to save him, for his name was now in the list of the proscribed commissioners. He says 'the scene shifts so fast here, that nobody scarce knows how to turn himself . . . Lord Sunderland restored to a public station must be congratulated and requested to serve his friends . . . that he has great power, everybody was satisfied before, and it is now manifest'. Evelyn is begged to write to him or my Lady to save his son's commission. To expedite the approach young John sent his

---

[1] Letter, J. Evelyn, jun., to J. Evelyn, 15 April 1697.
[2] Letter, J. Evelyn to Lord Galway, 19 April 1697 (Letter Book, p. 224).

servant to Wotton to bring his father's letter by eight the following morning. Even that hour might be too late; this very morning he could not contact Galway, 'being out before seven o'clock'.[1] One had to be up early to catch a patron.

Two days later, Lady Sunderland received him at eleven o'clock in her dressing room, after 'the crowd' had dispersed; she made him a great compliment saying that his name was enough to secure him; being sceptical, he said that a word from her Lord would put him out of danger, and this she promised if there be occasion. It would be a melancholy business, he laments to his father, 'to go five or six hundred miles only to démeuble', yet his dismission in Ireland 'will not be near so disadvantageous as here in the face of the world'. Evelyn must have made some reference to his own ill-luck with Godolphin, for young John goes on: 'I do not believe my Lord Godolphin shrinks from you, but you know he is lazy and now he is withdrawn is contented to be a spectator without medling with any business.'[2]

Young John found himself chasing the great ones in a circle. The following day Lady Sunderland called on him at Berkeley Street to tell him the Commission was bad and infirm and advised him to bid Evelyn write to Lord Galway. The latter, however, had gone with the King to see him embark at Margate; they must wait for his return. This disappointment was philosophically expressed: 'These ten days last passed have been a perpetual hurry and motion of the great men, who I think are but slaves in an higher sphere.' Yet still hopeful, he will learn when Galway sails for Ireland, 'if possible to take advantage of the same yachts and convoys'.[3]

A few days later Lady Sunderland again assured him of her assistance and advised him to sail with Galway. She also wrote to Evelyn. But by this time young John had had enough: 'I told her I would endeavour it, but I am sure I cannot do it; neither my health (tho' I look a little better in the face this warm weather) nor other circumstances can possibly admit of it so soon. I have too much reason to think the country will not agree with me in winter . . . it is some comfort not to be

[1] Letter, J. Evelyn, jun., to J. Evelyn, 21 April 1697.
[2] Letter, J. Evelyn, jun., to J. Evelyn, 23 April 1697.
[3] Letter, J. Evelyn, jun., to J. Evelyn, 26 April 1697.

dismissed on this side because I shall have wherewith to bear my expence thither and back again . . . my Lord Godolphin is gone to Newmarket, my Lady Sunderland's letter[1] [to Evelyn] is much in the strain of some I have seen of Oliver Cromwell's, who could chant and pray and yet was no Saint, though she may be one when she can bring herself to be brave.'[2] The sick and sad commissioner now realised that the second string was no substitute for the scratch man—Godolphin. If the latter had remained in office the desired equivalent position on this side would doubtless have been obtained.

[1] This has not survived.
[2] Letter, J. Evelyn, jun., to J. Evelyn, 1 May 1697.

CHAPTER XIII

The Wotton Settlement

~~~~~~

Evelyn had been somewhat slow in congratulating Lady Sunderland on her husband's new appointments; not until the first week of May did he write thus: 'The most welcome news of my Lord's appearing at Court again with a character so bright; as it receives lustre and estimation from his Lordship's merits (to which all that is great, is natural and but due) so it shows His Majesty's great discernment of persons the most worthy of his highest favours, and obliges me to come among the first with congratulations, though with this manner of confidence, that your Ladyship will so far condescend as to be my proxy, and answer for one who has ever been sincerely concerned in all those many providences through which Almighty God has exercised your virtue . . .'[1] Perhaps Evelyn's tardiness—and discretion—did him credit; perhaps, recalling Sunderland's part in the events of 1688 (not to mention his own role of adviser) he could not with indecent haste acclaim his alternative patron; Burnet would not be alone in thinking that Sunderland, by his 'dexterity of insinuating himself so entirely into the greatest degree of confidence with three succeeding princes who set up on very different interests . . . came . . . to lose his reputation so much that even those who esteemed his parts depended little on his promises'.[2]

However, by this time, Evelyn's son seemed to be beyond the

[1] Letter Book, p. 226 (Evelyn MS. 39).
[2] *Eng. Hist. Docs.*, vol. viii, 923.

cordial of favour. He was now ill, and restless. His uncle George invited him to Wotton in May; yet he stayed only a few days, being still anxious to continue his importunity of the great men in Whitehall. George wanted him to stay longer to breathe the country air, but he could not prevail with him. His letters to his parents ceased after 1 May. In August Mrs. Evelyn paid him a visit in Berkeley Street—probably to persuade him to return to Wotton; Evelyn records in the *Diary* that on 9 September his son arrived there. But no *Diary* entry or letter of this period tells us anything of his state of mind. We surmise that all hope of new employment or of better health was now abandoned.

Evelyn's anniversary letter on Margaret's death in September gave him the usual opportunity to remind Godolphin of his obligations, whose acknowledgment was decidedly cool: 'I am much obliged to you for your kind letter, and I assure you the constant continuance of them is no small satisfaction to me. I wish it had been in my power to do you as much service as my inclination would always carry me to, but since I have not had that good fortune, your kind acceptance of my best endeavours is however extremely obliging to yrs . . .'[1]

Evelyn, not wholly without hope, also continued to keep Lady Sunderland informed; he tells her that his son is recuperating at Wotton till the spring, 'in which interim he wholly depends on God and your ladyship's protection'.[2] Ten days later, Evelyn, undeterred by Godolphin's coolness, begged his mediation and assistance in the matter of naming a substitute to succeed his son in Ireland: no reply is known.

Numismata, announced to appear in November, was published about the 10 January 1698. It had given Evelyn no pleasurable anticipation. Despite Bentley's scholarly correction in the early stages—or, alternatively, because he corrected only the first two sheets (for there is no evidence that he corrected any others)—the book was doomed. Evelyn sent a copy to William Wotton, saying, 'Lying under two such great misfortunes, as were my not having such a generous and able friend to advise with, before I adventured on these subjects and my absence from the Town whilst more than half of it was wrought off, I should blush at the mean present I make you; had I not experience of

[1] Letter, S. Godolphin to J. Evelyn, 22 Sept. 1697.
[2] Letter, J. Evelyn to Lady Sunderland, 14 Oct. 1697.

your candour and indulgence, upon condition of my no more trespassing in this kind, and attempting things beyond my force and in my dotage.'[1] Similar excuses were inserted in a copy presented to Sir Hans Sloane. Apart from errors of fact and printing, the book deals with too many subjects other than medals. It is surprising that Bentley had been optimistic—at least in the early stages; he was of the opinion that Evelyn's last chapter on physiognomy 'will leave the reader with an appetite and a wish that the book was longer'.[2] Horace Walpole ridiculed the diversity of subjects indexed under the letter N: such as nails, narcotics, navigation, Neapolitans character, neck, negros, nightingale and nurses; many more equally irrelevant subjects could be quoted from other letters of the alphabet. There had been too many worrying distractions to the septuagenarian author. To Bohun he confessed: 'You know my mill was always grinding; but now I have lost my teeth, I must give over, when there comes nothing but chaff and bran.'[3]

Meantime, Admiral Benbow, at the King's wish, had sub-let Sayes Court to Peter, Tsar of Muscovy, who was on a visit to England to learn something of the art of shipbuilding. Thomas Gale (newly appointed Dean of York), of the Pepysian circle, tried to persuade Evelyn to meet him, for the Tsar desired to see 'some good honest country English gentleman'. But they never met. It was winter-time, and Evelyn was growing old, 'little curious', and with 'little inclination to stir from our warm fires here at Wotton till the weather be more inviting' as he wrote to Bohun.[4]

Just now a visit to his old house would have caused him deep displeasure. John Strickland, Evelyn's bailiff, described the Sayes Court scene under the royal tenant: 'There is a house full of people, and right nasty. The Tsar lies next your library, and dines in the parlour next your study. He dines at ten o'clock and six at night, is very seldom at home a whole day, very often in the King's yard, or by water, dressed in several dresses. The King is expected there this day, the best parlour

---

[1] Letter, J. Evelyn to W. Wotton, 23 Jan. 1698 (Evelyn MS. 39).

[2] Letter, R. Bentley to J. Evelyn, 15 Feb. 1695: Bentley's *Correspondence*, 1842.

[3] Letter, J. Evelyn to R. Bohun, 16 Feb. 1698.   [4] Ibid.

is pretty clean for him to be entertained in. The King pays for all he has.'[1]

For nearly three months the Tsar and his retinue treated the house and garden right nasty. Among other indoor items, paint, whiting, and tiles had to be renewed; three hundred window panes were broken; the kitchen dressers needed re-planing; Mrs. Evelyn's finest linen sheets were torn and spoiled; curtains were likewise treated; bedroom tables and chairs were broken; a warming-pan was burned beyond repair; valuable carved chairs were broken to pieces; twenty-five pictures suffered damage; several fine drafts and other designs relating to the sea were lost—these were valued by Benbow at £50.

In the garden their leaping and gymnastic tricks made pot-holes in the grass work and bowling-green. One hundred feet of garden border-board was damaged. There were pot-holes in the gravel walks. Branches of the wall-fruit trees were broken. The King's gardener George London, who surveyed for damages, reported these things; he also included: 'spoiling two or three of the finest true phylerias, breaking several hollies and other fine plants'; three wheelbarrows were broken and lost.[2]

The story has come down to us that the Tsar loved to be trundled in a wheelbarrow through Evelyn's beautiful holly hedges: we can now surmise how the story arose. The wheelbarrows and the hollies in George London's survey, and Evelyn's own somewhat ambiguous words, have been combined. He says, when speaking of holly: 'Is there under heaven a more glorious and refreshing object of the kind, than an impregnable hedge of about four hundred feet in length, nine feet high, and five in diameter, which I can shew in my now ruined gardens at Sayes Court (thanks to the Tsar of Muscovy) ... It mocks the rudest assaults of the weather, beasts, or hedge-breakers.'[3] Including, presumably, the assaults of the young barbarian Tsar. However, on the outskirts of the garden he would have found the less thickly planted hollies more vulnerable. The total damage cost the Treasury £300,[4] which was paid to Evelyn and Benbow.

[1] Letter, J. Strickland to J. Evelyn, 16 Feb. 1698.
[2] Cal. Treasury Papers, 1698; full details in Evelyn MS. 13, pp. 485–6.
[3] *Sylva*, 1706, p. 182.
[4] Cal. Treasury Books, 1697–8, p. 360.

On 20 March Godolphin's son Francis married Marlborough's daughter, Lady Henrietta Churchill. Six days later Evelyn wrote to young Jack, 'that there could not any thing come more seasonable, to show your regard and value for that young gentleman or so much oblige that worthy family, who upon all occasions so infinitely obliged both me and your father, than a copy of verses by way of Hymenikon to felicitate his late nuptials.' Evelyn then sets the scene for his composition, suggesting nymphs, cupids, and doves weaving a garland and filling their laps with flowers, all winging towards London to give him joy—to make his father, uncles, and the age happy, 'with a thousand other fine things your own invention will suggest, such as [giving him a few suggestions in Latin]; conclude that you will apply your study as fast as you can, that imitating him, you may get liberty to say much more of him. Show nobody this scribbled letter.'[1]

There was no alteration in young John's condition; the future welfare of the grandson became the dominant consideration in Evelyn's life. A month after the wedding he sent his grandson Scaliger's *Poetices*, 'for your composing not Epithalamias only but for all other occasions'. Apparently the young man's composition was held up for want of such an aid. It was a weapon which would help him to show his prowess to many. Evelyn tells him that his future good entirely depends on his early discretion, 'for the repairing of what the imprudence of others have so miserably shattered, and all for want of early prudence' —a remark apparently pointed at his brother's management of the estate. He again stresses that the reason for his grandson's lines on young Godolphin's marriage is the very great obligation he has to that family, and the use he will have of its continual favour and friendship in his behalf in due time. He tells him that his imitation of young Godolphin's virtues is very necessary; 'believe me, and follow my advice and the experience I have had in the world, and the sad event of your father's not hearkening to it, who had else been now as happy, as he is now miserable'.

He instructs him to be very careful into what company and places he goes whilst he is at London on account of the smallpox, play-houses especially being very dangerous, and any

[1] Letter, J. Evelyn to J. Evelyn III, 26 March 1698.

violent exercise which may over-heat him. When he visits Windsor, he instructs him to call on Mrs. Boscawen, Sir William Godolphin and the Provost of Eton. His verses for Francis 'may be sent . . . sealed up in a white paper and superscribed . . . afterwards visit him yourself and give him joy: these are manly, seasonable, and obliging civilities'. Such was Evelyn's good advice. Yet he would take no chances on the boy's Latin: 'What concerns Epithalamium you'll find in p. 381 of his [Scaliger's] *Idea*: I oblige you to nothing long or tedious, choose any topics you think best, and making a visit to Dr. Bentley (as from me) you may show him your composition, and securely rely on his judgement . . . it is not convenient this letter and hand be seen or lie about.'[1]

Evelyn was unable to spend many of the spring days at Wotton this year; instead, he had stayed with his son in Berkeley Street. Nor was he to enjoy the summer at Wotton: 'I came to pass the rest of the summer in Berkeley Street, during my brother's displeasure, because I could not assent to the alteration of a settlement of my brother's gift freely to me: which I pray God to reconcile.'[2]

This trouble may be said to have arisen in the previous year when George's twenty-six-year-old daughter Katherine married the Reverend Doctor George Fulham. He objected to the settlement of 1692 in which the Wotton estate would irrevocably pass to Evelyn and his male heirs—thus keeping it in the family name; Fulham insisted that, in the event of their death, the estate should become the property of George's heirs. This, of course, was a real risk; young John might die at any moment and smallpox might carry off the grandson. Evelyn at once refused to suffer this recovery, and quoted his brother's words of 1691: ''tis my comfort that you and my nephew are *in vivis*, to succeed me in the enjoyment of the estate our father left us'. Evelyn, angry, would seek legal advice. But he could not restrain his feelings with his hopes for his grandson clouded: 'Who will offer any advantageous match . . . when they find we are all but stewards, obnoxious to so many vexations, nay to be dispossessed, and accountable for the debts upon the estate, without any power of making the least provision for younger

[1] Letter, J. Evelyn to J. Evelyn III, 18 April 1698.
[2] *Diary*, 8 July 1698.

children?'[1] But with the support of Fulham, George persisted in his right to alter the settlement in favour of his own heirs. Evelyn appealed to Stillingfleet, the Bishop of Worcester, for his opinion on George's right to alter the settlement under which Lady Wyche would receive £6000 and all George's personal estate—after his death—to the value of £3000 more; the three grand-daughters nearly £3000 each to which Evelyn agreed to add £1500 to be equally divided. Stillingfleet declared that neither brother was obliged either in law or conscience to alter the present settlement. Glanville, in his downright fashion, incurred Evelyn's anger by suggesting that the case be no more put 'to the decision of fee'd lawyers and prepossessed Divines'—a remark Evelyn countered with: 'Pretty characters and censures of one of the most learned and worthy prelates of our Church.'

Thus the rest of the summer passed by with the two old unhappy brothers still apart; nor with the coming of winter was there any prospect of happiness: Evelyn practically homeless, George wracked with the stone, young John weaker and more despondent than ever, the house in Berkeley Street wrapped in gloom.

With the new year we find Evelyn still in Berkeley Street, his thoughts enlivened only by the virtue and progress of his grandson, who was about to go up to Balliol, and in whom all his hopes were centred. Evelyn wrote to Bohun—indeed there remained no one else in the family circle to whom he could unburden his heart—praising young Jack's 'ductile nature', his innocent cheerfulness, his industry, his being acquainted with the concerns of his family, 'which some are endeavouring to discompose and ruin through the instigation of one'. The unnamed one is, of course, the Rev. Dr. Fulham, 'the crafty serpent', who 'has crept in at Wotton, where he has abased my good and easy brother by a subtlety unparalleled'. Fulham's opposition, he says, 'damps all my remaining comforts, and would overwhelm me but for this dear, dear good child'.[2]

When George took his case to the House of Commons, desiring a Bill to re-settle the estate as proposed by Fulham, the petition was lost by over 300 votes. He then decided to be heard

[1] Letter, J. Evelyn to G. Evelyn, 3 May 1698.
[2] Letter, J. Evelyn to R. Bohun, 16 Feb. 1698.

in the House of Lords. Godolphin at once wrote to Evelyn: 'Your brother's bill being appointed for tomorrow . . . I am very desirous to let you know my present thoughts of that matter before the hearing comes on. If I am to believe his printed Case,[1] you have never yet stated the matter rightly to me, for you always told me, that in the voluntary Settlement made by your brother, he had omitted the clause usual in almost all Settlements, viz., that upon failure of those mentioned in the Settlement, the estate should revert to the right heirs of him that made it, and that this Bill was to supply that omission, whereas it appears that this clause is actually in the Settlement already, and no need of a Bill to supply its being omitted, but the Bill seems only to prevent you suffering of a recovery after the estate comes to be vested in you and that you may not have power to defeat the intent of that clause in your brother's Settlement; now this state being different from the first notion you gave me of it, I was uneasy till I had told you that in my opinion your brother's desire is very equitable, and if the thing proves upon the hearing to be as I have here stated it, I'm confident it will appear so to the House of Lords. I think therefore the best and most friendly advice I can give you is that you should agree this business with your brother as soon as you can, and I hope you will take this advice to be for your own service as sincerely as its intended.'[2]

Evelyn immediately informed Godolphin that he had obtained leave from the Lords (in Godolphin's absence and unknown to him) to defer the hearing for a week, and acknowledged that he had 'omitted to tell him of George's avowal that the estate should descend to himself without one word of female or other limitation, and that George had always intended it should go to the Name and family'. Evelyn goes on: 'Because I thought myself obliged to preserve an estate from being torn asunder,' he had now decided 'to bring them to terms of moderation'. Instead of £4500, the grandchildren were to receive £6000 within six years after his brother's death, and the entire inheritance is for Evelyn 'absolutely and without entail', and 'all pretence to reversion to cease'.[3]

[1] *The case of George Evelyn* [1698].
[2] Letter, S. Godolphin to J. Evelyn, 20 March 1698.
[3] Letter, J. Evelyn to S. Godolphin, 20 March 1699.

Although Evelyn was forced to be rather more generous to the grandchildren, the new settlement was equivalent to a surrender by George and Fulham. This being so, we are somewhat mystified—even after making allowances for Evelyn's patronal language—by his gratitude to Godolphin; it is a great satisfaction, he says, 'that I have brought it to the conclusion your Lordship advised I should', in which Godolphin has given him 'the noblest instance of your kindness a friend is capable of'.[1]

Any progress made by the lawyers was brought to a stop on 24 March by the death of Evelyn's son at the age of forty-four, 'worn, or rather emaciated to a skeleton'—as young Jack is told by his grandfather. In the same letter there is more precept than sympathy for the young man; having said that the death of his father will require some alteration in the deed of settlement, 'which will now be made an absolute estate to me and my disposure', Evelyn goes on: 'but you may be sure to your advantage, whilst you make yourself worthy of it . . .' Neither Evelyn nor his brother accompanied young John's hearse, Draper alone paying the last tribute of the senior members of the family. The bleak entry in the *Diary* tells us that his son was 'accompanied by several'.

Evelyn's memory failed him when he recorded in the *Diary*, 24 March, that his son's sickness was contracted in Ireland; in fact—as we remember—he was treated for what was probably a sinus by Dr. Ridgley in 1685, seven years before he went to Ireland. He repeated the mistake when applying to Lord Galway for a pension—for 'some favourable influence on his [son's] wife my daughter-in-law, and her loss thereby the more supportable'.[2] His son had been ill for so long that an inaccurate remembrance of his first attack is perhaps pardonable—though in any qualification for pension it was an important thing to remember.

We have noticed some variation in the amounts to be raised for debts and portions; and on 21 April Evelyn wrote to his lawyer, suggesting 'that when the Sussex land and that at Kingston is sold for discharging of the £9500, half of the estate remaining may be sufficient for the payment of the £6500, the debt lessening every year making so great security less necessary'.

[1] Op. cit.   [2] Letter, J. Evelyn to Lord Galway, 6 April 1699.

Presumably the larger amount was for the portions of Lady Wyche and the grand-daughters, the smaller for George's debts: we may ignore Evelyn's *Diary* figure (4 October) when he says that the grand-daughters received £15,000—impressive though it may be; we know that under the new settlement they were to receive only £6000. Nor is there any evidence that the figures agreed on in March had been altered; we may assume that they were unchanged on 28 June, when Evelyn was able to record in the *Diary*—after describing Fulham as 'a crafty and intriguing person'—'a settlement being made as strong as Law could do it, all was reconciled'.

With the usual discrepancy between the entries in his *Diary* and the less inhibited statements in his letters, little reconciliation however is noticed. Evelyn, finding occasions calling him so often to London, took over his son's lease of the house in Dover Street, 'my being at Wotton as yet inconvenient. So as I resolved . . . without removing my furniture at Wotton; having enough at Sayes Court, I furnished the house.' He concludes his account in the *Diary* of this troublesome affair: 'I pray God for his infinite mercy, whose gracious providence has hitherto so wonderfully extricated me out of this . . . to sanctify it to me, and to bless the remainder of my life and now very old age with peace and charity, and assist with his Grace to the end.'

Yet despite this hope, for some few months longer sanctification seems to have been witheld; Evelyn could not refrain from making a few more observations on his brother's former subjection by Fulham and Lady Wyche: 'I know very well who stood then by your elbow . . . the rancour, rage and eternal female clack, deafening you against all I could say or write.' It is a sad reflection that the affair continued to deprive Evelyn of the joys of Wotton: '. . . my too great desire to have ended my days where they began: I was fond of the place; but my taste is gone'.[1] In addition to the aftermath of ill-feeling, Lady Wyche remained in residence to prevent Evelyn's return.

The comparative boredom of his enforced retreat to London in the empty season is reflected in the *Diary*; there is little recorded except the long paraphrases of the sermons he listened

[1] Letter, J. Evelyn to G. Evelyn, undated (No. 1393).

to at Lee, Deptford, and Charlton, his visits to the new building
at Greenwich, and his drinking the purgative waters at Shooters
Hill. (His stay at his bailiff's villa in Greenwich for a fortnight
in August went unrecorded in the *Diary*.)

Of course young Jack was not forgotten—far from it. Hardly
a week went by at Oxford without his receiving a letter from
Evelyn, long pages of detailed advice and instruction on authors
and learning, similar to those he sent to his son in Paris in 1676,
and for which Margaret rebuked him with 'This is the ready
way to spoil him': there was a tiresome list of Greek and Latin
authors, with the advice to 'lay a solid foundation of mathematics, speculative and practical, the use of the spheres, sectors,
quadrants, perspective and *graphice*; get also some knowledge of
astronomy, oratorical exercises, logic, philosophy, that of
Descartes, Gassendus, and the new Baconian and Boilean
which is the only solid part'; mention is also made of chemistry,
anatomy, music and dancing; nor is he to forget his 'daily
exercise of body, as ball, boat, walking, riding, that thus
unbending you may come to them again with delight'.[1]

We are not sure whether the young man was reading the
right books, for his grandfather, when asked to send more,
objected: 'for how soon can you have read Herodotus, Thucydides, Polybius, Xenophon, Diodorus [all which Jack pos-
sessed], whilst you are learning and applying yourself to the
learning of those arts and things proper for the University?'
Again he tells him that the restoration of the Wotton estate
must be achieved by his diligence, adding, 'let not my hasty
scribble and letter to you lie neglected, to be seen by every
body: people are curious, and these matters are between you
and I only, though familiarly and negligently, not to be
despised, but dutifully observed'.[2]

Early in May Evelyn sent to the press the chapter (from his
abortive *Elizium Britannicum*) dealing with salads, called
Acetaria, and asked his grandson to supply for it some prefatory
Latin verses. He acquaints him with the subject-matter of the
book, and says that 'Mr. Cowley's works has a preface where
he writes of this subject which you may also consult: but let
none see what I write here'. (Cowley had flattered him.) 'I

[1] Letter, J. Evelyn to J. Evelyn III, 20 March 1699.
[2] Letter, J. Evelyn to J. Evelyn III, 8 April 1699.

declaim against the bloody shambles and the present luxury of all kinds . . . see Cowley's pindaric to me.'[1]

In due time—within a fortnight—the young scholar provided his grandafather with the verses. They proved unsatisfactory, perhaps for being too laudatory. In any case, Evelyn felt unable to use them, and in his letter of acknowledgment, discreetly 'changed the subject': he does not want to hurt the young man's feelings; he is well pleased with his grandson's performance 'at first sight; as to my work, which I think may answer the expectation of the vulgar, does not pretend to deserve the compliments you make me . . . I would not place your first essay and which is so good, before anything that should dishonour it: there is yet not above four or five sheets wrought off, and so much for that trifle: my great concern is the progress I find you make in your other more serious studies'.

We trust that the young man was not too badly piqued—whether his verses were rejected for lack of merit or by reason of Evelyn's regained sense of propriety.

There were more useful ways for his Latin. In the same letter Evelyn says: 'Your virtuous school-fellow Mr. Godolphin is made one of the Tellers of the Exchequer, which gives him an office worth £2000 a year, executed by a deputy.' (What a vision of the fruits of patronage!) He must congratulate him, that he be 'preserved in his memory and friendship: this in a Latin epistle would be well taken and may not be to your disadvantage, for he will certainly rise every day higher, to do you seasonable kindnesses in time . . . send me such an address open: I shall take care to seal and convey it'.[2]

At last the wind had changed at Wotton—and Evelyn passed on the good news to Jack. Apparently the signing of deeds was 'still in some suspense' due to the perverseness of Glanville who refused to show a deed in which both Evelyn and George were concerned, 'for what reason I know not', says Evelyn; 'the delay does yet so sweeten them at Wotton, that my brother has this day ordered his gentleman cook to visit us in his master's name, and is the first beginning of favour from that quarter this twelve-month'. Moreover Evelyn was feeling happier with his bargain; it was better than he had at first

[1] Letter, J. Evelyn to J. Evelyn III, 9 May 1699.
[2] Letter, J. Evelyn to J. Evelyn III, 26 May 1699.

judged it to be. He says 'it may be thought a rash concession of mine' in bringing the Wotton party to terms, 'but it now being considered what miserable havoc it was in the power of your uncle to make of the woods (which we find are valuable) and other spoils which the malice and rancour of our enemies would have caused by the letting long leases, raising fines, and bereaving us of so many other perquisites, there will be nothing lost by the bargain'.[1]

On the 12 June young Jack is told that his verse for Francis Godolphin is a tremendous success; Evelyn had showed it to some 'great judges' who would hardly believe that it was his own, because they acknowledged they could not mend it: 'style, matter, and contexture being so highly pleasing: "*macte, macte,*" they cried, and congratulate your progress to me.'

Young Jack sometimes complained of a pain in his side, and Evelyn, on learning of it, gave him his favourite dictum of *obsta principiis*: 'I am not a friend to physick nor save in extremity bear it with any kindness, and above all things ever dreaded the accustoming of myself to medicines: experience teaching that nature, youth, temperance, exercise, and especially the for-bearing what one observes to prejudice one's health, making the best doctor, that is, to be one's own physician.' Excellent advice though it is, we feel that some further enquiry concerning the nature of Jack's pain should have been made.

But Evelyn is thinking of other things, and looking forward to his grandson's assistance in the vacation; seven or eight large cases of his son's books have arrived from Ireland, 'which will take up some weeks to sort and catalogue; resolving to dispose of the duplicates, and to purge out many frivolous French books and other trash to exchange them for such books as we want, and are of more use'.[2] How stoutly his son had defended them! He had feared that they would need eloquence to save them; now, none was at hand.

The unpacking, however, was a task for the future. Mean-time, another Latin letter was desirable—this time for Pepys and 'the club' in York Buildings, 'who seldom fail of remem-bering you even to fondness: you may tell them that my acquainting you with the honours they often do you, requires

[1] Letter, J. Evelyn to J. Evelyn III, 26 May 1699.
[2] Letter, J. Evelyn to J. Evelyn III, 12 June 1699.

your acknowledgments, and that nothing would tempt you to leave Oxford, but the learned conversation of his house, which were to go from one university to another no less famous, for what passes of exquisite in all the sciences is to be met at his table'. Each member of the club is to have one short facetious epigram to celebrate his particular interest; Dr. Joseph Smith as the Divine, Bentley as critic and philologist, John Hutton as a botanist, Evelyn himself as the gardener and salad-maker, Bathurst as mathematician, and 'Pepys for his love of music, master of all the sciences in one, and worthy to be the President.' Pepys's 'inclination' Mrs. Skinner 'you may compare to some of Plato's female disciples, or rather a lady who could read lectures to Plato himself'.[1] (There is little doubt that Pepys's last and lasting choice of women was an affair of head and heart.) And although Pepys appreciated Jack's Latin, he reproved Evelyn who had 'long since taught him to make all Mr. Pepys's geese, swans'; in time, 'his own judgment will rectify him, though you won't'.[2] By his frankness Pepys showed his good friendship.

Three weeks later Jack's Latin skill is harnessed to Evelyn's own mill; he is asked to send an epistle to uncle George 'congratulating the union which is now brought to pass, and to hope that his kindness to your grandfather extending to you also shall not repent him, it being your endeavour to apply yourself to preserve the reputation of the family'—and so forth. Perhaps to spur the young man to the task, Evelyn adds: 'I am thinking myself to give him a short visit within a few days.'

In the summer vacation there was no relaxation of Evelyn's concern for his grandson's welfare. When his mother proposed to take him to Bath, Evelyn protested: 'My writing to you is at present not to stop your intention but to give you the sense and caution of many here'; there is 'nothing refreshing about the place, proper only for sick and infirm persons . . . I could wish him in some less suspicious air . . . this letter need go no further than between you and your entirely affectionate Father'.[3] Three days earlier he had written to the young man himself about 'that unpleasant and unwholesome aquey place', and how weary he had been—in his youth—'of its blue vapours

---

[1] Op. cit. The poem is in *Pepys' Correspondence*, ed. Tanner, i, 178–9.
[2] *Pepys' Correspondence*, ed. Tanner, ii, 72.
[3] Letter, J. Evelyn to Martha Evelyn, 8 Aug. 1699.

of the waters'; and suggests that he takes this opportunity of seeing Bristol, St. Vincent's Rock, and the fine seats of Sir Robert Southwell and the Duke of Beaufort.

Before going down from Oxford the Master of Balliol had instructed Jack to read *Commentarii Collegii Conimbricensis*—a commentary on Aristotle—of which Evelyn is very critical: 'I have sent young Tooke among all the old booksellers in Duckland, Little Britain, Holborn . . . to get Collegii Conimbricensis for you, but it is thought so very despicable a course of Logic and Philosophy that they sell them by weight as old paper to trunkmakers and grocers . . . so I cannot but wonder Dr. Masters [Mander] should desire such an old useless tedious bundle good for nothing to be sent you, there being a so much more noble and profitable method now used in the universities.'[1] Evelyn's derision of these commentaries on Aristotle, published between 1601–11, by the college of Coimbra in Portugal, was probably prompted by his friend the great scholar Bentley, who would consider them as out of date.

[1] Letter, J. Evelyn to J. Evelyn III, 5 Aug. 1699.

CHAPTER XIV

The Inheritance

$\infty\infty\infty\infty\infty\infty\infty\infty\infty\infty\infty\infty\infty\infty\infty\infty\infty\infty\infty$

GEORGE died on 4 October at the age of eighty-two. On the following day Evelyn wrote to Glanville: 'I do . . . deplore that to the rest of my unhappiness, I had not the satisfaction of declaring to him (as I intended) my unfeigned sorrow, for whatever real or other cause in my life I ever gave him of displeasure, and to beg his pardon, without any other apology to justify my own innocence (however esteemed by him, or others) conscious in myself of having done nothing that may justly reproach me, abating human passions, and such infirmities only as things of this nature unavoidably and surprisingly create, but for which I am heartily sorry.' He also asked Glanville not to give further credit 'to what has been mis-reported in aggravation of late unkindness', for he himself is now 'so disposed to reconciliation and perfect amnesty'. He says that 'the unhappy occasions of the dispute' have been caused by 'interest in some difference of judgment and (at least) appearing reason in others'. He reckons Glanville and himself 'of the latter, nor condemn I the former', hoping 'that after these storms and cloudy weather, a fair sky may break out'; his grandson's inheritance 'is the only remaining comfort'; and Evelyn himself will endeavour 'to recover a sedate and amicable composure of mind', suitable to his condition and great age.[1] There was no response from Glanville—as far as we know. The breach in their friendship following the death of Elizabeth had, in fact, never really healed.

[1] Letter, J. Evelyn to W. Glanville, 5 Oct. 1699.

Two days later, any promise there may have been in Evelyn's conciliatory assertion of the weakness of human nature came to naught, when he imparted to his grandson his thoughts of the gloomy prospects of Wotton: 'Your uncle Glanville having been there all this summer and his son very often, so as no doubt but all will be swept away save the walls, whether the Library or no, I know not, though I suspect it, myself being kept in ignorance of my good brother's danger . . . for had I known in what condition I should have visited him long since, and had me of any thing: but 'twas their interest to watch him to the last minute, and God be thanked, I coveted nothing but to have received some assurance of a perfect reconciliation'; Lady Wyche is to receive the Michaelmas rent and crop; 'whether the product of what is since sown, I am not lawyer enough to determine'.[1]

The presence of Lady Wyche and young Glanville, as executors, prevented Evelyn's immediate removal to Wotton; for the present he sent a servant or two to keep the house and garden in order. However, just now he could find pleasure in the appearance of his *Acetaria*, and in presenting copies to his friends. It would, in great part, wipe out the ill effects of *Numismata*; written in the 1660's, it showed—unlike the other—no sign of his dotage. It was an excellent idea to revive his prestige as a seventy-nine-year-old authority on gardening. 'It gave one so fresh an idea of its author,' said Thomas Gale. Evelyn was pleased, too, with his trimming choice of the Whig Lord Somers as dedicatee; next to Sunderland, he was the most influential man of the time. Evelyn only regretted that he could not give Somers a copy of the book with his own hands; but it was the custom not to be abroad between the death and the funeral of a relative.

Evelyn's fears of the executors' designs on George's personal estate were well founded; Lady Wyche and young Glanville would take all they could lay hands on: even the pigeons from the dovecots, the fish from the ponds, and the clock from its fixtures. On Evelyn's behalf Draper consulted—at the end of October—a solicitor who said 'fish in ponds, pigeons in dove houses always go with the inheritance, and that no fixed brewing vessel, coppers or cisterns are movable; as to the clock

[1] Letter, J. Evelyn to J. Evelyn III, 7 Oct. 1699.

he questions whether that may not be moved, leaving those irons which hold it . . . as to images and such things they are sometimes given the executor and sometimes to the heir'. The solicitor thought it 'a piece of unpracticed spite' to destroy the fish, 'and said upon a short Bill in Chancery suggesting that they have given out in speeches that they would take the fish and pigeons and pull down things fixed to the freehold, the Court would grant an injunction to stop them . . .' Nor can they pretend to any part of the Copse standing at George's death, but what of it was cut before.[1] Evelyn immediately forwarded this legal view to young Glanville.

Even throughout the early winter months Evelyn could make but little preparation for the taking over of Wotton; Lady Wyche was still there, 'busy as yet in appraising the rest of the goods, jealous of their not being set at higher prices . . . so as you must not think to find a joint stool left', he told his grandson. He also said: 'I have bought all the tackle, carts, and other utensils belonging to the husbandry, with the oxen, 50 sheep to eat up the remaining pasture, hay, and other provender, 2 cows, 2 sows, I boar, I being obliged by custom of the manor to keep a boar and a bull: so you see I am of necessity forced to become a motley husbandman or farmer, at least till the spring, when, as I find it answer, I shall put it all off to others, and only reserve what may be necessary for the economy when we are there, and that will be a bailiff, one maid, a gardener and helper, and perhaps some other drudge which must constantly reside there.'[2]

Evelyn had been unduly sceptical that the library would be 'swept away'; in fact, in the will it was left—with three family portraits—to him entirely. It comprised about 600 volumes of Travel, History, Law, Theology, Classics, and Literature, including many fine copies of the works of Boyle, Browne, Donne, Milton and Randolph. A large gilt cup and cover was bequeathed to Mrs. Evelyn; 'more doubtless would my good brother left us, had not they who feared it, industriously hid my brother's decaying condition from us, to prevent my coming till he was past altering any thing'. (But, surely, it was the Fulham opposition and 'the eternal female clack' that kept him

[1] Letter, W. Draper to J. Evelyn, 31 Oct. 1699.
[2] Letter, J. Evelyn to J. Evelyn III, 15 Nov. 1699.

away.) Nothing but the books and pictures were left for him; 'cocks, hen, hog, and ducks are all flown already, so as we are to go as to a new plantation . . . and thus you have the state of our affairs for improvement of which you will have need of all your mathematics, especially mensuration of superficies and solids that you may know how to deal with crafty clowns as well as law to defend your title . . . adieu, dear child, serve God, and have a care of your health'.[1]

On the 25 January of the new year Evelyn paid a visit to Wotton: his *Diary* entry for that day is remarkable for its propriety and restraint: 'to furnish the house with necessarys through my Lady Wyche and nephew Glanville being executors, having sold and disposed of what goods were left of my brothers'.

There is little doubt that Evelyn was unfortunate in his dealings with Lady Wyche. Progress had been made in the payment of debts and some of the portions; Northstoke was sold for £2045, Denton for £3622, but full details of the Wotton timber sales are not known. By 31 March young Glanville had received £2261 for money borrowed by Evelyn's son, Fulham received £1894 for his wife's portion, and Sir J. Arundel—to whom George had owed money—£2136. In fact the Arundel money was designed for Lady Wyche, but being called in by Arundel's executors Evelyn was forced to postpone her Ladyship's portion. The heat engendered on both sides burns through a letter which Evelyn wrote—but never sent—to her Ladyship's lawyer; after disappointing her, Evelyn met 'with reproaches, rude and undecent language in the street'. He says that she and the grand-daughters had defamed George 'or me as if we had used them like bastards (which is their language) after above £20000 [*sic*] has been divided among children'. As for Lady Wyche, 'you and your lady would do a blessed work to mitigate this bitter spirit of hers, by representing to her, how unbecoming her sex and youth this immodest and provoking passion is: how long I and my wife have lain under that envenomed tongue of hers, she well knows. Envy and avarice make her lean . . .'[2]

Evelyn paid another visit to Wotton after Easter. As expected, he found little except the empty house and the desolation of the

---

[1] Op. cit.   [2] Letter, J. Evelyn to — Willis, 31 March 1700.

outbuildings. Not a cock was left to crow a welcome. It was impossible to restrain his feelings; to any neighbour he chanced to meet he would say, 'my brother hath not left me estate enough to keep a coach; the executors, contrary to law hath sold my brother's goods and personal estate fixed to the freehold, and left me an empty house'. He told Love the malt-man of George's letter of 1691 in which he had been promised the whole estate without any reservation. 'Look at the woods!' he would exclaim; 'instead of timber I have nothing but hedge-rows.' He lamented to many neighbours that his brother, though a very good man, was managed and governed by those about him. There was the question of Lady Wyche's unhurried valuation; 'my son-in-law Draper says I would do well to sue her for a quarter's rent!' The servants—still paid by Lady Wyche—answered some useful questions regarding the burning of any papers or the tearing off of any seals.[1]

Unfortunately, her Ladyship came to learn of Evelyn's conversation and inquiries; perhaps he wrote to one of the Glanvilles after his visit. Her comments—her last to survive—begin: 'I wonder that your wife and governess (in her own conceit so well-bred) should suffer you to trouble your friends with long letters so full of ingratitude, malice, folly, falsehood and hypocrisy, virtues which have sufficiently discovered you to the world to be a couple of very religious, sincere, and good Christians.' Evelyn's conversation with the neighbours took place, she points out, after his 'Lent devotion and Easter Communion'; and she has heard of what he discussed. If George was managed and governed, 'never did any knave in plainer words call his brother fool'—which seems a reasonable remark; 'the servants you call mine—when you pretend in respect to me you suffer to stay in the house—pray discharge now; you have kept 'em long enough to drain 'em to be your informers: that I have burnt any papers or torn off any seals of writings belonging to you is a lie'. Perhaps the final thrust cut the deepest: 'You will do me a great favour to let me see the letter which my Lord Godolphin wrote you before the throwing out of my father's Bill.'[2] Doubtless Lady Wyche conjectured that there

---

[1] Letter, Lady Wyche to J. Evelyn: copy in W. Glanville's hand, *c.* April 1700.
[2] Op. cit.

was some connection between the lawfulness of the reversion
—which Godolphin affirmed—and Evelyn's new pacifying
proposals for the Settlement. Evelyn must have guessed that
Lady Wyche's astute request could only have emanated from
young Glanville's divulgence of what Godolphin wrote. Thus
the rift between himself and the executors tended to widen.

Evelyn's rock-like resolution to further his grandson's advancement acted like a breakwater, reducing all Lady Wyche's
thunderous waves to harmless spray: 'This being now the seed-
time', he would say to his grandson, 'cultivate the field, as
you do, the Harvest will be yours.'

On 24 May Evelyn left Dover Street to spend the rest of the
summer at Wotton. During the next few weeks the remainder
of the books and furniture were sent from Sayes Court. Thirty
large cases, trunks, and barrels containing the books, and a
hundred bales of furniture travelled by a 'great Western barge'
to near Kingston and thence by road. Of the Dover Street
books, 900 were sold a year later for £60 to young Tooke,
(£50 being offered by Brown at the Black Swan, and Bateman
of Paternoster Row, 'the greatest dealers of the Tribe').[1] Some
hundreds were sent to Wotton to be added to the main library,
leaving the rest of the son's books to be weeded by young Jack,
'and prepared for another auction'. Wotton now looked 'like
a merchant's store-house'. The existing shelving proved inadequate and forced upon Evelyn 'another purgation to make
room for better books'. Altogether, he must have disposed of
nearly 1500 volumes.[2]

For the greater part of Evelyn's first month at Wotton peace
was denied him, suffering badly from a strangury and a feverish
attack. Pepys advised him to leave off malt-drink and to take
barley-water, blanched with almonds and sweetened with a
little sugar. A month later, he was writing to Pepys like a
farmer: 'I pass the day in the fields, among horses and oxen,
sheep and cows, bulls and sows.'[3] Perhaps a little belatedly—
on the 11 August—he records that he was well enough to go
to church and give God thanks for his recovery. During the

---

[1] Letter, J. Evelyn to J. Evelyn III, 2 July 1701.

[2] Evelyn's 1687 Catalogue lists nearly 5000; a catalogue made in 1707
only 3700.

[3] *Pepys' Private Correspondence*, ed. Tanner, vol. II, 20.

following month he visited Draper at Adscomb near Croydon and Pepys at Clapham—whilst the masons and carpenters made necessary alterations at Wotton.

At the end of September, a month before his eightieth birthday, Evelyn returned. He was in a generous mood, and allowed a tenant some timber for the repair of a copyhold; a concession, said George's bailiff, never hitherto allowed where no timber grew on the premises.[1]

Towards the end of October young Jack fell ill of the smallpox. Evelyn's fears, intensified by his bitter memories of Mary and Elizabeth, were so great and oppressive that he could hardly handle a pen to write to him. He was completely dejected at the thought that all his hopes might yet be dashed. Dr. Mander (now Vice-Chancellor) took the utmost care of the patient, lodged him in his own apartment, and employed his own physician. Daily bulletins were sent by Mander or Jack's tutor, Strong. Happily, by the 26 October all danger had passed, and Evelyn was able to tell his grandson that his 'most earnest prayers to Almighty God were heard'. To show his own gratitude, young Jack is instructed to send some verses to Mander and Uncle Harcourt (who sent £15 towards the medical expenses); 'you'll meet admirable examples in Erasmus . . . all which you know better than myself'. ('Uncle' Harcourt was the father of young Jack's sister Elizabeth's husband, Simon, Viscount Harcourt.)

Meantime—with the days so short—the repairs and renovations at Wotton were brought to a halt till the spring, and Evelyn had returned to Dover Street for the winter. With the shock of his grandson's illness and another attack of his strangury, he himself was enfeebled: '. . . glad therefore shall I be to see my dear child, whose assistance I daily need more and more . . . I am so very weak that I can hardly stand . . . you may see by my almost illegible scribble how feeble I am become.'[2]

Yet, by the 12 December all his troubles and ailments were forgotten; on that day Godolphin returned to the Treasury as First Lord—the result of the Tory victories at the general election. As Mrs. Evelyn said on a former occasion, 'a little

[1] Letter, J. Evelyn to — Sherwood, 9 Oct. 1700.
[2] Letter, J. Evelyn to J. Evelyn III, 26 Oct. 1700.

luck is a good cordial'. Evelyn must have felt that the restoration of his broken family—for which he lived—would now be accomplished. He could now more clearly visualise Godolphin's niece, Anne Boscawen, as the future mistress of Wotton. That was the great goal.

One of his first tasks in the new year was to compile a list of the names of all his tenants and their respective rents, and the acreage of his estates under the headings arable, meadow, woods, and coppices, farmhouses and tenements, heath and common: the total rent from tenants came to £1150, and the total acreage was 7500.[1] The Living of Wotton was worth £140 a year with the tithes, 'though near £200 if paid all in kind', said Evelyn when he offered it to Bohun—who had already held a New College living—in February; but the higher value had not been reached for many years; 'the care and fatigue of scholars turning farmers not suiting with the late incumbents'. The Parsonage house, he says, 'is so despicable and fit only for the farmer who is in it . . . as to your accommodation, if poor Wotton (left me almost in as ill a plight) stands, you may be sure of welcome there'.[2]

In March Mrs. Evelyn tried to secure a Salisbury prebend for Bohun, making her application to Bishop Burnet's wife (who was related to Bohun). Evelyn followed this up by calling on Burnet, who did all the talking; 'overwhelmed with rhetoric so natural to him . . . I parted from the man of the world, who following me down [stairs], left me nothing to reply . . . the bishop is a courtier: verbum sap', writes Evelyn to Bohun.[3] However, the latter got his prebend before the summer was over.

To add to Evelyn's anxieties, Mrs. Evelyn's health began to decline with recurrent coughing and rheumatism. From Dover Street she would walk to Hyde Park, where she found that the air did 'her more good than all the prescriptions of physicians'. In April she went to Greenwich (perhaps to John Strickland's house) to recuperate and take the waters at Shooters Hill. Evelyn, too, still needed medical attention; on 14 April she wrote, 'I am not a little concerned you are indisposed; I wish you would send for Mr. Garnier and take some gentle purge

[1] Evelyn MS. misc.   [2] Letter, J. Evelyn to R. Bohun, 13 Feb. 1701.
[3] Letter, J. Evelyn to R. Bohun, 25 March 1701.

that may clear the way, and pray do not meddle with the old remains of physic.' On 26 May Mrs. Evelyn, sensible of the expense of her convalescence, wrote: 'I am heartily sorry I am not with you, and do not stay here for diversion, but to confirm an unsteady constitution very much altered from my former way; I am sensible of the expense and would help if I could: I wish by being restored to tolerable health I may signify to the good of the family. It shall not be want of endeavours if I fail, of which I am persuaded you are convinced.'

At Dover Street Evelyn was in a muddle; having forgotten which of the books were for disposal he sent his grandson 'a rude draught of the Chamber' so that the shelves containing duplicates could be marked. He was worried about Bohun, now at Wotton, '*captus pedibus* in some sort, as not able to stand in a pulpit, which is very unfortunate now at his first appearance: but what remedy?' he asks on 13 May. In the middle of June, Mrs. Evelyn, sufficiently recovered, went to Wotton; she described her eventful journey: 'When we were in the remotest part of Banstead Downs the axel tree and one of the fore wheels fired almost to a flame. The wheel was so hot it melted the fat of some meat we had left, and we were constrained to throw on some sack to quench it which was all the liquid we could come by. The wheel was set on again and hoped to reach Leatherhead there to secure it better, but it heat again after a little driving; obliged to stop again where we found a puddle of water and quenched it. We held safe to Leatherhead, the whole set examined and secured.'[1]

From Wotton Mrs. Evelyn sent her husband an account of the building alterations in a manner suggesting that any deterioration of her health had had no effect on her ideas of house planning: 'I have visited every place within doors; the dairy answers beyond expectation . . . I shall be glad to have a stillhouse . . . I have given orders to set up shelves in the closets . . . your new study is much improved by the addition of the chimney . . . the walls may be lined with slit deal to secure the hangings . . . there will be a want of more deals to finish what is in hand. My brother's chamber chimney is not, I fear, to be cured; when it rains it pours a stream into the room, and has changed the colour of the stones of the hearth; I never saw the

[1] Mrs. Evelyn to J. Evelyn, 14 June 1701.

gardens lie so rough: Nick lays it on the dry weather; I have expressed my dislike . . . I cannot but wish you here and must acknowledge the freshness of the air and perfect quiet of the country is very charming now all parts are so very green and pleasant.'¹ A week later she tells Evelyn that Bohun 'is just the same man as ever, cautious, inquisitive, ailing, and unsteady'; she also says, 'I am a little uneasy to see twelve men daily drinking in the house, besides the family. I wish it hold out.'

Evelyn continued to send young Jack long newsy letters which included, as usual, further hints for his heterogeneous education. John Keill of Hart Hall, Oxford, had reported his progress in mathematics; now Evelyn wishes his grandson to proceed to perspective and architecture, and suggested that Dean Aldrich of Christ Church might act as 'a good master and director . . . to whom I will get you recommended if you think fit'. He must also learn to draw: 'I think it is best to design human bodies, for one that draws the head, hand, and feet &c (that is, the naked) has overcome the main difficulty (Other animals are easy) and then to design them clothed, and to begin with the eye, ear, mouth, nose, not too small but pretty large and near the life; with all the postures of the hand . . . for all which Palma's Book of Design is the best . . . Landscape and other graceful accessories come in with perspective. The only danger is you distort your body, now every day growing . . . it therefore requires placing your breast just before your copy, and to be no longer at it than is consistent with your health and other studies of importance. Figures and statues and drawing after rounds, solids . . . are reserved for the last, and so much for *Graphice* at present.' Another Latin verse was called for, this time in acknowledgment for a book given to him by the Bishop of Norwich; Evelyn suggests, as usual, the matter; thanks for the rare book, the glorious sight of the bishop's richly stored library which is enough to incite a young student to apply himself to learning—to this Athens, or something to this effect. The verse is to be sent to Evelyn open, of course, who will seal and cause it to be delivered.

Young Jack's sister played the harpsichord, and told Evelyn that she was challenged by her brother with the flute. Evelyn disliked his grandson's wood-wind prowess; 'I had rather you

¹ Op. cit.

exercised your voice (as much healthier) and learnt so much of the rudiments of music as to be able to sing a plain bass, which in a month or two may be learned.' Evelyn also advised him to read Greek History; 'it is much more useful than Greek verse. Herodotus is counted easy as well as pure; but one who conquers Thucydides is master of all the rest.'[1] As we shall see presently, Gale and Bentley gave much better advice on the reading of Greek.

Pepys growing old, too, was advised to leave York Buildings; 'being much impaired in his health finds London air so inconvenient, that his physicians have advised him to quit the town altogether, and reside at Clapham to which his age and infirmities incline him; so as he is letting his fine house, and translating all his goods and curiosities thither, which will break up our Saturdays assembly, much to his regret . . . such a weaning I myself must think of shortly'.[2] In three weeks' time Evelyn would leave for Wotton, travelling in his new coach with its modern flat roof. (But no real 'weaning' happened, for he continued to spend the winters in London.)

Having consulted Gale and Bentley concerning the Greek poets, Evelyn told Jack that they advised him to acquaint himself with Homer and the Greek poets, which alone would render all other Greek authors easy, and that the reading of Greek historians was a false method and could come from none but the ignorant and lazy.[3]

For Evelyn the fine summer weather passed at Wotton with something of its old magic. The garden was flourishing, the builders had finished the alterations—and his new cork shoes were comfortable. Lady Wyche's tongue was silent, her portion paid, and he would soon settle all accounts with the Glanvilles. He was in 'tolerable health', approaching his eighty-first birthday. Admittedly he could not always find the books he wanted without Jack's help. Bohun, despite his snuffling melancholy, managed to preach every Sunday (except when he went to Salisbury to be installed into his prebend). If Evelyn could no longer walk the three-quarters of a mile to Wotton church, he could travel in his fine new coach.

In letters, he and Pepys would muse on the past delights of

[1] Letter, J. Evelyn to J. Evelyn III, 14 June 1701.   [2] Op. cit.
[3] Letter, J. Evelyn to J. Evelyn III, 2 July 1701.

York Buildings. Pepys must have cheered him with 'As much as I am (I bless God) in perfect present ease here as to my health; 'tis little less, however, than a very burial to me, as to what of all worldly goods I put most price upon, I mean the few old and learned friends I had flattered myself with the hopes of closing the little residue of my life in the continued enjoyment of, and at the head of them all, the most inestimable Mr. Evelyn.'[1]

At the end of November Evelyn returned to Dover Street for the winter; Mrs. Evelyn remaining behind to do a little coaching in the kitchen, putting the cook in the way of making hog puddings and suchlike—'to put her in a way of sending us sometimes such varieties as might be expected from one's own farm'—as she put it. Three days later she says: 'I am pretty well but apparently want the Bath waters . . . I look after the workmen to the best of my skill, and do not leave doing something that seems necessary till ten at night.' Bohun 'is ailing, melancholy, silent and thoughtful according to custom'.

In London Evelyn, without friends, felt his loneliness, and his inevitable lack of mobility. Pepys was his last surviving friend—perhaps the only real friend he ever had. There had been others, of course, such as Jeremy Taylor, who went to Ireland and passed out of Evelyn's life in 1658; Abraham Cowley, who died in 1667. There were many faithful correspondents—we cannnot call them friends—Robert Boyle, and garrulous John Beale of Yeovil to whom Evelyn wrote regularly for twenty years—though they never met. Now he missed the company and cheer of his only remaining friend. 'I pass not by York Buildings without serious regret. Saturday which was wont to be a Jubilee . . . the most diverting of the weekly circles is from a real Sabbath now become wholly saturnine, lugubrious, and solitary,'[2] he said to Pepys. Raillery and William Glanville had parted; he was 84, 'decaying apace and willing to die having done as much good and as much ill as he desired'—so Mrs. Evelyn told Bohun.

But Evelyn would soon have the company of Jack, who

[1] Letter, S. Pepys to J. Evelyn, 19 Nov. 1701. Evelyn MS. 3; Vol. II, p. 124.

[2] Letter, J. Evelyn to S. Pepys, 10 Dec. 1701. (Tanner, II, 237.) Evelyn's copy is dated 9 Dec.

proposed to leave Oxford at the end of the year. Evelyn suggested the usual civilities: a handsome compliment to the Master of Balliol to be delivered with Evelyn's own acknowledgments 'of his kindness and care of you'. There was 'a guinea extraordinary' for the tutor Strong: 'these last civilities leave their effects and impression accordingly. Why should you not take leave of the Dean of Christ Church and though you have little acquaintance with him, you could not leave the university without doing your duty to him whom you have heard your grandfather speak of with so much respect.'[1]

On the political horizon appeared a cloud. The elections at the end of the year resulted in an even representation of Whig and Tory. On 30 December Godolphin resigned. Evelyn heard the ominous rumour earlier in the month, and had said to Pepys: 'you hear my noble and bosom friend has laid down his office, for which I am sorry and as I look on it, an ill omen'.[2] The sad news went unrecorded in the *Diary*.

In the new year, Bohun, though able to entertain himself so well at Wotton 'as not to regret his solitary way', proposed a visit to London. It was not easy to find accommodation in the Dover Street locality; 'The town is full,' said Mrs. Evelyn, 'and this neighbourhood especially being so near Kensington never wants lodgers.' However, for three shillings a week a room was found. Mrs. Evelyn so informed Bohun, and gave him some news of their servants' love affairs. The Wotton bailiff's son had married Strickland's maid, having done her 'justice and taken away slander'. One of Mrs. Evelyn's maids had owned her marriage to the coachman: an unequal match, to the girl's loss; 'a better tempered good natured maid I never knew, but love masters all discretion'.[3] Inevitably, Mrs. Evelyn was reminded of her own daughter Elizabeth.

[1] Letter, J. Evelyn to J. Evelyn III, 13 Dec. 1701.
[2] Tanner, II, 237.
[3] Letter, Mrs. Evelyn to R. Bohun, 8 Jan. 1702.

CHAPTER XV

The Fruits of Patronage

〜〜〜〜〜〜〜〜〜〜〜〜〜〜〜〜〜〜〜〜〜〜〜〜〜〜〜〜〜〜〜〜

T HE death of King William on 20 February brought Anne
—as Mrs. Evelyn put it, 'an English Queen with an English
heart'[1]—to the throne. It also brought the Tories back to power.
Their witty toast 'to the little gentleman in black velvet' was a
tribute to the mole that caused King William's horse to fall.

Young Glanville of the Treasury expressed 'an odd fancy in
saying a greater loss could not have come to the nation next
to the crucifixion of Jesus Christ . . . zeal one may allow', com-
mented Mrs. Evelyn when she told Bohun. The Glanville
antagonism is manifest in her story that when his daughter saw
her father so concerned, she said, 'Papa, would to God my
grandfather had died in the room of the good King.'[2]

Evelyn's 'ill omen' on Godolphin's resignation in December
was completely dissipated when he came back in May as Lord
Treasurer, Marlborough as Captain General and Master of the
Ordnance. By his choice of patron, and by Francis Godolphin's
marriage to Marlborough's daughter, Evelyn was fortunately
placed, and deeply satisfied when these happy appointments
were made.

Meantime, in April, Glanville senior had died. We know
something of his admiration for Mrs. Evelyn, and of his support
of Fulham in the matter of the settlement; yet Evelyn could
say in the *Diary*, 12 April, 'Our relation and friendship had been
long and great, but much interrupted by a displeasure he took

[1] Letter, Mrs. Evelyn to R. Bohun, 13 March 1702.   [2] Op. cit.

both at me and my wife, the cause of which I could never learn or imagine, unless my not concurring with him as to his opinion of the Trinity.' That is most impressive. On second thoughts perhaps, he adds: 'I pray God of his infinite goodness pardon whatever passed between us during the late Settlement: et R.I.P.' Glanville directed that his body be wrapped in lead and thrown into the sea between Dungeness and Dover near the Goodwins: an element, as far as is known, to which he had no relation; it afforded Jack a subject for a Latin verse— doubtless at Evelyn's suggestion.

On the day of the announcement of Godolphin's appointment as Lord High Treasurer Evelyn wrote a long letter to him. He told him of his financial position, the full obligations under the Settlement; the portions, his son's debt, his brother's debts, all of which made a total 'near £15000' (without mentioning, however, that the greater part of the money had been found by the sale of his two farms and the Wotton timber); he goes on, 'that how to discharge the heavy burden and leave my grandson for a competency . . . I am utterly unable to find out what remedy to apply'. Sayes Court, he says, being settled between his wife and his son's widow, is not in his power to sell. A year ago his Wotton rental was £1150; now he has £1200 income per annum. His problem is to pay taxes, interest, and for repairs; for present subsistence; and to make a marriage settlement for his grandson: 'Your Lordship will easily compute how small a pittance can remain to make a . . . settlement.' Therefore he seeks Godolphin's goodness and counsel to assist him by either obtaining the payment of the sum due from the Crown to the estate of Sir Richard Browne, or, 'which we would rather choose', Godolphin's taking his grandson into his favour and patronage—for which his education and parts fit him: 'I shall not deceive you . . . who is so perfect a judge.'

What did this 'perfect judge' think of the manner in which he was again held with the pistol to his promises of friendship, of Evelyn's being 'left to your Lordship's care for twenty years by a Saint now in Heaven and for her sake, to a promise of continuing it as long as I live'? Thus he begs for some expedient 'which should heal and save a sinking family; not by importuning your Lordship for any sudden operation, but what may come spontaneously from you as a mark of that generous, and by me, never-to-be-forgotten Friendship'. (Evelyn has some reputation for care in the use of words; but we may question how a solicited benefit can come spontaneously.) Then, recalling the former benefits obtained, he confesses that he is ashamed and too presumptuous. (It was something habitual in Evelyn to express his regret after a misdeed.) He goes on to quote one of Godolphin's letters written after Margaret's death in which he said 'anything I can do for you, shall always be most welcome to me'. This reminder can be justified: 'My Lord, I challenge Plato himself . . . to show me such a generous and obliging period! Thus . . . I hold myself discharged from an impudence unparalleled, were not this and other passages of your uncommon kindnesses to me as deeply engraven in my heart, as conspicuously under your own hand.'[1] Godolphin made no reply.

A month later Evelyn asked him for some employment for Draper—an application which enabled him to lead into 'as for my dear grandson I have said and I hope done enough in wholly referring him to your Lordship's care . . . you sometime entrusted me with your Lordship's and dear Lady's treasure, to some little care of mine, and I well remember, that having once occasion of asking you about something which concerned the little man, you replied, "who should take care of him but you?": but my Lord I make no application: the parallel is not just'. From this dissembling he leads into another suit, none other than his expenses—still unpaid—incurred in the Second Dutch War: 'I had all the ties in the world to your Lordship and to one you loved: whilst your Lordship's favours to me are supernumerary and the free emanation of your good nature, which encourages me to continue my supplication.'[2] But Evelyn forfeited his chances of payment by setting his expenses against the five or six thousand pounds owing by the Crown to his wife as heiress to the estate of Sir Richard Browne: and again there was no reply.

Therefore little progress—known to us—was made in Evelyn's plans and ambitions. He had tried to secure Godolphin's patronage for his grandson, having first acquainted his Lordship with the poor prospects of a marriage settlement.

[1] Letter, J. Evelyn to S. Godolphin, 7 May 1702.
[2] Letter, J. Evelyn to S. Godolphin, 12 June 1702.

Now he approached the young man's prospective mother-in-law, Mrs. Boscawen, Godolphin's widowed sister. He begins by dissembling on the identity of the proposer of the marriage —though it seems an easy guess: 'The value which we have ever had for your noble family must needs create in us an unexpressable satisfaction, were it possible for us to hope for so near a relation to it, as that which some kind friend has, we find, discovered of their good wishes for my grandson.' Unfortunately, 'there are other inequalities which forbids us the hopes . . . of so great a blessing'; these are, of course, his present financial embarrassments. Yet 'it still were in the compass of an illustrious friend to make it possible by a just expedient in his Lordship's power . . . by an act of a signal friendship'. But whatever happens, 'there will appear an estate of near £2500 a year after some leases (near expiring) are determined and the jointures free'. To strengthen his side of the proposal he gives Mrs. Boscawen a catalogue of the merits—actual and potential —of the Wotton estate, and goes on: 'And now, madam, why I cannot obtain of my self, the proposing anything of this to my Lord Treasurer myself, neither modesty will suffer, nor the effects of the least repulse, should his Lordship seem uneasy, or frown upon it. You may therefore do with this letter as you think fit; I am not ashamed you should show it him, but not as if I desired you should. I know I am safe in your conduct, prudence, and kindness, to which I absolutely leave it.'[1]

Mrs. Boscawen's reply, four days later, was disappointing. 'My wishes are not bent upon great things either of quality or estate; what I desire in the disposing of my child is a good family, a sober, virtuous young man and a competent fortune, and these things I take to meet in your grandson, and I like him much the better for being yours and Mrs. Evelyn's.' But she thought that the persons most concerned were young enough to wait a little. (Her daughter was seventeen, young Jack twenty.) Meantime, 'when you've tried the kindness and assistance of the friend you rely upon for the relief of your present circumstances I shall be ready to enter into a closer treaty'.[2]

Thus by Mrs. Boscawen's prudence Evelyn was thrown back upon his own resources.

[1] Letter, J. Evelyn to Mrs. Boscawen, 22 June 1702.
[2] Letter, Mrs. Boscawen to J. Evelyn, 26 June 1702.

As usual, he and his wife spent the summer at Wotton, where they had the company of the Drapers, whose new house at Addiscombe was not yet ready for occupation. With the good and easy harvest, and Bohun's excellent sermons, they could enjoy a wonderfully calm August.

As the anniversary of Margaret's death drew near Evelyn decided that it must be specially commemorated; his usual twelve lines or so on her virtues would be, in this year of Godolphin's return to the Treasury, an inadequate congratulation. Moreover, his grandson's need of patronage still remained unsatisfied, his own financial embarrassments unaltered. Yes, the 8 September 1702 must be made unforgettable. *The Life of Mrs. Godolphin* had never yet been sent to Godolphin. Was this not the occasion for it? Evelyn had re-read it so often, each time with less critical sense and more liking—as is an author's way with a manuscript laid by. He was now inured to its shortcomings, its omissions, its equivocation. Besides, he was encouraged by his conviction of Margaret's silence, of her loyalty to himself which the passage of the years had strengthened. Godolphin, since her death, had fulfilled his promises—when opportunities allowed. If he now knew more about Evelyn than he did in 1678, it did not matter; as a man of honour, Godolphin would continue to fulfil his promises. Therefore, Evelyn ran no risk in presenting the manuscript to him. As we know, Lady Sylvius had received the first manuscript version in 1684. She either lent or related the story to Godolphin's sisters, who, knowing the truth of it, may well have lifted their eyebrows and conveyed their doubts of Evelyn's veracity to their brother. But any disbelief in the manuscript would not be allowed to prejudice his promises of 1678. In due time—on the never-to-be-forgotten day, Evelyn sent the manuscript. Ominously, no acknowledgment survives; whatever Godolphin said in acceptance of the work, it could hardly have been commensurate with Evelyn's idea of its importance, or considered worth preserving.

The year dragged on to Evelyn's birthday, 31 October. Instead of recording in the *Diary* his usual thanks to God for his preservation, once more he listened to the voice of conscience. Twenty-two years ago, after confessing his sins, he had pleaded to God for mercy and acceptance. Had he found acceptance? Life had gone very hard with him since 1680.

The benefits of patronage now seemed strangely delayed. Perhaps he was not yet accepted. He would try again. Taking the 1680 confession from his scrittoire he brought it up to date—at least as far as the little remaining space on the single sheet of paper allowed; two legible entries are '1693 Nup. daughter Draper', and '1698–9 concerning the Case'—Susan's marriage, and his brother's Case regarding the Settlement. But what the paper could not contain was doubtless revealed in his heart. By this action—as in 1680 he comes to life, and impresses us. In the *Diary* he wrote: 'humbly imploring the pardon of my past life, sins, and particularly of the incursions and frailties &c. not yet fully subdued; but that by the assistance of his Grace I may yet be more than conqueror'. By this second purgation he would find acceptance and a quiet conscience. He would trust that in the deserved attainment of this new spiritual state his outstanding problems would be solved. It was a curious coincidence that, a fortnight later, Bohun preached in Wotton church on the danger of a death-bed repentance. Oh how gratifying to have escaped that danger! Evelyn returned to Dover Street in peace because he had once more taken God into his confidence and allowed Him to look into his heart. Repentance, if sincere, can never be too late.

In the new year Evelyn made another application to Godolphin for his Dutch War expenses, again subtracting them from the Sayes Court debt owing by the Crown. He had told Godolphin of his present sharp nephritic pains which detained him from being able to wait upon his Lordship, and implored him 'not to abandon' him altogether. He also asked that Draper might succeed him as Treasurer of Greenwich Hospital; Evelyn wanted no more official offices. But he would continue his prayers for his Lordship, 'and carry the effects of them to a better world'.[1] Again no reply arrives. As he said to Lady Sunderland on 9 March, 'we are every moment declining . . . not unmindful of more lasting and better habitations . . . in the meantime endeavouring not to be wanting to a family . . . that God Almighty will leave it a blessing, whose Providence and protection has hitherto supported it'.

The return journey to Wotton on 14 May was broken at

[1] Letter, J. Evelyn to S. Godolphin, 18 Jan. 1703.

Clapham to allow Evelyn to visit his old friend Pepys, lying
seriously ill. When Evelyn saw him and heard that there was
small hope of his recovery he was 'much affected'. He never
saw him again, for twelve days later he died. Evelyn's uncertain
health and old age prevented his attendance at the funeral.

Evelyn's own end was undoubtedly drawing near. In July
he had a feverish attack during which he nearly expired. But
his work was not yet done, the reward of Grace still to come,
the marriage of his grandson not a certainty. He had again
been in correspondence with Mrs. Boscawen on the matter of
his financial contribution to any marriage settlement. The
Wotton rental, in round figures, is down to £1000 per annum,
'to which I can only add,' he says, 'goodness of the Title,
improvements of the woods and copses, leases, and advowsons,
accommodation as a gentleman of the best rank would much
value, but becomes us not to do so'. After the present jointures
(that is after both he and his wife are gone) 'there would be
better than £22,000 per annum remaining to the family, very
modestly computed'. Again he stresses the importance of
Godolphin's receiving young Jack into his patronage, 'by
reserving some employment for him' with, of course, a competent maintenance: this, however, is still but a hope. There
was more hope in the greater issue; in that Mrs. Boscawen had
no objection to giving her daughter in marriage—which Evelyn
spoke of as 'most obliging inclinations'.[1]

No further development took place during the following six
months, apart from Mrs. Boscawen's making a second attempt
to persuade Godolphin to alleviate Evelyn's financial embarrassments. On 5 August he thanked her for her support, adding,
'what cannot be accomplished without some extraordinary
providence, we humbly acquiesce in (as Christians should do)'.
None the less Evelyn, anxious and fretful, could not refrain from
writing to Francis Godolphin asking him to encourage his
grandson's 'humble addresses and speak kindly of him to my
Lord your father' and so 'exceedingly oblige your dying friend'.[2]

The great gale which struck the south of England at the end
of November tore down more than 2000 of Evelyn's precious
trees, including growing timber and the fine, old specimens

[1] Letter, J. Evelyn to Mrs. Boscawen, 17 June 1703.
[2] Letter, J. Evelyn to F. Godolphin, n.d. [1703].

reprieved from the axe for shelter and ornament. The Garden Mount with the young promising trees of his own planting lay prostrate. The damage to his tenants' farms, houses, barns, and outhouses was so serious 'as twice £500, I fear, will barely compensate', he said to William Wotton on 27 November. Acknowledging God's justice, Evelyn looked upon the gale as a chastisement for our national sins, 'and my own, who yet have not suffered as I deserved to', he recorded in the *Diary*, 26 November. As if it were a symbol, he resolved to replant some of his fallen elms; writing to young Jack, he says he is 'resolved to set them up again disbranched, not pollard, if we have the strength to effect it: for an elm will grow and recover marvellously above all other trees, willows and alders excepted'.[1] Evelyn possessed the longevity and recuperative powers of an elm; he, too, would yet grow and recover.

Nor had he finished with his pen. At this time he began to prepare new editions of *Sylva*, and of *The Parallel of Architecture*. Of the latter, Wotton said: 'I know you have noble materials for another impression by you, which the public greedily longs for.' The first edition—which was handsome enough—would be improved; and he would dedicate it to Sir Christopher Wren. *Sylva*, too, would outdo all the earlier editions; *Acetaria*, so well received, could appear with it among the subsidiary tracts. Young Jack would see it all through the press. And he would include Nanteuil's portrait of himself, drawn in 1650, when he was in his thirtieth year. Now he was in his eighty-fourth! The old and ageing President of Trinity, Dr. Bathurst, rather envied him; he told Bohun that Evelyn had 'little reason to complain who is able to study and put out new editions of books at these years'.[2]

With the new year came the first answer to Evelyn's prayers, the first sign of absolution; young Jack was appointed receiver-general for the Stamp Duties on 16 January at a salary of £300 per annum. It was an earnest of Godolphin's good will. Evelyn was now convinced that his patron would further the marriage settlement; he would catch him again on this wave of generosity; he applied for the balance of his Dutch War expenses. But again

[1] Letter, J. Evelyn to J. Evelyn III, 29 Nov. 1703.
[2] Letter, R. Bathurst to R. Bohun, 31 Dec. 1703.

he was too optimistic; instead of the Treasury being in his debt, he was now pressed for £244; his expenses, having been charged at too high a rate, had become an overpayment! (These doubtful expenses must not be confused with his overcharged Sick and Wounded Prisoners Account to which he had confessed in 1680.) On 26 January he therefore protested to Godolphin that it was agreed that expenses should not exceed forty shillings a day—the rate allowed to his fellow commissioners; he was 'much surprised he should alone be singled out for a precedent to others of somewhat inferior rank and credit to serve at a cheaper rate'. It was a clear case of adding insult to injury. Obviously, during the Dutch War, when money was irregularly paid, authorisation for the rates of payment was also irregular. As before, he asked Godolphin to acquit him of the 'burden or to instal it upon the great [Sayes Court] debt still remaining as due'. Again the Treasury declined, and the debt remained unpaid during Evelyn's lifetime, though Godolphin showed his sympathy now, by signing a stay of process against him for the recovery of the £244. Evelyn felt certain that he would never be deserted by his Lordship.

Nevertheless, eight months were to pass by with no word from Mrs. Boscawen or Godolphin. Evelyn—who could always find employment—began to write his last work, *Memoires for my Grand-son*—excellent advice for the health of the young man's soul and for increasing the wealth of his earthly estate—through which shines the writer's deep and sincere affection. But this task, performed in failing health, did little to allay the anxiety that possessed him.

At the end of April he recorded a week's affliction with many infirmities. It was a race between the grave and the marriage. When Bathurst, his oldest acquaintance, died in June, 'it was a serious alarm to me; God of his mercy grant that I may profit by it'. Midsummer came with the silence unbroken. Perhaps the celebrations of the victory of Blenheim in August brought home to Evelyn that Godolphin—as the financial mainstay of Marlborough and his armies—had employments other than the manipulation of marriage settlements.

Yet soon after the battle, Godolphin found time to make proposals that would resolve all Evelyn's anxieties. Mrs. Boscawen passed them on, beginning, however, with an ambiguous sentence which must have damped all Evelyn's hopes: 'If my daughter had a portion that would clear your estate, I should think it well bestowed in your family, but since the case is far otherwise with us, we must not flatter ourselves any longer with hopes of what may never be.' What may never be! Evelyn might well have had a heart attack. She then says that Godolphin is positive "twas impossible for him to help you upon that foot of your pretension to an old debt from the Crown'. But Godolphin approved of the marriage, and the employment given to young Jack 'was rather done with the prospect of it'—which was certainly more encouraging.

Now Evelyn must have bristled; she actually criticised the account of his estate and debt, 'which altogether amounted to £11,000, but I observed there was only £3000 of it charged by your brother remaining upon the estate' and the £11,000 included—'quite justly—a portion for your granddaughter: but for that part of it you can yet pay no interest and I suppose the principal lessens every year.' Blenheim had done nothing to lessen the acumen of the Lord Treasurer.

But more pleasing and positive proposals followed: 'if upon paying down £4000, any part of the estate could be so cleared as to make a reasonable jointure for such a portion, and that my Lord Treasurer should think fit to add to your grandson's present salary so much in some other employment as would make that £500 or £600 a year, I don't see why a young couple no way extravagant, might not live comfortably upon that for the present, as a part of your family, which is what I shall insist upon for many reasons and upon nothing else from you, but let the whole estate remain in your management as long as pleases God, and you to go on in paying the debt as fast as you can, and long may you live to enjoy it in so doing: this I offer as the only expedient I can think of, to finish an affair which has been now a good while depending, in case you and Mrs. Evelyn approve of it, and that the young people should like the conclusion as well as the old.'[1] He had almost found acceptance; it only remained for him to provide an adequate jointure for the future mistress of Wotton. At the rate usual in this period—£1000 portion to £100 jointure—it would be £400; roughly a third of the expected income of the estate.

[1] Letter, Mrs. Boscawen to J. Evelyn, 21 Sept. 1704.

Evelyn's health at once appeared to improve; apart from his usual drowsiness at afternoon sermons, during the rest of the year he recorded but one indisposition. Therefore his wife had no hesitation in leaving him at Wotton, whilst she attended the birth of another of Susan's babies at Surrey Street: 'she grows so big I can scarce think she reckons right', said Mrs. Evelyn.

The repercussions of the marriage settlement had little effect upon Mrs. Evelyn. She had always maintained an economical standard of housewifery. Before Evelyn joined her in London for the winter, she wrote: 'I hope you do not spare any of the good things I left in the closet for your use. When the next hog is killed, the butcher should cut a little more flesh to the chine, and not chop off the hog's snout from the head. I shall be glad Margaret should send some part of the sauce when she sends the [hog] puddings, spare rib and chine. Let the gardener know the apples were very well packed and kept from bruising, but he laid too much hay between the rows so that we have fewer apples than he might have sent. I would not have him send any of the apples which were bought; they being gathered before the time have little taste; they were better spent at home in apple pies mixed with others.'[1] How Evelyn must have missed the prolific fruit trees of Sayes Court, and deplored the purchase of apples.

It is unfortunate that the pages of the *Diary* for December and January are missing, and that only one letter of the period throws any light on the progress of the marriage settlement. Apparently Evelyn had not been idle. He had persuaded the affluent Draper to lend him £9000 on mortgage, of which £5000 paid off the debt owing to young Glanville. This pleased Mrs. Boscawen: 'I'm glad that you have cleared a part of your estate so as to make a competent jointure, since that appears to be the chief occasion of the delay, and though I neither expect nor desire it without some addition to your grandson's present income, I must suppose that this addition depends entirely upon the other part, which is first to be adjusted by friends and counsel, and then I can't doubt but my Lord Treasurer will comply with his part when he has an opportunity, since I had his leave to propose it to you.'[2]

[1] Letter, Mrs. Evelyn to J. Evelyn, 25 Nov. 1704.
[2] Letter, Mrs. Boscawen to J. Evelyn, 5 Feb. 1705.

In due time—in July—Godolphin appointed young Jack to be one of the Commissioners of the Prizes at £500 per annum. The marriage settlement could be completed. If Evelyn's mind was now at rest, he still suffered intermittently great pain with the stone, and on occasion could only 'creep' to church. At the end of the month he spent a few days at Wotton, where the subject of Bohun's sermons might have been embarrassing; on 5 August Evelyn heard him preach concerning the necessity of serious repentance and danger of procrastination, 'upon which he insisted every Sunday I was in the country'. Now, of course, such admonition was unnecessary. Evelyn could return to London for the engrossing of the marriage settlement with a good conscience.

The entire estate would be left to young Jack, reserving Evelyn's possession of it during his life, with the disposal of his personal estate by will; the lease and furniture of the Dover Street house to Mrs. Evelyn. The interest on Draper's £9000 would have to be paid out of the £1000 or so of the Wotton rental, leaving little more than £500 for subsistence. As Mrs. Evelyn said to Bohun 'we must contract and live as discreetly as we can'.[1]

Jack and Anne were to be married on 18 September by Evelyn's friend, the Archbishop of Canterbury, Dr. Tenison, in Lambeth Chapel. To Evelyn's last letter—which has not survived—to Mrs. Boscawen, wherein he apparently suggested it was time the wedding was arranged and that the young couple should receive the Holy Communion on the Sunday before the ceremony, she replied: 'I think, good and worthy sir, you are generally in the right, and particularly so when you desire an end to a business that has been so long depending. There shall be no obstacle on my part whenever a day is agreed upon between them and you, and there can't be a better preparative [the Holy Communion] and I find her well disposed for that duty upon the next Sunday at St. James's Chapel where the Communion is constantly celebrated at noon and is our place of resort to it. After this I think there needs only time and place to be adjusted for the ceremony, and as great a gadder as I am, you may set me where and when you please, for this affair I

---

[1] Letter, Mrs. Evelyn to R. Bohun, 29 Sept. 1705.

dare not brag of being so fine as you pretend [it] to be, but I expect to be as well pleased as any body.'[1]

Mrs. Evelyn related the events of the wedding-day to Bohun —and explained why he had not been invited: 'It was on the Lady's part to set the wedding day, to choose the person that should join their hands and invite the guests; we had no concern but to comply with their desires.' The guests included Sir William Godolphin, Dr. Henry Godolphin (the Provost of Eton) and his wife, Charles Godolphin and his wife, Sir Philip Medows and his wife, a Mrs. Jane Boscawen (whose husband was in Cornwall), Mrs. Jael Boscawen, Evelyn and his wife, young John's widow and her daughter Betty, Draper, and Susan, 'and no one person besides the solicitor, in all 18 persons' (with the bride and bridegroom) 'and if it had been desired no one person more could have sat at the table, so small are Mrs. Boscawen's rooms . . . the entertainment was great and plentiful, quietly and kindly performed: we left the young couple in bed, and so we returned to our own beds . . . I am thus particular that you may know it was neither want of kindness or respect that we did not invite you to be a witness, knowing you do not care for trouble and that we might be free with so good a friend . . . the young couple seem very well pleased with one another . . . all relations express great kindness and satisfaction on both sides'.[2]

Only one circumstance was to be regretted: the absence of the Lord Treasurer. Yet Evelyn could die in peace. He had created a fine garden; he had written a Diary—which would be a main source for seventeenth-century English history—and that great book *Sylva*; he had made this marriage that would ensure the social status of his descendants for half a century. And his conscience was clear: he had opened his heart to God. Most important of all, he had acknowledged his affection for Margaret—the affection that well-nigh robbed Godolphin of a wife. Her silence, her loyalty, led to Godolphin's acceptance of his proffered friendship. By Godolphin's promises—honourably fulfilled—he gathered the fruits of patronage, attained the great goal, the marriage, the reward of Grace.

[1] Letter, Mrs. Boscawen to J. Evelyn, 12 Sept. 1705.
[2] Letter, Mrs. Evelyn to R. Bohun, 29 Sept. 1705.

Evelyn died at his Dover Street house on 27 February 1706, five months after the marriage, in his eighty-sixth year.

*　　　　*　　　　*

It has often been said of Evelyn that in giving us his *Diary* he hid from us his character; that he lost himself in the panorama he depicted. Comparison with Pepys is always forthcoming; one revealed his humanity and became to all but the squeamish a warm friend; the other by withholding the secrets of his heart proved but a distant acquaintance.

William Bray, the Evelyn family solicitor and the first editor of the *Diary*, must be held largely responsible for keeping Evelyn aloof from us. The letters he chose and appended to the *Diary* did nothing to release Evelyn's character from cold storage; not one letter did he print that might have allowed us to learn of Evelyn's loves, hates, aspirations, and failings. Little more than his relations with the great and the *virtuosi*, and the measure of his piety, were illustrated in Bray's carefully selected letters. The letters printed from or to those with whom he was most intimate, Mrs. Evelyn, his son John, Sidney Godolphin, Samuel Pepys, and George Evelyn, contained nothing to discount the righteous self-portrait of the *Diary*. No hint of junketings with Pepys, or any word of love and friendship uttered by Margaret Blagge or Evelyn, was allowed to appear.

The publication, in 1818, of the confession would have been unthinkable. Yet what effect might not its appearance and certain letters have made upon Evelyn's place in our hearts? To have added the knowledge of his strivings, weaknesses, his occasional intemperance, and particularly his excessive affection for Margaret to our notion of his piety would have brought him nearer to ourselves.

The same obscurantist policy was continued throughout the nineteenth century by W. J. Evelyn of Wotton who firmly refused all access to the unprinted material. His action, however, may be justified by his legitimately acquired fear of scholars; the autograph collector William Upcott, who assisted Bray in the printing of the *Diary*, made away from Wotton with scores of books and manuscripts, and hundreds of letters, many of which

W. J. Evelyn bought back at Upcott's sale in 1848 at a cost of many hundreds of pounds.[1]

So it comes to be our privilege to use the new material like a broom to sweep away—or at least to disturb—the unhealthy surface piety under which Evelyn has been allowed to shelter. Now, surely, with his personality adjusted he is silhouetted more sanely and sharply against his seventeenth-century background. His friendship with such diverse characters as Jeremy Taylor and Samuel Pepys is the more readily comprehended. His toleration of Pepys's association with Mary Skinner is now acceptable. Evelyn could discuss seraphic love with Boyle;[2] we may now assume his discussion of profane with Pepys.

Perfectionist that he was, Evelyn knew well his own shortcomings: on the inside cover of his *Hooker*[3] we find the following quoted sentences:

'Our very vertues may bee snares unto us.'

'The enemy . . . hath found it harder to overthrow an humble sinner than a proud Saint.'

'There is no man's case so dangerous as his whom Sathan hath persuaded that his own righteousness shall present him pure and blameless in the sight of God.'

'Nothing good or perfect in the very best Saints.'

In his friendship with Margaret, Evelyn's saintly strength was sometimes wanting, indeed we may think that the friendship was wrecked by the lack of it. Even the saintly Margaret had to contend with 'cheap' thoughts. If their friendship seems a tangled, ill-explored forest, through it ran a path to Evelyn's patron Godolphin. It would have been foolish, if not criminal, if Evelyn had failed to exploit that association; patronage was in the air that Evelyn breathed, and upon which he was expected to sustain his friends and relatives.

In the *Diary* he was posterity-conscious, and the possibility of its eventual appearance in print governed all personal entries. The reason why such happenings as his dismissal of Richard Hoare for intemperance went unrecorded, and of our being

---

[1] See *Times Lit. Suppl.*, 6 April 1951, for an account—by the present writer—of Evelyn's Library.

[2] Evelyn's *Diary*, 1854 ed., III, 121–6.

[3] Press-mark d. 95: Evelyn Library.

told that William Glanville contested on a matter of the Trinity rather than on the Wotton Settlement may be found in Sir Thomas Clarges' letter to Evelyn: 'I know your civility to all mankind is such that you will not make any man blush to read his own miscarriages.'[1] Therefore the whole truth is rarely to be found in any personal entry in the *Diary*. It is otherwise in his letters. There he is uninhibited, giving us his real image, a rounded personality. Perfectionist he may have been with concomitant susceptibilities, trying at times to servant, friend, or relation. But he was as jealous of the nation's reputation as for the spiritual health and survival of his name and family. His children, the gardeners, the builders, the Navy, the *virtuosi* were all enriched by his varied endeavours. He was 'a man so much above others', said Pepys: with our fuller knowledge we cannot but agree.

[1] 8 Dec. 1664.

Bibliography

General

Ashley, M.: *England in the Seventeenth Century*.
Bacon, Sir Francis: 'Of Gardens' (*Essays*).
Bryant, A.: *Pepys*, 3 vols.
Burnet, G.: *History of My Own Time*.
Cambridge Modern History, Vol. IV, Chs. IX–XI, XV, XIX.
Cambridge Modern History, Vol. V, Chs. V, VIII.
Churchill, W. S.: *Marlborough*, Vol. I.
Clark, G. N.: *The Later Stuarts*.
D'Arcy, M. C.: *The Mind and Heart of Love*.
Elliot, Hon. H.: *Life of Sidney, Earl of Godolphin*.
English Historical Documents, Vol. VIII, 1660–1714.
Faber, A. O.: *De Auro Potabile Medicinali*, 1677.
Feiling, K.: *A History of the Tory Party*.
Fussell, G. E.: *The Old English Farming Books, 1523–1730*.
Habbukuk, H. J.: 'Marriage Settlements in the Eighteenth Century' (*Trans. R. Hist. Soc.*, 1950).
Hammond, H.: *A Practical Catechism*, 5th ed., 1649.
Hanford, J. H.: 'Pepys and the Skinner Family' (*R.E.S.*, VII, 257).
Hanmer, Sir T.: *The Garden Book*.
Hind, A. M.: *History of Engraving and Etching*.
Hooker, R.: *Of the Lawes of Ecclesiastical Politie*, 1639.
Lambert, U.: *Godstone*.
Lever, Sir T.: *Godolphin: His Life and Times*.
Macaulay, T. B.: *History of England*, Vol. III.
Ogg, D.: *England in the Reign of Charles II*.
Ogilby, J.: *Britannia*.
Parkinson, J.: *Paradisi in Sole*, 1629.
Pepys, S.: *Diary*.
Ranke, L. von.: *History of England*, Vol. IV.
Rea, J.: *Flora, Ceres, et Pomona*, 1665.
Tanner, J. R.: *Private Correspondence and Misc. Papers of S. Pepys*.
Trevelyan, G. M.: *England under the Stuarts*.

Bibliography

Trevelyan, G. M.: *English Social History.*
Trevor-Roper, H. R.: *The Gentry: 1540–1640.*

EVELYN: *Printed*

Of Liberty and Servitude, 1649.
The State of France, 1652.
Essay on the First Book of Lucretius; English verse by J. E., 1656.
The French Gardiner (by N. de Bonnefons), transl. by J. E., 1659.
The Golden Book of St. John Chrysostom, transl. by J. E., 1659.
A Character of England, 1659.
An Apologie for the Royal Party, 1659.
Late News from Bruxels Unmasked, 1660.
A Panegyric to Charles the Second, 1661.
Fumifugium, 1661.
'A faithful and impartial narrative of what pass'd at the landing of the Swedish Ambassador' (in Sir Richard Baker's *Chronicle of the Kings of England,* 1665).
Instructions concerning erecting of a Library, by G. Naudeus, interpreted by J. E., 1661.
Tyrannus, or The Mode, 1661.
Sculptura, 1662.
Μνστήριον τῆς Ἀνομίας . . . *The Mysterie of Jesuitism,* 1664.
Sylva, 1664 ⎫
Pomona, 1664 ⎬
Kalendarium Hortense, 1664 ⎭
A Parallel of the Antient Architecture with the Modern, by R. Fréart de Chambray, made English. To which is added an Account of architects and architecture, by J. E., 1664.
The Pernicious Consequences of the New Heresie of the Jesuites against the King and State, 1666.
The English Vineyard vindicated, by John Rose, 1666.
Public Employment and an Active Life prefer'd to Solitude, 1667.
An Idea of the Perfection of Painting, by R. Fréart, and rendered English by J. E., 1668.
The History of the Three Late Famous Imposters, 1669.
Navigation and Commerce, 1674.
A Philosophical Discourse of Earth, 1676.
Mundus Muliebris: or The Ladies dressing-room unlock'd, 1690, by Mary Evelyn; preface by J. E.
The Compleat Gard'ner, by De la Quintinye (transl. by George London, supervised by J. E.), 1693.
Numismata, 1697.
Acetaria, A discourse of sallets, 1699.

Bibliography

Posthumous

Diary, ed. by W. Bray, 1818, and later eds.
Diary, ed. by J. Forster, 1854, repr. by Bohn, 1859.
Diary, ed. by E. S. de Beer.
The Life of Mrs. Godolphin, ed. by S. Wilberforce, 1847.
The Life of Mrs. Godolphin, ed. by H. Sampson, 1939.
The History of Religion, ed. by R. M. Evanson, 1850.
Seven Letters of John Evelyn, 1914.
Memoires for my Grand-son, transcribed &c. by G. Keynes, 1926.
Directions for the Gardiner at Says-Court, ed. by G. Keynes, 1932.
A Devotionarie Book, Intr. by W. Frere, 1936.

Doubtful attribution

The Manner of ordering Fruit-trees. By the Sieur Le Gendre, 1660,
    transl. by J. E.

In *R.E.S.*, XIV, 1938, Mr. F. E. Budd attributes this translation
to Evelyn on stylistic grounds and on parallels of translation in it
and *The French Gardiner*. The argument is somewhat weakened by
citing further parallels in *The Compleat Gard'ner* which we know now
to be the work of George London. Moreover, it is curious that
Evelyn did not possess a copy of the translation. It does not appear
in his list of publications sent to Dr. Plot on 16 March 1683 (Letter
Book, Evelyn MS. 39, p. 37).

MRS. EVELYN

The Picture of the Princesse Henrietta, 1660.

Manuscripts

Letter Book: Evelyn's copies 16 April 1679—4 February 1698
    (Evelyn MS. 39).
Elysium Britannicum (Evelyn MS. 45).
Inventory of Pictures (Evelyn MS. 53).
Abstract of leases and rents, Deptford, 1690, 1694–1703, with note
    of debts (Evelyn MS. 62).
Account Book 1673–81 (Evelyn MS. 64).
Trades: secrets and receipts mechanical (Evelyn MS. 65).
Meditation for Michaelmas Day (Evelyn MS. 72).
Meditation for Monday–Thursday (Evelyn MSS. 73, 82, 84, 85).
Meditation upon the Advents (Evelyn MS. 76).
Office for Trinity Sunday (Evelyn MS. 83).
Office for All Saints (Evelyn MS. 86).
Office for the Lord's Day (with Mental Communion) (Evelyn MSS.
    90, 130).

Bibliography

Testamentum in procinctu: advice to his son (Evelyn MS. 93).
Officium Sanctae & individuae Trinitatis (Evelyn MS. 96).
An Eucharistical Office (Evelyn MS. 97).
Œconomics to a newly married friend (Evelyn MS. 106) and B.M.
    Add. MS. 15950.
A new yeares gift for [M. Blagge] (Evelyn MS. 110).
Office for Fridays (Evelyn MS. 116).
Officium Poenitentiae (Evelyn MS. 117).
The trimming of the lamp, or a short Eucharistical Office (Evelyn
    MS. 120).
Otium Evelyni (Evelyn MS. 124).
Office for Nativity & Epiphany (Evelyn MS. 125).
Office for Pentecost (Evelyn MS. 126).
Instructions œconomique (Evelyn MS. 143).
The Legend of the Pearle (Evelyn MS. 304).
Meditations by J. E. and Margaret Blagge (Evelyn MS. 305).
Confession (Evelyn MS. misc.)
Directions for the employment of your time: for his daughter Mary
    Evelyn (Evelyn MS. misc.).
A faithfull and impartial Narrative of what pass'd at the Landing
    of the Swedish Ambassador (Evelyn MS. misc.).
Evelyn (Mary): Rules for spending my pretious tyme well (Evelyn
    MS. 92).
Necessary additions to those Directions of my Father when I was
    at Sayes Court (Evelyn MS. misc.).
Coventry Papers, Vol. XLI, ff. 464, 487, 503.

Evelyniana

Evelyn estate deeds, transcriptions from (Evelyn MS. 252).
Evelyn estate accounts and Oxford education, 1634–41 (Evelyn
    MS. 131).
Foljambe, C. G. S.: *Evelyn Pedigree and Memoranda*, 1893.
Bell, C. F., ed.: *Sculptura*, 1906.
Evelyn, Helen: *History of the Evelyn Family*, 1915.
Levis, H. C.: *Extracts from . . . Evelyn and Pepys relating to Engraving*,
    1915.
Woolf, Virginia: 'Rambling round Evelyn' (*The Common Reader*, 1st
    ser., 1925).
Ponsonby, Lord: *John Evelyn*, 1933.
Keynes, G.: *John Evelyn: a study in bibliophily*, 1937.
Hiscock, W. G.: *John Evelyn and Mrs. Godolphin*, 1951.
Budd, F. E.: 'A Translation attributed to Evelyn' (*R.E.S.*, XIV,
    1938).

Bibliography

de Beer, E. S.: (Two articles on Evelyn's and Morley's part at the Restoration, *Sussex Record Soc.*, Vols. XIV, XIX).

Treasury Papers, May 9, 11, 1698: Damage to Sayes Court.

Calendar of Treasury Books, v.d., appointments and financial matters, J. E. and J. E. jun.

The Case of George Evelyn (1698), Wing E3476, 7.

The Declaration of George Evelyn, 1699. Not in Wing.

Sunderland, Earl of: Letter to a friend, 1689, Wing S6177.

—— Anr. ed. In Christ Church Library. Not in Wing.

Wotton House Accounts, 1692–95: in W. Glanville, jun.'s, hand (Evelyn MS. 262).

Sherwood Taylor, F.: 'The Chemical Studies of John Evelyn' (*Annals of Science*, VIII, 1952).

Letters

John Evelyn's Letter Book: his own copies, 1679–98.

All original letters in the Evelyn Collection to and from the following correspondents:

Arlington, Henry Bennet, Earl of.

Bathurst, Ralph.

Berkeley, Christian Riccard, Lady.

Berkeley, John Lord.

Blagge, Margaret (later Mrs. Godolphin).

Bohun, Ralph.

Boscawen, Mrs. Jael.

Browne, Sir Richard.

Bullack, John.

Clarendon, Edward Hyde, Earl of.

Danby, Earl of (Sir Thomas Osborne)

Draper, William.

Evelyn, George,

—— John.

—— John, jun.

—— Mary (daughter to John).

—— Mary (daughter to George).

—— Mrs.

—— Richard (brother to John).

—— Susan (later Mrs. Draper).

Gibbons, Grinling.

Glanville, William, the elder.

—— William, the younger.

Godolphin, Francis.

—— Sidney.

Henshaw, Thomas.
Howard, Anne (later Lady Sylvius).
Pepys, Samuel.
Strickland, John.
Sunderland, Dorothy, Countess of.
—— Robert Spencer, Earl of.
Taylor, Jeremy.
Thicknesse, James.
Tuke, Lady.
—— Sir Samuel.
Wren, Sir Christopher

Index

Abingdon, 150
Abinger Hammer, 1
  Shipwalk, 3
Acetaria, 207–8, 213, 232
Addiscombe, 229
Albemarle, Duke of, *see* Monck, George
Albury, 71
Aldrich, Henry, 49, 221, 224
Allestree, Richard: *The Whole Duty of Man*, 68
Anne, Queen, 225
Apology for the Royal Party, An, 40
Apsley, Capt., 13
Argyll, Archibald Campbell, Marquis of, 29
Arlington, Earl of, 59, 63–4, 120
Arnauld, Antoine, 55
Arundel, Sir J., 215
Arundel, Thomas, Earl of, 13
Arundel Marbles 71
Ashe, George, 172
Ashmole, Elias, 49, 113
Aubrey, John, 8
Aurum potabile, 114–15

Bacon, Sir Francis, 28, 30–1
Bagshot, 148
Bagwell, Mrs., 57
Baker, Sir Richard, 47
Barlet, A., 16
Bartolozzi, F., 155
Bateman, —, of Paternoster Row, 217
Bath, 158–9, 190–1, 210–11
Bathurst, Ralph, 73, 210, 232–3
Bayley, Lewis: *The Practice of Piety*, 68

Baynards, 12, 15
Beale, John, 49, 51, 223
Beale, Mary, 96–7
Beaver, Lord, 186
Beck, M. Blagge's maid, 84, 99
Benbow, John, 187, 199, 200
Bentley, Richard, 177–8, 198–9, 202, 210–11, 222
Berkeley, Christian Riccard, Lady, 84–5, 88–9, 93–6, 99, 100
Berkeley, George, Earl of, 42
Berkeley, John, Lord, 88, 100–6, 109, 110
Berwick, Duke of, 150
Blagge, Margaret, later Mrs. Godolphin, her scheme of devotion, 80; friendship with Evelyn begins, 81; leaves Court, 84; at Berkeley House, 84–5; visits Sayes Court, 88; portrait by Dixon, 88; at Twickenham, 88–9, 92; desires to live at Hereford, 92; visits Southborough, etc., 94; returns to Berkeley House, 95; portrait by Mary Beale, 96–7; acts in *Calisto*, 97; Evelyn sups with her, 98; marriage, 99; in Paris, 103–4; returns to England, 106; marriage revealed, 107; in Scotland Yard, 109; honeymoon, 110; conception, 112; illness and death, 113–15; will, 115–16; letters to Godolphin, 134; in Evelyn's will, 141; in Evelyn's confession, 126, 237–9
Blagge, Thomas, 80
Blake, Robert, admiral, 33

247

Index

Blake, Stephen, 31-2
Blith, Walter, 32
Bohun, Ralph, 56, 66, 71-6, 91, 143, 146, 219-24, 230
Bolney Court, 20
Bonnefons, N. de, 37
Booth, George, 39, 40
Boscawen, Anne, 178, 184, 219, 228, 231, 234, 236-7
Boscawen, Mrs. Jael, 141-2, 153, 172, 178, 184, 228, 231, 233-5, 237
Boscawen, Jane, 237
Boyer, Abel, 98
Boyle, Hon. Robert, 52, 55, 223
Bradshaw, George, 7
Bradshaw, John, 22
Bragge, T., 155
Bray, William, 238
Bretton, Dr., 58
Brockelsbye, —, 2 n.
Brouncker, Lord, 56
Brown, bookseller at The Black Swan, London, 217
Browne, Lady, 26, 33
Browne, Sir Richard, 16, 44, 57, 59, 62, 64, 66, 121, 125, 130, 226-7
Buckingham, Duke of: glass-works, 109
Budd, F. E., 243
Bugdane, John, 155
Bullack, John, 61
Burnet, Gilbert, 150, 194, 197, 219

Caldwell, Mary, see Evelyn, Mary, 1st wife of George
Cambridge: Pembroke College, 52
Catherine, wife of Charles II, 49, 136
Cave, William, 141
Challenors, 2
Chamberlain, Peter, 114
Character of England, A, 39, 186
Charles I at Oxford, 6, 7; at Hampton Court, 18-9; execution, 22
Charles II, 20; report of being a R.C., 40; 42, 46, 52, 55; borrows money, 59; encourages Evelyn, 63; 77, 80, 135-6

Chesterfield, Philip Stanhope, Earl of, 46
Chiffinch, Thomas, 59
Church lands, 19
Church of England Service in Paris, 23
Churchill, Lady Henrietta, 201
Churchill, Sir Winston, 98
Circumcision or New-Years-Day Office, 83
Clarendon, Earl of, 64, 71, 143-4, 172
Clarges, Sir Thomas, 240
Clayton, Sir Robert, 120
Clifford, Lord, 190
Cobb, tailor, 69
Cocke, Capt. George, 56, 59, 60
Coimbra: Commentarii Collegii Conimbricensis, 211
Compleat Gardner, The, 168-9, 243
Compton, Sir F., 150
Convulsions, treatment of, 181
Cornbury, Lord, 57, 64, 150
Courtin, A. de, 129n.
Coventry, Sir William, 57, 59, 63
Cowley, Abraham, 51, 207-8, 223
    The Cutter of Colman Street, 75
Cranborne, 148
Creation, Story of the, 95-7
Crew, Sir Clipsby, 20
Crisp, Sir Nicholas, 35
Crowne, John, 97

Danby, 1st Earl of (Sir Thos. Osborne), 105
Dawe, George, 3
Dawe, Robert, 3
Denham, Sir John, 51, 65
Denton, 2, 215
Devonshire, Duke of, 190
Diodati, G., 140
Directions for the Gardiner at Says-Court, 147
Dixon, Matthew, 88-9, 176
Doyly, Sir William, 56
Draper, Sir Thomas, 170

Index

Draper, William, 170, 175, 183, 192, 205, 227, 230, 235, 237
Drayton, Bucks, 144
Drogheda, Earl of, 171–2
Dryden, John: *The Siege of Granada*, 74–5
Dublin: Trinity College, 172
Ducie, William, 20
Du Guernier, Alexandre, 33

Earnly, Lady, 190
Œconomics to a newly married friend, 108, 113, 123
Electra, see Blagge, Margaret, 80, 85
Elysium Britannicum, 32–3, 51
Evelyn, Eliza, 3
Evelyn, Elizabeth, dau. of John, 71, 86, 131, 136–7; marriage, 140; 141–3
Evelyn, George, grandfather of John, 1
Evelyn, George, brother of John, 2; at Oxford, 4–9; at Middle Temple, 9, 15; marriage, 10; refuses office of High Sheriff, 12, 16, 31; loss of children, 34, 39; 45, 53–4, 61, 65, 67; advice to daughter, 68–9; clothes for children, 69; 120, 147, 156; on inheritance of Wotton, 157, 159–62; loan to Evelyn's son, 163; ill-health, 174; alters Wotton Settlement, 202–4; accepts modification, 204–6; death, 212; library, 214; 238
Evelyn, George, son of George, 53, 60–1, 65–6, 151, 156–7
Evelyn, Capt. George, 23
Evelyn, Jane, 3, 12, 15; on Civil War, 15, 16; marriage, 19; 23; death, 24–5
Evelyn, John, birth, 2; at school, 3, 4, 7; at Oxford, 7–10; at Middle Temple, 10–11; in Holland, 12, 13; portrait by van der Borcht, 13; part in Civil War, 13, 14; travels abroad, 14–16; in Paris, 22–5; fashion, 23; returns to

England, 25; cost of living, 26; settles at Sayes Court, 27; plans garden, 28–32; loss of children, 34–5, 38–9; moves for Charles II's restoration, 40–1; elected to Council of Royal Soc., 47; Commr. for Sick and Wounded Prisoners, 52, 56–67, 72, 119, 126; receives Holy Communion in Exeter House Chapel, 56; his Plague amulet, 56; dines with Pepys and company, 56–7; reads his poems to Pepys, 60; praised by Council, 61; his fruit trees stolen, 61–2; project for Naval Infirmary, 63–4, 179; thanked by Charles II, 63–4; excused office of J.P., 66; excused election to Council of R. Soc., 67; describes Fire of London, 67; plan of St. Paul's, 67; on Dutch War, 70; Arundel Marbles, 71; receives *Marmora Oxon.*, 71; Albury terraces, 71; dines with Maids of Honour, 73; describes his wife, 78, 188; friendship with Anne Howard, 79, 80; meets M. Blagge, 80; friendship with her, 81 ff.; Christmas gifts at Whitehall, 83; pentacle, 84; arranges for Dixon's portrait of Margaret, 88; query advises her to marry, 92, 96, 99; devises her daily spiritual routine, 93; 94, 95; sups with her, 98; manages Berkeley's affairs, 102–5, 106; ceases to pray with Margaret, 112; writes last Office for her, 113; describes her death, 114–115; origin of Godolphin's patronage, 116–17; visits Pepys in Tower, 121–2; advice on sexual intercourse, 122–3; his son's drunkenness, 124; advises him against living in London, 124; on patronage, 125; confession of his sins, 126, 238; on

249

Index

Court appointments, 127; his industry, 130; friendship with Pepys, 131; part in daughter's marriage proposal, 132–3; forgives his son, 135; in Council chamber after death of Charles II, 136; compares daughter Mary with Margaret, 138; his will (1685), 140–2; advises wife on religious reading, 140–1; hope of alliance with Godolphin family, 141–2; Commr. of Privy Seal, 143–4; library, 146; advises Sunderland, 149; acts for Sunderland's return, 152–3; on Tunbridge, 154–5; portrait by Kneller, 155; declines presidency of R. Soc., 156; 157; criticises Wotton Settlement, 160–2; invites himself to Wotton, 163, 166; financial position, 167, 176–7; on transl. of *The Compleat Gardner*, 168–9; on Susan's marriage, 170–1; invited to live at Wotton, 174; leaves Sayes Court, 175; presents copy of Margaret's portrait to Godolphin, 178; elected to Council of R. Soc., 178; Treasurer of Greenwich Hospital, 179; constipation, 181–2, 187; his coach, 182; dines at Lambeth, 186; on monetary situation, 188–9; congratulates Lady Sunderland on S.'s return to office, 197; postmortem on *Numismata*, 198–9; suggests Latin verse on F. Godolphin's marriage, 201; disputes Wotton Settlement, 202–204; new Settlement, 204–6; criticism of Wotton circle, 206; advice to grandson, 207; optimism on Wotton Settlement, 208–9; aversion to medicines, 209; on Bath, 210–11; desires reconciliation with Glanville, 212; fears for brother's

personal estate, 213–6; sale of books, 217; strangury, 217; rental of Wotton (1701), 219; advises grandson on drawing, 221; on Greek, 222; loss of Pepys's hospitality, 223; on Godolphin's resignation (1701), 224; his death desired by Glanville II's daughter, 225; on W. Glanville, 225–6; seeks Godolphin's patronage for his grandson, 226–7; match with grandson and Anne Boscawen, 228, 231, 233–5; sends *The Life of Mrs. Godolphin* to Godolphin, 229; second confession, 229–30, 232; applies for Dutch War expenses, 230, 232; damage in 1703 gale at Wotton, 231–2; his debt to Treasury, 233; disposal of Wotton estate, 236; achievements, 237; death, 238; character, 238–40

Evelyn, John, son of John, 35; presented to Charles II, 66; health, 73; at Oxford, 73, 100; in Paris, 103–4; 119, 120, 122–4, 126–7, 131–2, 137; medical treatment, 144, 154, 188, 190, 193; symptoms of illness, 145, 164, 186, 195; 146, 149–52, 156–7, 159; Commr. of Revenue in Ireland, 162–5, 167–8, 171–4, 177, 180–2, 184–6; protests against sale of his books, 167–8; financial position, 171; on Lady Wyche, 173; on Wotton, 174, 177; attacks the Glanvilles, 184; returns to England, 186; his reading, 188; criticism of *Othello* and *The Comical Revenge*, 188; Bath news, 190–1; seeks patronage of Sunderland, 193; retires, 198; death, 205; his French books, 209; 238

Evelyn, John, grandson of John, 155, 163, 172, 177–8, 180–1, 201, 207–9, 217–18, 220–24,

226-7; Receiver-General for Stamp Duties, 232; Commr. of Prizes, 236; marriage, 237

Evelyn, John, son of George, 144, 147

Evelyn, Katherine, 202

Evelyn, Martha, 237

Evelyn, Mary, wife of John, marriage, 16-17; 23, 25; health in first pregnancy, 26-7; 33; at Court, 45-6; letters to W. Glanville, 49, 50, 63, 65; childbearing, 71; friendship with W. Glanville, 72-3, 76-8, 89, 90, 98; as dramatic critic, 74-5; her character, 78-9, 91; criticism of *Calisto*, 97; entertains the Queen, 107; 132; on Mary's death, 139; 147, 155, 158, 187, 189; secures prebend for Bohun, 219; ill-health, 219, 220; on Wotton alterations, 220-1, 223-224; on Q. Anne, 225; 235; describes grandson's marriage, 237; 238

Evelyn, Mary, dau. of John, 127-9, 131; marriage proposal, 132-3; death, 136-9; her poem, 137-8; 140-2, 155-6

Evelyn, Mary, 1st wife of George, 10, 15; death, 15

Evelyn, Mary, 2nd wife of George, 39, 52

Evelyn, Mary, dau. of George, 21, 53, 65; marriage proposals, 66-67; cost of board in London, 68; habits and reading, 68-70; 120, 127; marriage, 163-6; 173-5, 203, 206, 213-16; on Evelyn and his wife, 216

Evelyn, Richard, father of John, 1, 2, 6; illness, 10; 11; death, 11; will, 12

Evelyn, Richard, brother of John, 2, 8; at Oxford, 10, 12, 15; marriage, 21; 22, 31, 34

Evelyn, Richard, son of John, 27, 38, 141

Evelyn, Susan, 71, 145, 154, 158-9; marriage, 170-1; her painting, 176, 184; 185-6, 235, 237

Evelyn, W. J., 238-9

Faithful and impartial narrative of what pass'd at the Landing of the Swedish Ambassador, 47

Feiling, K. G., 192

Fenwick, Sir John, 191-2

Fitzharding, Lady, 94

Floyd, David, 192

Fowler, Capt. Thomas, 146

Fox, Sir Stephen, 130, 165, 179, 181, 192

Francis I, story of, in tapestry, 84

Fréart, Roland, de Chambray, 52

French Gardener, The, 37, 243

Fulham, Rev. George, 202-3, 205-206, 215

Fumifugium, 46

Galations, 129

Gale, Thomas, 199, 213, 222

Galway, Lord, 193, 195

Gerrard, Lady, 53, 65, 69

Gibbons, Grinling, 77

Glanville, William, marriage, 19, 20; appearance, 49; letters to Mrs. Evelyn, 50, 72-76, 78, 82; on seraphic love, 89; 90, 98, 109, 120-1, 139, 146; 56, 71, 132, 143; on the Axe and the Rod, 145; character, 145; 156-157, 203, 212-13, 223; death, 225-6

Glanville, William, son of William, 69, 70, 144, 157, 179, 181, 183, 185, 189, 190, 213-15, 217, 225

Godolphin, Charles, 237

Godolphin, Francis, 141-2, 172, 178, 180-1, 184, 201, 208-9, 225, 231

Godolphin, Henry, 237

Godolphin, Sidney, 80; Charles II's description of him, 81; at Goring House, 84-6; visits Sayes Court, 88; at Twickenham, 88-

89, 92; proposes marriage, 92; moves against Evelyn, 98; marriage, 99; character, 109, 138; 109–12; Master of the King's Robes, 112; grief at Margaret's illness and death, 114–15; at Treasury, 119; 121; disposal of posts, 130; illness, 134; barony and First Commr. of Treasury, 135; in Evelyn's will, 141–142; 144, 146–8, 156; re-marriage rumours, 159; 162, 165, 177–80, 184; resignation, 191; implicated in Fenwick Trial, 191–2; still in Whitehall, 192–194; leaves Treasury, 194; laziness, 195; at Newmarket, 196; 198; advises on Wotton Settlement, 204–5, 216–17; returns to Treasury, 218; resigns, 224; returns as Lord Treasurer, 225; ignores Evelyn's letters, 227, 230; ignores copy of *The Life of Mrs. Godolphin*, 229; 232–9

Godolphin, Sir William, 153, 237
Golden Book concerning the Education of Children, 39
Gosterwood, 1
Graham, Mrs., 106
Greenville, Sir John, 41, 43
Guido Reni, 97
Gunson, Benjamin, 44

Halford, Lady, 183
Hammond, Henry, 126, 140
Hanmer, Sir Thomas, 30–2, 51
Harcourt, Simon, Viscount, 218
Harvey, Sir Daniel, 62
Heathie Land, 3
Heigham, John, 9
Heigham, Mrs., 53, 58, 68–9
Henrietta Anne, Duchess of Orleans, 45
Henshaw, Thomas, 33
Herbert, Arthur, admiral, 152
Herbert, Sir Henry, 67–8
Herbert, Lady, 53, 67–8

Herbert, Mary, 69
Herbert, Richard, 69
Hill, Thomas, 32
History of Religion, 130
History of the Grand Visiers, The, 119
History of the Three Imposters, The, 78
Hoare, Richard, 22, 24, 34, 239
Hobbs, William, 4–5, 8–9
Holden, Rev., 143
Homefield, The, 2
Hooke, Robert, 109
Hooker, Richard: *Of the Lawes of Ecclesiastical Politie*, 1639, 239
Hortensia, 82–3
Hoskins, John, 21
Howard, Anne, 79, 80, 86; verse on Evelyn household, 87; 112, 134, 141–2, 193, 229
Howard, Dorothy, 79
Howard, Henry, 66, 71
Howard, Henry, 7th Duke of Norfolk, 129
Howard, Mrs. William, 79, 106
Hurcott Manor, 20
Hussey, John, 132–3
Hutton, John, 210

Idea of the Perfection of Painting, An, 78
Instructions concerning erecting of a Library, 46
Instructions œconomique, 20, 21, 23
Ireland, 164, 171–2, 177, 180, 182, 185
Ireton, Henry, 21

James, Duke of York, *see* James II
James II, 44, 63–5, 129, 133, 143, 148–150
Jeffreys, Sir George, 132
Jenkins, Sir Leoline, 100
Jermyn, Henry, 44
Josephus, 129
Jones, Inigo, 52
Jonson, Cornelius, younger, 21
Juniper berry ale, 69

Kalendarium Hortense, 51, 165
Keill, John, 221
Keynes, Sir G., vi, 24

Kingston, Earl of, 190
Klosterman, N., 178, 180
Kneller, Sir Godfrey, 155

Lambert, John, 39, 40
La Mothe le Vayer, Sieur de, 22
Late News from Brussels unmasked, 41
Laud, William, archbp., 6–8
Lawson, William, 132
Leeds Castle, Kent, 61–2
Le Febure, N., 16
Legend of the Pearle, The, 78
Le Gendre, Sieur de: *The Manner of
   ordering Fruit-trees,* 243
Leigh Farm, Sussex, 12
Lewkenor, Lady, 76–8, 108–9
Life of J. B. Colbert, 185
Life of Mrs. Godolphin, The, 80, 117–
   118 and *passim*
Littleton, Lady, 159
London, George, 168–9, 200
London: Berkeley House, 84 and
   passim
   Black Lion, The, 67
   Black Swan, The, 217
   Covent Garden, 68
   Devonshire House, 84
   Dover Street, 177
   Duckland, 211
   Ely House, 171
   Euston, 120
   Exeter House, 56
   Goring House, 84–6
   Greyhound, The, Whitehall, 69
   Holborn, 211
   Hyde Park, 128
   Lambeth, 68, 109, 113
   Little Britain, 211
   Middle Temple, 9, 10
   New Palace Yard, 128
   Pall Mall, 132
   Paternoster Row, 217
   St. James's Park, 128
   St. Paul's, 67
   Scotland Yard, 108
   Sun, The, 61
   Surrey St., 182
   Temple Church, 99

Tuttle St., 67
Villiers St., 131
Westminster Hall, 128
York Bldgs., 131
London, Fire of, 67
Long, Mrs., 190
Lovelace, John, Lord, 150
Lower, Richard, 114
Lucretius, 32
Lucretius, transl., 37
Luttrell, Col. Henry, 190

Macaulay, T. B., Lord, 191
Mackenzie, George, *A moral essay,
   preferring solitude to public employ-
   ment,* 70
Malling, South, 2, 12
Mander, Roger, 211, 218, 224
Manwood, 1
Maratti, Carlo, 14
Markham, Gervase, 32
Marlborough, John Churchill, Duke
   of, 191–2, 225
Mascall, Leonard, 32
Meditation for Michaelmas Day, 89, 90
Medlicott, Mr., 150
Medows, Sir Philip, 237
Memoires for my Grand-son, 233
Mennes, Sir John, 56–7
Mental or Spiritual Communion, 91
Milton, 1
Monck, George, 40–1, 43, 59, 62–3,
   66
Monmouth, Duchess of, 94
Monmouth, Duke of, 129
Montagu, Charles, 192, 194
Moor Park, 94
Moore, John, bp., 221
Moray, Sir Robert, 55
Mordaunt, Col., 190
Mordaunt, Elizabeth Carey, Lady,
   114
Mordaunt, John, Lord, 44, 46
Morley, Herbert, 27, 40–1
Morin, Pierre, 29, 31–2, 37
Mountagu, Edward, see Sandwich,
   Earl of
Mundus Muliebris, 155

Index

Murillo, Bartolomé Esteban, picture by, 184
Mysterie of Jesuitism, 55

Nanteuil, Robert, 232
Naudé, Gabriel, 46
Navigation and Commerce, 95
Needham, Gasper, 114
Needham, Marchamont, 41
Nether Wallop, 144
Newmarket, in 1663, 72
Nicole, Pierre, 55, 64
Nimeguen, Congress of, 100, 106
North, Sir Francis, 80
North, Roger, 31
Northstoke, 2, 215
Numismata, 176–8, 198–9, 213

Of Liberty and Servitude, 22
Office for Nativity, 83
Office for Pentecost, 88
Office for the Lord's Day, An, 91–2, 111–12
Office for Trinity Sunday and Octaves after Pentecost, 113
Offley, Mary, *see* Evelyn, Mary, 2nd wife of George
Oliver, Peter, 21
Orange man, The, 166
Ornithia, *see* Howard, Anne, 80, 82, 87
Oughtred, William, 5
Oxford, Earl of, 150
Oxford: Balliol College, 7–10, 211
    Exeter College, 9
    Magdalen College, 148–9
    New College, 151
    Sheldonian Theatre, 52
    Trinity College, 4, 8, 73
Oxford University Statutes (1636), 6

Packer, Philip, 117
Paddington in Abinger, 1, 11
Palma, Jacopo, the younger: Book of design, 221
Panegyric to Charles II, 46
Parallel of the Antient Architecture, 52, 232

Parker, Samuel, 141
Parkinson, John, 30–2
Pasture Wood, 3
Patrick, Simon, 122, 140–1
Pearse, John, 59
Penthea, *see* Howard, Anne, 80, 88
Pepys, Samuel, collector of prints, 49; sups at Greenwich, 56–7; naval profit, 59; visits Sayes Court, 60; approves Chatham Hospital project, 64; opinion of Albemarle, 66; 70, 73, 77; at Windsor, 94; opinion of Evelyn's son, 119; in Tower, 121–2; 131; obliges Mrs. Evelyn, 146; receives portrait of Evelyn, 155; suggested as tenant of Sayes Court, 158; entertains Evelyn, 167; presents *Memoirs* to Evelyn's son, 168; 172; his 'inclination' Mrs. Skinner, 183; The Club, 209–10; 217–18, advised to leave York Buildings, 222; tribute to The Club by Evelyn, 223; illness and death, 231; 238–40
Pernicious Consequences of the New Heresie . . ., 64
Peter the Great, 199, 200
Peter, Daniel, 3
Philips, Edward, 172
Philaretes, *see* Evelyn, John, 80, 82
Philosophical Discourse of Earth, 99
Picture of the Princess Henrietta, The, 45
Pierrepont, Mrs., 190
Plague at Chatham, 58; Chelsea, 58; Deptford, 55–6, 58, 65; East Horsley, 65; Greenwich, 58; Kingston, 65; Reigate, 65; Westminster, 67–8; Woodcote, 55–6
Plume, Dr., 56, 60
Plutarch: *Lives*, 144
Pomona, 50
Ponsonby, Lord, v, 108, 175
Pope, Walter, 53
Prettyman, William, 19, 25, 147–8
Prideaux, Humphrey, 71

Index

Public employment and an active life prefer'd to solitude, 70

Quintinye, Monsieur de la, 168

Rea, John, 28, 32, 52
Ridgeley, Dr., 145-6, 205
Rose, John, 67
Royal Society, 47, 130, 178
Rules for spending my pretious tyme well, 128
Rupert, Prince, 47-9
Russell, Lord William, 191
Rusthall, 129
Ruyter, Michael de, 56, 66

St. Albans, Earl of, 64
St. Albans, Henry, Earl of, see Jermyn, Henry
St. John Chrysostom, 39
Sales, Francis de, 20
Sanders, cousin, 68
Sandwich, Earl of, 44
Sandwich, 1st Earl of, 56, 59, 62
Sayes Court, 19, 20; garden, 27-32; 33, 147-8; building leases, 34-35; Grant, 125, 135-6, 144, 147-8; holiday-makers at, 175; let to Benbow, 187; sub-let to Tsar, 199, 200; debt of the Crown, 226, 230, 233
Scaliger, Julius Caesar: Poetices, 201-2
Scarlet fever, 155
Scrope, Lady, 45
Sculptura, 47
Serlio, Sebastiano, 52
Sherwood, Joseph, 218
Shooters Hill, 207, 219
Short, Thomas, 114
Shrewsbury, Charles Talbot, Earl of, 191
Sidney, Lord, 156, 163, 192-3
Siegen, Ludwig von, 48-9
Skinner, Mary, 183, 210, 239
Sloane, Sir Hans, 199
Smallpox, 5, 142, 218
Smith, Joseph, 210

Somers, Lord, 213
Southborough, 94, 129
Spencer, Martha, 122-3
Squerryes, Westerham, 35
Standish, Arthur, 32
Stansfield, Eleanor, 2
State of France, The, 33
Stillingfleet, Edward, 203
Stonehouse, Sir John, 122, 150-1
Strafford, Earl of, 12
Strickland, John, 199, 200, 207
Strong, Edward, 218, 224
Sunderland, Dorothy, Countess of, 106, 121, 148-9, 152-3, 156, 159, 162, 193-7, 230
Sunderland, Robert Spencer, 2nd Earl of, 148-9, 152-3, 192-5 197
   Letter to a Friend, 152
Sussex, Lord, 190
Swallowfield, 148
Sylva, 50-1, 67, 155, 165, 232, 237
Sylvius, Lady, see Howard, Anne
Sylvius, Sir Gabriel, 112, 127, 193

Tate, Nahum: Poems by Several Hands, 1685, 144
Taylor, Jeremy, 51, 223, 239
Temple, Sir John, 165
Temple, Sir William, 100
Tenison, Thomas, 126, 153, 186
Thynne, Henry Frederick, 112
Tillotson, John: Sermon before the Queen, 8 March, 1689, 173
Tintoretto, Jacopo Robusti, 77
Tippets, Sir John, 140
Tooke, Benjamin, 175
Tooke, Benjamin II, 211, 217
Tories, 129, 164
Trades: Secrets & Receipts mechanical, 4
Trumball, Sir William, 192
Tuke, Sir Samuel, 71-2; at Norwich, 72; in Paris, 72; 73, 74n., 91
Tunbridge Wells, 27, 129, 154, 158, 190
Tusser, Thomas, 32

255

Index

Twickenham Park, 85, 88-9, 94-5
Tyrannus, 46

Upcott, William, 238-9

Valentines, 69, 70
Vaughan, Henry: *The Mount of Olives*, 83; 86
Vincent, Mrs., 165
Vitruvius Pollio, Marcus, 52

Waller, Edmund, 51
Walpole, Horace, 199
Warwick, Sir Philip, 57
Westcott, 1, 11
Weston, Henry, 45
Wharton, Lady, 190
Whigs, 129
Whole Duty of Man, The, 129
Wilkins, John, 29, 141
William III, 148-52, 191, 225

Williamson, Sir Joseph, 59
Winchelsea, Lord, 190
Windsor, 148
Woodcote, 21, 55-6
Woolf, Virginia, v, 21, 179
Worlidge, John, 31
Wotton, Sir Henry, 49, 52
Wotton, manor purchased, 1; income, 2, 219, 226, 231, 236; sale of produce, 3, 4; garden temple, 23
Wotton, William, 198-9, 232
Wren, Sir Christopher, 35, 52, 67, 77, 179
Wyche, Lady, *see* Evelyn, Mary, dau. of George
Wyche, Sir Cyril, 163-6, 171, 173, 175

Yarborough, Henrietta Maria Blagge, Lady, 106-7
Yarnton cheese, 146